THE UPPER NIGER REGION

1 Bambara /Bamana/
2 Marka
3 Soninke
4 Malinke
5 Bozo
6 Dogon
7 Bobo
8 Bwa
9 Gurunsi
10 Mossi
11 Kurumba-Nioniosi
12 Senufo /Siena/
13 Nafana
14 Kulango
15 Tussian
16 Lobi
17 Ligbe

THE WEST GUINEA COAST

18 Bijogo
19 Nalu
20 Landuman
21 Baga
22 Mende
23 Vai
24 Gola
25 Temne
26 Toma /Loma/
27 Kru
28 Grebo
29 Kpelle
30 Dan
31 Ngere /Guerze/
32 Ngere-Wobe
33 Bete
34 Guro
35 Baule
36 Baule-Yaure
37 Attie
38 Adioukrou
39 Alagya
40 Ebrie
41 Asante
42 Anyi /Agni/
43 Abron
44 Fante

THE EAST GUINEA COAST

The Republic of Benin and Western Nigeria
45 Ewe
46 Fon
47 Yoruba
48 Yoruba-Ekiti
49 Bini
50 Urhobo
51 Ishan

South-Eastern Nigeria
52 Ijo
53 Kalabari
54 Anyang
55 Widekum
56 Ekoi /Ejagham/
57 Keaka
58 Bokyi
59 Ibibio
60 Ibibio-Oron
61 Ibibio-Anang
62 Kana /Ogoni/
63 Ibo
64 Ibo-Afikpo

The Benue River Basin
65 Igala
66 Idoma
67 Tiv
68 Jukun
69 Chamba
70 Mumuye
71 Mambila
72 Kaka
73 Wurkun
74 Goemai
75 Montol
76 Kantana /Mama/
77 Ham /Jaba/
78 Koro
79 Afo
80 Basa-Nge
81 Basa Komo
82 Igbira
83 Nupe

The Cameroon Grasslands
84 Bamileke
85 Bangwa
86 Tikar
87 Bekom
88 Bamum
89 Bali
90 Bafo
91 Bakundu
92 Duala

EQUAT AFRIC

The Og
93 F
94 B
95 Bu
96 Yaunde
97 Yabassi
98 Bakota
99 Mahongwe
100 Ambete
101 Mitsogho
102 Balumbo
103 Mashango
104 Ashira
105 Bapunu
106 Bavuvi

Northern and Eastern Zaire
107 Bakwele
108 Bwaka /Ngbaka/
109 Mangbetu
110 Azande
111 Bambole
112 Balega /Warega/

The Lower Congo Basin
113 Bavili
114 Bawoyo
115 Basundi
116 Basolongo
117 Babembe
118 Bateke-Sise
119 Bateke-Fumu
120 Kuyu

Southern Zaire
121 Bayaka
122 Basuku
123 Bambala
124 Bahuana /Bahuangana/
125 Bapende /West/
126 Bapende /East/
127 Bakuba /Bushongo/
128 Bashilele
129 Bawongo
130 Bashobwa
131 Babindji
132 Bakete
133 Ndengese
134 Bena Biombo
135 Bena Lulua
136 Balwawa
137 Basalampasu
138 Bena Kanioka
139 Bachokwe
140 Ovimbundu
141 Baholo

The Lualaba Basin
142 Baluba
143 Basikasingo
144 Babembe
145 Babuye
146 Baholoholo
147 Batabwa
148 Basongye
149 Batetela

OUTH
153 Ometo
154 Wassiba /Haya/
155 Wakerewe
156 Wassukuma
157 Abaha /Ha/
158 Wabende
159 Wanyamwezi
160 Wagogo
161 Washambala
162 Wazaramo
163 Doe
164 Wabondei
165 Makonde
166 Wamuera
167 Mawia
168 Wayayo
169 Lomwe
170 Barotse /Lozi/
171 Masubia
172 Bathonga
173 Zulu

LEGEND TO THE REGIONAL MAPS OF TRIBES

african ART

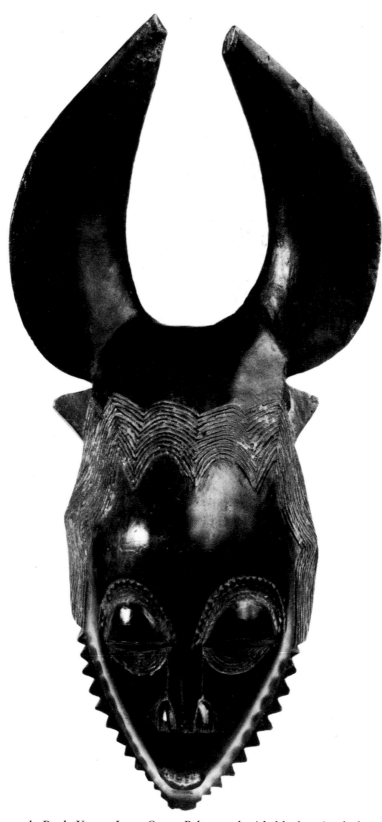

**Buffalo mask. Baule-Yaure, Ivory Coast. Pale wood with black-stained glossy surface.
Crust of ochre patina in grooves. Points of horn painted with ochre.
The Yaure sub-tribe dwells on the northern border of the Baule territory, in a hilly region between two arms of the Bandama river.
Their art is partly influenced by the style and technique of the neighbouring Guro. In most cases,
the masks of animal demons do not take the form of stylized animal heads here, as they do among other Baule sub-tribes,
but are represented by human faces, supplemented by characteristic attributes of the animals in question.
Height 38.5 cm.** Náprstek Museum, Prague.

african ART

ERICH HEROLD

HAMLYN

Contents

English language edition first published 1990
by The Hamlyn Publishing Group Limited,
A Division of The Octopus Publishing Group,
Michelin House, 81 Fulham Road,
London SW3 6RB

© Artia, Prague 1989
© Aventinum, Prague 1990

Translated by Dušan Zbavitel
Photographs by Jan Pícha
Drawings by Ivan Zpěvák
Graphic design by Karel Vilgus

ISBN 0 600 56094 5
Printed in Czechoslovakia by Tisk, Brno
2/99/80/51-01

ACKNOWLEDGEMENTS

The publishers wish to express their thanks to the Prague museums (Náprstkovo muzeum, Národní muzeum) and all the individuals who were kind enough to permit the photographing and reproduction of the artefacts belonging to them or of their property.

The following museums have kindly given permission for their photographs to be reproduced: Koninklijk Museum voor Midden-Afrika, Tervuren; Linden-Museum, Stuttgart; Musée Barbier-Müller, Geneva; Museu de Etnologia do Ultramar, Lisbon; Museum für Völkerkunde, Berlin; Museum of Mankind, London; Néprajzi Múzeum, Budapest; Rautenstrauch Joest-Museum, Cologne; Übersee-Museum, Bremen.

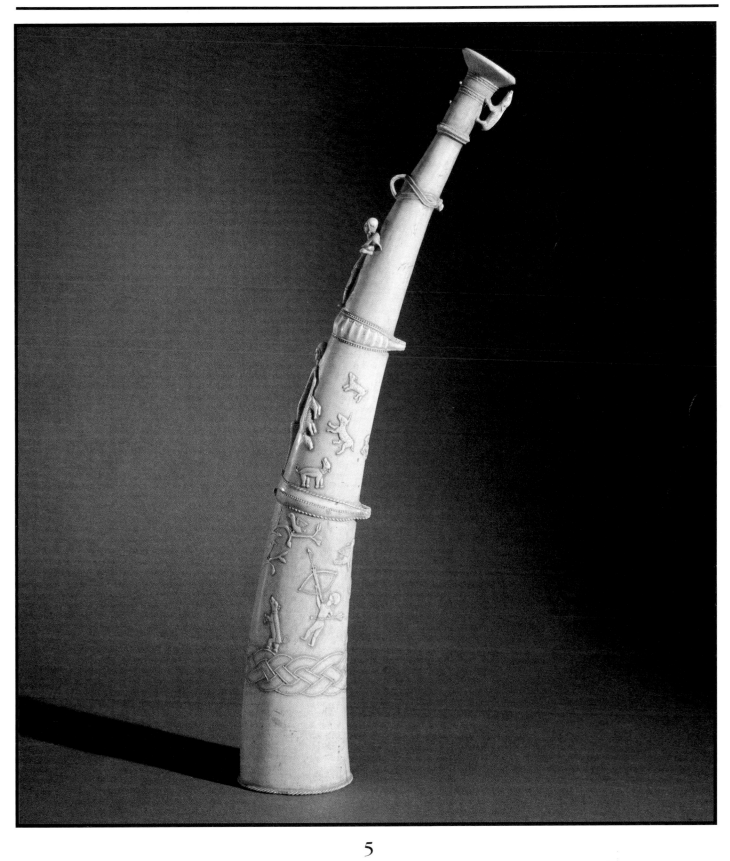

Every general statement about African art needs to be heavily qualified, and this is true of even the most fundamental categories. For example, it is common to discuss sculpture in traditional African society as if it existed throughout the Black Continent, playing the same role everywhere, whereas it is in fact found only within strict geographical limits, as the product of a certain type of society. The locus of African sculpture is the western Sudan and the vast continental belt bordering the Gulf of Guinea, from Guinea-Bissau in the north-west to Angola in the south, including the Congo Basin. The south-eastern section of this vast area takes in parts of Tanzania, Mozambique and territories further south. African sculpture is native to the basins of both large and small rivers leading into the Gulf of Guinea in the west and the Indian Ocean in the south-east. It is the product of the rain forest and the adjacent zones of forest-steppes, that is, regions suitable for agriculture, since traditional African sculpture is the art of a society based on the cultivation of the soil. Among the hunting and food-gathering populations of tropical forests and sub-deserts, and the pastoralists of the African savannahs, sculpture is non-existent.

As we shall see, African sculpture did not develop to the same extent in all the areas where it appeared. At this point we need only note that it is much poorer in the south-east of the continent than in the west, although even there it must once have been richer than now appears to be the case. The lesser importance of figure carving in the eastern half of Africa is usually attributed to the prevailing pastoral economy, since pastoralists' main forms of artistic expression are in what might be called the applied arts.

The term 'traditional' crops up again and again in this book: traditional society, traditional art, traditional sculpture, traditional design. In most instances this term might be replaced by 'tribal'. The farmers who produced African sculpture were organized in clans and tribes based on the principle of kinship. Political authority rested with village chiefs, and given this situation a great deal of African sculpture could be described as village art. However, in some places, political

1, 2 Hunting-horn. Afro-Portuguese ivory. Sherbro, Sierra Leone, 16th century. This once included another figure of a quadruped, carved below the mouthpiece on the point of the tusk; the hoofs, which are still in place, indicate that this was a wild boar. The two European figures on the convex side of the tusk are carrying a dead boar. The lower decora-

power was centralized at tribal level or even became a state apparatus, extending beyond the framework of a single tribe. Such a state was headed by a monarch who not only wielded political power but also performed vital religious functions ('sacred kingship'). This system still survives; it is incorporated into the modern state organization, although it is disintegrating under the influence of new forms, and the old division into tribes is gradually giving way to a broader consciousness of belonging to a nation or state. This is, of course, a slow process, effected through all sorts of compromises and influenced by many economic and political factors. Tribal society has existed in Africa for millennia, experiencing its first shocks only as a result of its contact with Europeans. It nevertheless succeeded in surviving the period of early Euro-

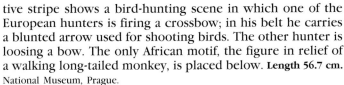

tive stripe shows a bird-hunting scene in which one of the European hunters is firing a crossbow; in his belt he carries a blunted arrow used for shooting birds. The other hunter is loosing a bow. The only African motif, the figure in relief of a walking long-tailed monkey, is placed below. **Length 56.7 cm.** National Museum, Prague.

3 Spoon with a handle decorated with figures of a cock and a horn-bill (?). Afro-Portuguese ivory. Benin (?), 16th century. This spoon and the hunting-horn in plate 1 are survivors from the collection of Rudolph II (1552-1612), which was seized in Prague by the Swedish army. National Museum, Prague.

pean attempts at Christianization, the centuries of slave-hunting which devastated large areas, and even the long period of colonial exploitation and direct political domination by foreign powers. (However, foreign domination did not always undermine the tribal system: British colonial administrations often utilized it for their own purposes, thus helping to prolong its existence.)

The tribal system has drawn its power of resistance from the conservative traditionalism which is one of its characteristic traits. Clinging to political, religious and cultural traditions helps tribal society to survive, although inevitably hindering any developments within it that might lead to economic and social advancement. It is therefore entirely proper to call tribal society traditional, and to equate traditional with tribal art.

The religious outlook of African tribal society is based on a belief in the posthumous existence of ancestors, who continue to play a part in the life of subsequent generations. Manifestations of this belief are called ancestor worship, and the practices connected with it are intended to regulate the interference of the dead with living so that it is beneficial rather than negative in its effects. The majority of African figure sculptures have been made in the service of this cult. The figure is on one level an expression of pious regard for the dead ancestor which may be offered gifts, propitiated by oblations, won by offerings or begged for advice or help. But it is much more than that: it is also the seat of the ancestor's soul, which must be bound to the figure so that it cannot wander around freely among the living, with harmful effects.

Both the fundamental belief and the practices and customs connected with ancestor worship have undergone many ethnic and regional variations and modifications, with the result that there are many differences in the meanings of cult figures. In some communities they represent the first parents of the clan or tribe, or the founders of the village, whereas in other instances they signify purely mythical ancestors. The latter may even be of totemic animal character, as in the Congo; but in other places they are idealized representations of personalities who actually lived many generations ago. By contrast, the Baule of the Ivory Coast used to make figures portraying recently deceased persons. In a number of tribes in Gabon, idealized portraits of the dead were made in the form of masks which were used during funeral and propitiatory rites. Other objects of ancestor worship and consequently of figure sculpture include heroes of the tribe who died long ago (for example, in the Bajokwe tribe of northern Angola or the tribes inhabiting the Calabar Coast of Nigeria), although these cults are not motivated by kinship ties.

There was a time when ancestor worship was practised by tribal communities all over the world. But in Africa it is characterized by certain peculiar features. One of these is the cult of the deceased twin, motivated by a belief in the supernatural origin of twins. Its artistic result is that the same attention is paid to the figure of the dead child as to its living counterpart; for example, when the surviving twin marries, a figure of the dead twin will also be 'married' to another figure. This practice, extant among the Yoruba of Nigeria, was also known in some other tribes, but it was

4 Figure of a seated woman. Bambara, Mali, Segou City region. Pale wood with black-stained, slightly glossy surface. The eyes are made of nails with convex brass heads. A small circle made of iron wire passes through the nose partition. The figure originated in the eastern part of the Bambara territory. Five identical figures may be found in collections elsewhere, undoubtedly made by the same anonymous carver, who was appropriately called the Master of the Rapacious Profile (*Maestro del profilo di rapace*) by Ezio Bassani. Shovel-shaped hands and a convex profile are the characteristics of this personal style. Nothing is known concerning the purpose of these figures. **Height 61.5 cm.**
Náprstek Museum, Prague.

5 *Nomoli* human figure seated on a backed stool, the hands placed on the knees. Steatite. Sherbro, Sierra Leone, 16th century (?). Despite the surface deterioration, which has obliterated the detail, it is possible to discern the bulging eyes and nose, which are stylistic traits identical with those of Afro-Portuguese ivories. **Height 17.8 cm.**
Private collection, Prague.

learn the practical knowledge needed for hunting or housekeeping, obtain a sort of sexual education as a preparation for family life, and become acquainted with tribal traditions and customs.

This 'bush school' is one of the most effective means of preserving the continuity and immutability of tribal traditions. Its course, and especially the ritualized conclusion, involves much use of masks. In Angola and southern Zaire, for example, the camp of the young people under initiation is watched over by guardians wearing large masks and close-fitting woven costumes. In the river-basin of the Kwango in Zaire, after the initiation is finished, the boys return to the village in a procession with masks which are expected to arouse mirth by their inventiveness. In some tribes in the western part of the Ivory Coast and in Liberia, a masked functionary maintains communications between the village and the camp of boys. And so on.

Closely connected with the initiation is the institution of the secret society. In some tribes the ritualized transition from child to adult is automatically connected with the admission of the initiated boy into the lowest age grade of a secret society. These organizations are a significant means of maintaining the social order and the traditional rules of the community. Sometimes they are endowed with judicial authority, even using terror to impose their will on other members of the tribe. In tribes where political authority does not extend beyond the boundaries of the village, such an organization may serve as a means of inter-tribal understanding. This is because the membership of a secret society is not always confined to a single tribe and may have a more or less 'international' character, even enabling it to solve inter-ethnic problems. The most famous organization of this kind is the secret society *poro*, which exists in a number of tribes in Liberia and the adjacent parts of neighbouring countries. Among ethnic elements which have formed tribal and urban states, such as the Bakuba of Zaire or the Yoruba of Nigeria, some secret societies even play the role of police. Most of these organizations are confined to men; only in Liberia, Sierra Leone and the north of Ivory

not universal. In some tribes belief in the supernatural origin of twins resulted in the opposite attitude, and they were killed.

It was probably African masks that did most to make the art of the continent known in the West. To a very great extent these are connected with the second important source of inspiration for African art: the initiation. The African young, both boys and girls, must submit at a certain age to an institutionalized preparation for life among the adult members of the tribe. This takes the form of a rite representing the transition from childhood to adult status. Young people spend a couple of weeks, or even months, in a camp outside the village — a kind of school at which they are strictly segregated from the uninitiated and from members of the opposite sex. Here they

6 Stool with a caryatid in the form of a seated woman. Bambara, Mali. Pale wood with a geometric ornament on the seat painted green. Vertical surfaces blackened by burning; the eyes, nipples and scarification marks represented by brass hobnails. A similar piece was reproduced in an advertisement of a Paris curio shop in 1982 (*African Arts*, XV, 4, p. 85). Although both objects can be only a few decades old, they are masterpieces of African 'cubism'. The manipulation of spatial geometry while preserving an organic wholeness has hardly been surpassed anywhere in Africa. **Height 36 cm.** Private collection, Prague.

7 Free-standing figure of a woman. Bambara, Mali. Brown heavy wood with the surface stained brown-black. Rounded eyes made of flattened aluminium wire. The conical breasts on a level with the shoulders are found in most of the female figures from this art province. Neither its function nor the exact place of its origin are recorded. It seems to be a *flanitokele*, a figure carved in memory of a deceased twin. Ten years ago this practice was described in an article by J. P. Imperato, an American doctor who was studying Bambara culture. By contrast with *ibeji*, the well-known Yoruba figures of a dead twin, the Bambara *flanitokele* may also feature a 'husband' or 'wife' of the dead. The reason is that when the surviving twin is married, the figure of the dead brother or sister 'marries' a figure of the opposite sex. **Height 63 cm.** Náprstek Museum, Prague.

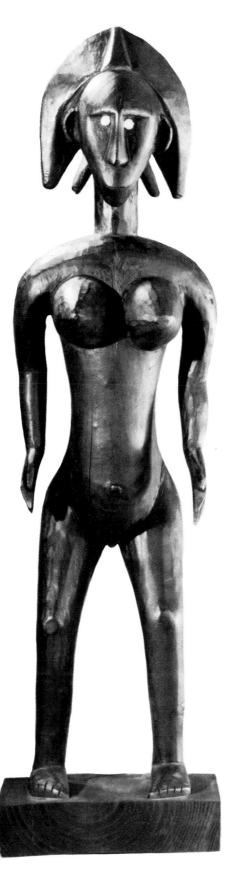

Coast does there exist a female secret society, known under the name of *bundu* or *sande*, which functions on similar lines to the male *poro*.

It is these societies that occasion much African art. Their important personages and officials appear in masks of a prescribed type while carrying out their functions. Ordinary members wear masks at the funerals of their fellows, and also on other occasions, for example, during the festival of the first harvest and other celebrations connected with the annual agricultural cycle. It is virtually impossible to enumerate all of the occasions on which the masks appear, and all of the practices connected with them. They differ from tribe to tribe and from one village to another.

Masks are not the only objects made by African artists for secret societies. There are also various insignia, carved from wood or cast from brass, as well as musical instruments used during the society's ceremonies, dance staffs, and other impedimenta. The severe enforcement of discipline within these societies is testified to by figures of hanged offenders (fig. 35) used at the initiation ceremony of new members in a secret society of the Zaire tribe of Bambole. They served to remind initiates of the punishment to be expected by those who broke the laws of the secret society.

A very different kind of African sculpture was produced in order to strengthen the prestige of the ruler and the state, and has some traits characteristic of court art. Benin bronze-casting was an example of such a court art. In Benin, and also in the Abomey kingdom in the territory of the present-day Republic of Benin, bronze-casters were organized in a guild which worked exclusively for the court. Similar guilds are also known among the Nigerian Yoruba and the Bakuba of Zaire. Court wood-carving existed, in a very developed form, in Cameroon, where it served a number of urban sultanates (in fact hardly more than village sultanates). It was needed not only for making many types of masks and commemorative figures of the ruler's ancestors, but also to decorate the palace and its luxurious fittings. Court wood-carvers were set to make items such as

11

8 *Chi-wara* dance head-dress. Bambara, Mali. Pale light wood. The surface is dark-stained, partly blackened by burning. There is a metal collar round the neck, cut from a European tin. Unlike the essentially two-dimensional dance head-dresses of a vertical type, those made in the area of Bamako are horizontal and have the character of three-dimensional sculpture. The head and trunk are carved from separate pieces of wood, which is unusual in Africa. The two parts are connected in the middle of the neck, in older examples with iron clamps or a leather collar; more recently a tin collar is often used. This example was probably made in the 1950s. **Height 25 cm, length 57.5 cm.**
Náprstek Museum, Prague.

royal sceptres, stools and thrones decorated with human and animal caryatids, the figured tops of ceremonial umbrellas, and also the symbolic insignia of court dignitaries and masters of ceremonies. Generally speaking, the more complicated the structure of the society in question, and the larger the number of social institutions it had created, the more it needed works of art for representative and ritualistic purposes hallowed by centuries-long traditions. Hence the contrast between, for example, the small tribe of Nafana in the north-eastern part of the Ivory Coast, which had no central political authority and

9 *Chi-wara* dance head-dress. Bambara, Mali. Pale wood with dark patina. This is the best known of several types of Bambara dance head-dresses in the form of stylized antelopes. It comes from the territory between Bamako and Sikasso, and in recent decades has become a popular symbol of Africa. These head-dresses are attached to a small cap which is made of vegetable materials and tied to the dancer's head under the chin. The antelope head-dresses are carved in pairs. The male's characteristics are an ornamental openwork mane and long horns curved in a bow. The female has straight horns, no mane, and is usually accompanied by a calf standing behind her or directly on her back. The antelope is said to have taught the Bambara how to cultivate the soil, and young men who dance, wearing these head-dresses at the beginning and end of the agricultural year, imitate the movements of an antelope. **Height 96.5 cm.** Náprstek Museum, Prague.

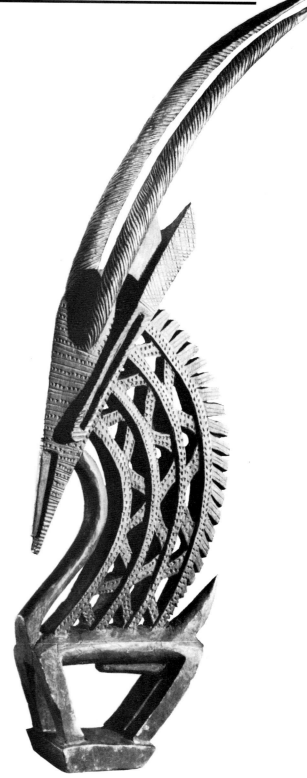

no known art but flat painted masks, and the Yoruba, who created a number of urban states and several secret societies in western Nigeria, and are famous as the most prolific African carvers, with no rivals except perhaps the Baule of the Ivory Coast. Which does not, of course, mean that all Yoruba carvings can be called court art, although certain stylistic traits are common to all Yoruba works. The court art of Benin, for example, is clearly different in style from the 'folk-art' of the Bini tribe.

Leaving aside figures connected with ancestor worship, only a small proportion of African wood-carvings serve purely religious purposes. Figures which represent gods and demons are almost a rarity, met with only

10 Face mask surmounted by a figure. Bambara, Mali. Pale wood with dark-stained glossy surface. These masks, provided with a human face and a human or animal superstructure, are used at the boys' initiation ritual in the *n'tomo* society, one of the six secret societies which boys belong to from the age of seven. **Height 56 cm.** Náprstek Museum, Prague.

11 Cross-bolt. Bambara, Mali. Pale wood with a patina created by use. The bolt is in the form of a stylized female body. A predilection for connecting planes at right angles, apparent in this piece, is typical of the entire art province from which it comes. Cross-bolts were invented in ancient Mesopotamia and spread among the West African tribes by the Arabs. The Dogon too made bolts, either in figural form or decorated. **Height 47.4 cm.** Náprstek Museum, Prague.

12 Rider on horseback; marionette. Bambara, Mali. Pale wood with dark-stained surface. Puppet-shows with marionettes carved in wood and clad in fabric costumes take place in the Mopti and San regions. The plays are farcical in character. **Height 33 cm, length 35.5 cm.**
Náprstek Museum, Prague.

here and there in the territories bordering the northern coast of the Bay of Guinea — most frequently among the Yoruba, who created a large pantheon. Supernatural beings are more often the subject of ceremonial masks, as in the buffalo masks frequently found through-

13 Figure of a standing woman. Dogon, Mali. Hard pale wood with patinated surface. Characteristic of the Dogon style are the dart-shaped nose, the elongated upper parts of the arms and trunk, the legs bent at the knees, and the hands placed on the thighs.
Height 57.3 cm.
Náprstek Museum, Prague.

out West Africa, personifying a spirit who takes the form of this animal, and the mask in the form of a large female bust, representing the goddess of fertility Nimba, made by the small Guinean tribe of Baga. On the other hand, the Congo Basin produced a larger number of figures of fetishes, based on beliefs about the influence of magic forces and serving to control them. These supernatural forces appear mostly in the shape of sexless human figures; animal figures, though known, are relatively rare. Magical practices make it possible to release these forces and to give them the desired direction, for example, against some enemy of the fetish owner. The figure form is not essential in a fetish; the same goal may be served even by a simple stone or some other object, whether animate or lifeless. It is the magical force which is of significance and which the figure has to be invested with. This is done by inserting part of a placenta or a paste consisting of various magic ingredients into a pocket carved into the trunk, top of the head or anus of the figure, or by driving nails into the surface of the body. This last custom is based on the general belief in the magical power of iron, a power shaped by antelope horns, which are stuck into the top of the head of a fetish figure or attached to its necklace.

To sum up, then, African sculpture is closely connected with traditional tribal society, and its purposes are defined by tribal cults, ceremonies and other social needs. It is based on a belief in the posthumous existence of ancestors, the existence of supernatural beings — especially spirits inhabiting the surrounding world — and the conviction that the course of events can be influenced by magical practices.

TRIBAL AND INDIVIDUAL STYLES IN AFRICAN ART

At first sight an African sculpture may appear to be an artless, almost childish attempt to give form to a given subject or idea. Thanks to this false impression, the arts of African and other tribal societies used to be described,

15

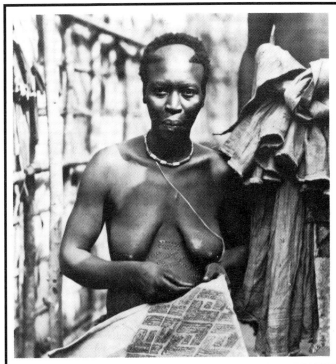

14, 15 Vessel with figures decorating the lid. Dogon, Mali. Light brown wood with dark-stained surface and patina resulting from use. The cracked lid is held together by two iron clamps. Vessels of this type served ritual purposes. The figures on the lid probably represent the Dogon Adam and Eve. The indentation round the perimeter of the base indicates that the base was formerly the lid of another vessel. The heads of both the figures are carved in the second Dogon style, characteristic of which is a sharply ridged nose which continues over the forehead and into the ridge-shaped hairstyle. **Height 43.5 cm.**

Náprstek Museum, Prague.

16 A postcard photograph from the 1930s, taken in the former Belgian Congo. It shows a woman embroidering the well-known 'Kasai velvet'; the hair above the woman's forehead is shaved off in a traditional manner.

without further distinctions, as 'primitive'. In fact, however, there is nothing primitive about them, since none of their characteristics are the result of immaturity, lack of skill, or chance. On the contrary: everything is well thought out, full of meaning and suited to its purpose — the product of a definite intention, expressed by adequate formal means, and often executed with a surprising degree of technical skill.

African figures are mostly rigid and, with a few exceptions, strictly symmetrical in relation to the vertical axis. The proportioning of the individual parts does not usually correspond to that of real figures. The heads are too large or too small, the necks are overlong, the trunks are either log-like or, contrariwise, are

reduced to a minimal structural element holding together the limbs and head. But the head itself is usually carved with admirable care, full of unexpected details and perfectly finished on the surface in stark contrast to the seemingly negligent treatment or outright omission of the limbs. The African artist gave the eyes, ears and noses of his figures stylized geometrical forms, but portrayed with naturalistic precision the hairstyle and the ritual scars on the face, forehead and other parts of the body. (This practice is known as scarification.) He treated the mouth as a regular oval or quadrangle, but showed the upper incisors realistically, filed into triangles according to the age-old tribal custom, a practice carried out on the young as part of their initiation.

None of these features are expressions of artlessness or primitivism. Each deviation from the realism that until recently dominated Western art is fully justified. It is motivated by a different scale not only of aesthetic but also of moral and social values, and by an urge to express the elements that mattered

17, 18 Free-standing female figure. Bwa (?), Burkina Faso (former Upper Volta). Pale wood covered with brown European oil-paint, eyes and loin-string made of cowries. This undocumented figure was part of the collection of Hloucha, who probably acquired it in 1930. Its attribution is hypothetical, based on some traits (the posture, the position of the arms with bracelets above the elbows, and the belly with a tattoo in the form of a cross, the navel at its centre) identical with those of the documented figure from the Museum of Ouagadougou (see William Fagg, *African Sculpture*, 1970). The face, with its very large nose, is closer in style to Bobo-Fing masks. **Height 61 cm.** Náprstek Museum, Prague.

18

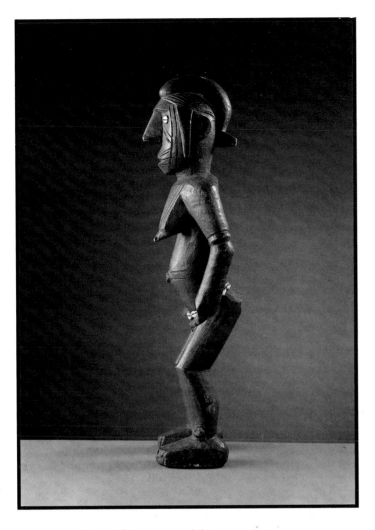

sense, or higher will develop from it ... It is an utterly perfect style, completely finished in itself.'

A tribal art style is a set of principles and creative means, canonized by tradition, which the artist of the tribal society has to respect and apply in his work. Only if he observes a generally agreed code can his work be understood, accepted, and fulfil its social function. Such canonized artistic means include the general posture of the figure, its proportions, the shape of its head, the stylized rendering of its eyebrows, eyes, nose, mouth and ears, the shape of its shoulders, the way in which its legs are connected with its trunk, and so on. As the character of these petrified stylistic features is bound up with a given community, it in fact plays a similar role to the traditional hairstyle, scarification, tattooing or mutilation of teeth; all of these, too, are symbols whose function is to maintain the tribe's identity and integrity. This is why the hairstyle and scarification are usually not stylized, even where the human figure and its individual parts are executed in a highly non-naturalistic fashion. They are fixed, stylized marks of identification which cannot be changed in any way.

They may be changed, however, by a neighbouring tribe which has taken them over and used them in its sculpture, not as a primary mark of identification but as a stylistic or decorative element. A typical example of this phenomenon is the characteristic line dividing the forehead from the hair, to be seen on the masks and figures of the Bakuba in central Zaire. This is considered to be one of the most significant elements of the Bakuba style. In fact, as documented by a photograph of a Bakuba woman from the 1930s (plate 16), this is simply an accurate, realistic reproduction of the traditional way of shaving the hair above the forehead. But in the carvings of neighbouring tribes we may meet it as a mere element of style, not founded on local practice. Many instances of this kind occur in African art.

The people who created this art lived in a small world, restricted to the territory of a single village, or at most a single tribe. This world ended at its boundaries and a new one

most to the African and his society, suppressing the irrelevant and inessential. The sum of these priorities and modes of expression comprised the traditional style, the style developed by the tribe, village or larger unit, although stylistic boundaries are not necessarily identical with ethnic or linguistic frontiers or the present political arrangement of the continent. A couple of hundred styles of this kind are known in Africa.

The African tribal style was excellently characterized by the Czech painter Josef Čapek (1887—1945), brother of the more famous writer Karel Čapek. In 1938 he wrote of this style that 'it is neither primitive in relation to anything higher ... nor has it led ... to anything higher, similar to "European work". It is fundamental, it towers simply and naturally on its own basis and nothing else. Nothing more perfect has degenerated in it ... and hardly anything better, in the European

19

19 *Numtiri* dance head-dress. Kurumba, Burkina Faso. Yellow-white light wood, coloured with white and brick-red on the brown bottom. The right horn was carved from another piece of wood. This beautiful mask, showing traces of use, is somewhat different from currently published *numtiri* dance head-dresses, since it was not attached to a basketwork cap, but rested directly on the top of the dancer's head; this was made possible by a concave hollow made in the bottom of the neck, which is coloured with brown clay. Fringes were tied to holes drilled along the edge of this hollow. The ears are erect, not curved, and do not touch the points of the horns. The head is relatively massive, and a sharp edge passes from the neck over the rounded top of the head, up to the muzzle, which is not flattened. The geometric ornament is a cosmogonic symbol.
Height 81 cm.
Private collection, Prague.

20 Pendant in the form of a buffalo. Tussian, Burkina Faso. Lost-wax casting in brass. The object's provenance is revealed by the stylization of the head, which is a miniature replica of this tribe's wooden masks.
Height 5.3 cm, length 7.6 cm. Náprstek Museum, Prague.

21 Pendant in the form of a horn-bill. Tussian, Burkina Faso. Lost-wax casting in brass. According to Herta Haselberger, these pendants were used as initiation badges by the *do* secret society, the members of which bore animal names and were organized in grades on that basis. The pendants were carried suspended from a belt. **Height 6.5 cm, length 12.5 cm.** Náprstek Museum, Prague.

began there, inhabited not only by hostile aliens but also by hostile spirits and demons. At this level of development, people were dominated by xenophobia, an ingrained dislike of foreigners; and if anything in African art can justifiably be called primitive, it is this xenophobia, which it partly reflects.

An African work of art is not, of course, a mere mechanical compound of stylistic elements petrified by tradition, just as a Gothic cathedral is more than a sum of buttresses, pointed arches, gargoyles and finials. Like a Gothic cathedral, an African figure or mask may be a masterpiece, a unique work, or, on the contrary, a product of mediocre craftsmanship or provincial imitation. In the case of African sculpture, it may even be a beginner's effort or an example of mass plagiarism.

Tribal styles of African art are in fact comparable with the historic styles of European art, at least in so far as they concerned the activity of individual artists. The traditional tribal style dictated to and imposed limitations on the African carver, in much the same way as the existence of a dominant historic style restrained and directed the European artist. The difference is that the tribal community and its tradition go beyond stylistic prescriptions, deciding which objects are to be treated by the artist (although even in this respect there are analogous situations to be found in European art). It is obvious that, in such circumstances, little scope remains for the individuality of the artist, especially as far as the choice of subjects is concerned.

Tribal styles are also different from European historic styles in the dimension of time. European styles have developed relatively quickly, and have frequently been replaced by new styles; and over the centuries this process has accelerated. By contrast, the styles of tribal communities may last for long ages, even though changing fashions and the strong individualities of carvers may cause a certain movement. The impression of stylistic immobility is undoubtedly strengthened by the fact that only very few extant works of traditional African carving can be proved to be more than a hundred or a hundred and fifty years old. Nevertheless some works which have been preserved by chance, for example in old European collections, prove that before tribal integration was distorted by western influences, tribal styles were liable to change, albeit only slightly. It is only in our century — particularly its second half — that the gradual disintegration of the tribal system and the abandonment of cultural traditions have

22 Free-standing male figure. Lobi, Burkina Faso. Hard brown wood with glossy patina on the protruding parts. The left arm is missing. This figure is one of the rare Lobi carvings known in Europe before the Second World War. It was a part of the small collection of the Czech writer Karel Čapek, who acquired it in Paris towards the end of the 1920s. This is the tenth known piece from the hand of one particular carver, including a two-faced figure (Janus figure) in the famous collection of Charles Ratton in Paris. This personal style is characterized by almond-shaped eyes with emphasized upper and lower lids and semicircular eyebrows. The glossy patina and framing of the slightly bulging eyes give these figures an extraordinarily vivid expression. A suitable title for this anonymous carver might be 'the Master of the semicircular eyebrows'. The head is shaven except for one or more strips of hair in the former traditional style of the Lobi. **Height 38.5 cm.** Private collection, Prague.

led to the neglect of the old and especially the formal prescriptions of the canonized style; the process can be traced in the datable works of 20th century carvers. As well as encouraging new forms and new aesthetic impulses, this has also often led to corrupt versions of the old art; created to satisfy the inner needs of tribal societies, it is being produced in distorted form, as artless artifacts for the tourist mass-market.

Despite what has been said above, the tribal world has not everywhere been hermetically sealed off. Until the 19th century, in Africa as perhaps nowhere else in the world, there were extensive migrations and interpenetrations of ethnic units, a process only brought to an end by the partition of the continent between the colonial powers and the creation of firm, albeit artificial, state frontiers. In earlier times there may have been constant tension and latent hostility between neighbouring tribes; but practical needs brought about trade relations based on the exchange of produce, fish, salt, textiles, iron and other goods. In some cases, even works of art became commodities of inter-tribal commerce. Trade roads necessarily crossed the territories of, and enforced contact with, other tribes. Furthermore, foreign refugees and exiles were received as welcome reinforcements by communities that felt threatened by more powerful and bellicose neighbours; and in some cases these fugitives created new, heterogeneous communities made up of various ethnic and cultural elements. Thanks to these phenomena, artistic ideas and subjects spread; elements of style were taken over and mixed together; larger stylistic areas, exceeding the framework of a single tribe, were created; and new styles and sub-styles developed. Later, in colonial and post-colonial times, the process was immeasurably speeded up. The spread of modern methods of work (for example the plantation economy), large public undertakings, transport, the development of central administration — all these result in ethnic shifts and mingling, with an accompanying cultural interchange. And so a mask of a certain type, which in its original ethnic milieu served a serious ritual purpose, is often accepted in a new environment as a

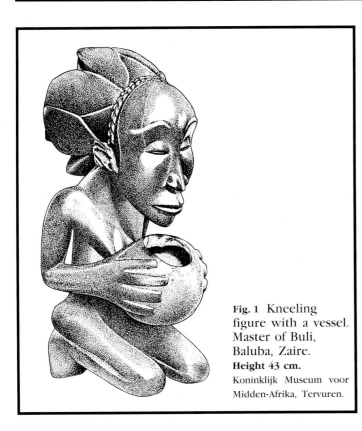

Fig. 1 Kneeling figure with a vessel. Master of Buli, Baluba, Zaire. **Height 43 cm.** Koninklijk Museum voor Midden-Afrika, Tervuren.

Fig. 2 Headrest with caryatids. Master of the Cascade Coiffures, Baluba-Shankadi, Zaire. **Height 17 cm.** Collection J. and R. Studer-Kuh, Switzerland.

comic requisite of general amusement. And sometimes, as we have seen, alien iconographic elements are taken over and applied in local carving because of their decorative appeal, without retaining any of their original significance. The spread of a style beyond its original ethnic frontier is also promoted by the migration of popular carvers who work for a larger geographical market. But cases are also known in which the carvers of a particular community work to order for the neighbouring community, complying with the alien canons of style and taste.

In such ways, tribal styles often pass beyond the boundaries of a tribe, thus ceasing to fulfil their original conservative social mission. However, it has been established that despite the genetic connection between African art and tribal society, that art did not become extinct because it crossed the boundaries of the tribe, or because the community left behind the tribal stage of development. Like all great art, African art has proved capable of surviving independently of the social organization which gave birth to it and the functions it originally performed. This fact may even provide the answer to the frequently

discussed question of the future of African art in an age of continuing detribalization and developing nation-states. There is nothing in the makeup of African art to prevent its further development. Its present degeneration, caused by the death of some social institutions which were the source of its traditional themes, and by the commercialization resulting from foreign demand, may prove to be a transitory phenomenon.

Since the 1920s African tribal styles have been intensively studied because accurate stylistic analysis made it possible to classify and determine the provenance of the quantities of undocumented African material accumulated in museums and flooding the European and American curiosity market. But although our knowledge of African art has since been expanded enormously, it is not yet comprehensive. Even now, new and hitherto unknown works and styles appear, their very existence unsuspected until a short time ago; and on the other hand we are sometimes surprised to find that traditional carving still flourishes in places where it was widely imagined to have died out early in the present century.

In some areas, however, our knowledge of African art — formerly supposed to be an entirely anonymous product — has become so extensive that we are able to name not only the style but the carver, even one active a couple of decades ago, or at least the workshop or the carver's family. Thanks to William Fagg, the greatest advances have taken place in the study of Yoruba art. As well as familiarity with the terrain, the expert arrives at his knowledge through a comparative study of large amounts of material, along with all the available data concerning the location and other circumstances in which exhibits were acquired. It is only such an approach to African works of art which may enable us to discern, within a particular tribal style, characteristic individual differences between the means, techniques and skills of different carvers — in short, to determine the master, though unnamed, whose hand is revealed by his personal style. In classifying anonymous medieval European paintings, we use such terms as 'the Master of Flémalle' or 'the Master of the Female-Half-Lengths'; and similarly in African art we refer to a master defined by the name of the place where his works have been found, or by his characteristic style. Such a master was identified for the first time in the Baluba territory in Zaire. He is called the Master of Buli (fig. 1), after the village or area where the only two documented carvings by him were found, although he may have worked in a quite different place. His works are mostly chiefs' stools with human caryatids. (Incidentally, one such stool with two caryatids was bought towards the end of the 1970s by the Metropolitan Museum of Art in New York for one million dollars, the highest price ever paid for a work of tribal art.) Another anonymous carver with a personal style, called the Master of the Cascade Coiffures (fig. 2), was identified in the Shankadi tribe of the Baluba. His finely carved figures are smaller than those of the Master of Buli, and although also mostly caryatids, are not stools but head-

23 Mask with a flat superstructure. Nafana (?), Ivory Coast. Soft painted wood. Heavily damaged by insects. The mask was acquired by the museum in an exchange with H. L. Diamond of Vienna in 1968. It is said to have been collected in Ghana and to have originated among the Dagari, neighbours of the Gurunsi, in Burkina Faso. The colour combination is untraditional and seems to have been inspired by the French tricolour, which suggests that the mask came from one of the former French colonies; it might therefore be the work of the Dagari in Burkina Faso, or of the Nafana in the Ivory Coast. They are worn once a year in pairs at nocturnal purification dances called *bedu*. The male mask has a superstructure in the form of a horizontal crescent; the rounded superstructure of the female mask probably represents the full moon. **Height 121 cm.**
Náprstek Museum, Prague.

24

rests, and are characterized by peculiar two-storey coiffures. Later on, William Fagg traced such anonymous masters in Benin and Yoruba art. Towards the end of the 1970s the Italian Africanist Ezio Bassani attempted to assign Bambara figures and masks of a certain type from the southern part of the Republic of Mali to three anonymous carvers. One of the carvings, a sitting female figure assigned to the hypothetical carver whom Bassani calls the Master of the Rapacious Profile (Maestro del profilo di rapace), is reproduced in the present book (plate 4). With ever-increasing research, the number of masters ascertained in this way will undoubtedly grow; and although we shall never learn their names, what they looked like, or the stories of their lives, we shall be able to know them through the works they created in their own individual styles.

THE AFRICAN ARTIST AND HIS WORK

Like tribal art in general, African art is usually described as being of anonymous authorship. It was perhaps this designation that led to a long-standing lack of interest in its creators, the African artists. One reason for this was that the first collectors of masks, figures and other works of African art, in the 19th century, did not think of what they were collecting as art, let alone recognize the superiority of its masterpieces to the academic European art of their own time. In so far as their interest went beyond souvenir-hunting, it

24 Figure of a seated woman. Senufo (Siena), Ivory Coast. Pale wood with black-stained patinated surface. An initiated young woman seated on a four-legged stool is one of the most frequent subjects of Senufo carving. Explanations of the function of these figures vary; according to some writers, they represent a reward for the young man who proves himself fastest in a hoeing contest. This example is a masterpiece from a workshop whose carvings are characterized by a peculiar treatment of the human body. This is treated as two intersecting vertical flat surfaces; the area of the shoulders is flattened breadthwise, whereas the belly and chest are flattened as if intended to be viewed from the side. The headdress is in the form of a guinea-fowl sitting on eggs.
Height 28.5 cm. Náprstek Museum, Prague.

was directed towards the religious or cultic significance of these objects rather than their aesthetic quality. Such an attitude resulted from their 'primitive' appearance, and perhaps also from the fact that these first collectors seldom came into direct contact with African artists. Wood-carvings and other works of art were often acquired by Europeans by chance and indirectly — through the mediation of coastal tribes, sometimes as spoils or, later on, from travelling Muslim merchants who had neither religious nor aesthetic sympathy with these works.

In the early 1900s, when the development of European taste made it possible to recognize the artistic qualities of African sculptures, they were at first treated as something resembling natural phenomena rather than works made by men. This was doubtless encouraged by the fact that in public collections African works of art used to be included in general ethnographic collections, which in turn belonged to departments in museums of natural history. Vestiges of a 'natural history' approach were also observable until quite recently in many a book on African art. The result was that individual works of art used to be treated not as separate human creations, conditioned by historical developments, but in a similar way to unchanging types of flora and fauna.

This situation changed only slowly. From the 19th century onwards, scholars and travellers did record various remarks about African works of art; but these remarks were either too fragmentary or too generalized and superficial to be very useful. It is only since the 1930s that attention has been systematically paid to the creators of African art, the development of which has become the subject of specialized research. We still do not know the position of artists and their conditions of work in all African tribal communities, and we shall probably never know them in places where this work has ended; but African art has at least ceased to be a mysterious continent of which only the outlines are known, and in many cases has shed its anonymity.

It is true, however, that African society itself never attached as much importance as

Fig. 3 Male *bieri* reliquary figure. Fang, Gabon. **Height 39.4 cm.** Former collection of Dr. Emanuel Klein, New York.

Europeans do to the personality of the artist as an individual. Nor, of course, was there an art-conscious élite of the sort that can only arise in a society with a much more complicated structure than that of any tribal community. But the African did not care any less about the personality of an artist in his society than, for instance, an ordinary Christian cared (or cares even today) about the identity of the artist who painted the altarpiece in front of which he prayed. Such a believer rarely questions whether he is kneeling to a masterpiece by a renowned master or a piece of work by an ordinary craftsman, a copyist or a plagiarist; the name makes no difference as far as the efficacy of the prayer is concerned. Similarly from the African's point of view it is of no importance who has made a figure of the tribal ancestor, a mask or a politico-ritual symbol of which he makes use. Unlike the European, however, he usually knows the author of these artifacts, who is almost always a contemporary member of the same community. Moreover he is often aware of the artist's competence (or otherwise), since he may wish to have commissions of his own carried out.

In this respect the situation described by Fernandez in the Fang tribe of Gabon is particularly illuminating. Undoubtedly one of

the loveliest and most sought-after works of African art is the *bieri* (fig. 3), a type of figure connected with the Fang cult of ancestors. *Bieri* statuettes represent both male and female figures; by means of protrusions at the lower end of the trunk they were slotted into cylindrically shaped reliquaries made of bark in which the ancestors' bones were kept. As well as many *bieri* that are veritable master-pieces of carving, however, there are nume-rous mediocre or even poor examples. These were made because most pious Fang tribes-men did not care about aesthetic criteria, but for cultic reasons preferred to have a figure of the dead carved by a relative. Nevertheless the Fang were capable of appreciating exceptional talent, and this is why some of them ordered figures from renowned carvers, irrespective of kinship considerations. With-out such orders, the outstanding artists who created the finest *bieri* could hardly have de-veloped among the Fang.

The plastic arts, carving and bronze-casting are all male prerogatives in traditional African art. However, an excellent carver among the Dan described the organization of his work as follows: his apprentice prepared the wood, one of the carver's wives did the rough car-ving, and he himself only added the fine detail and finishing. This case, recorded by Hans Himmelheber, is probably the exception that proves the rule.

Making pottery, on the other hand, is a traditional occupation of African women, but the division of work according to gender va-ries from place to place. In some tribes, men even take part in the lowly task of making domestic pots, whereas in others, their

25 Figure of a rider on horseback (*bandéguélé*). Senufo (Siena), Ivory Coast. Pale wood with surface stained black. Before being stained with black, the surface was covered with red geometric decoration. This figure comes from the same workshop as the example in plate 20. Senufo figures of riders holding in their right hands what may be a stylized gun, as in this case, or a spear or knife, personify the spirits who assist the diviners in their operations. The figure of the horse is always smaller than that of the rider. The horse's head is in the same style as Senufo animal masks; the legs are rendered schematically as two moulded slabs, much as in European folk toys.
Height 41 cm, length 19 cm.
Náprstek Museum, Prague.

participation is confined to the manufacture of ritual wares; among the Asante of Ghana, and also among the Nigerian Tiv, men were the sole producers of figure pipes. However, both vessels decorated with figures and independent ceramic figures made by women are known (for example from Nigeria). These works prove that women share the extraordinary talent for the plastic arts.

The discussion that follows will be restricted to carving, which is the most significant of the three-dimensional African arts and one about which we possess the fullest information. It is an art made for, and also by, farmers, since most African artists are themselves at least partly dependent on crops that they grow in their own fields. When they devote all of their time to carving, all the work in the fields is done by their wives and children, or by apprentices. An exception occurs in Calabar in Nigeria, where the people live among mangrove swamps on small islands; here the main occupation of the carvers is naturally the same as that of their fellow-tribesmen, namely fishing. This exceptional case confirms the observation that in traditional society the African carver could not make his living exclusively by practising his craft.

Nor was his vocation always self-chosen. Some tribes in the western Sudan, for example, are divided into castes that probably reflect their polyethnic origins; and his caste determines whether or not a man shall become a carver. Among the Yoruba in Nigeria, carving is usually associated with the craft of the joiner. In the large Bambara tribe, in the

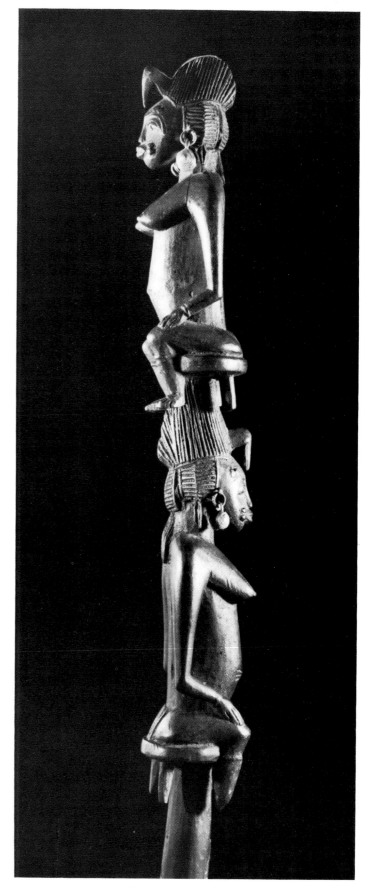

26 *Daleu* ceremonial staff. Senufo (Siena), Ivory Coast. Pale wood, dark-stained, bells cast in brass, brass sheet, and a forged metal point at the end. Slightly crusty patina on the top. According to Holas these staffs are carried by boys returning to the village after being initiated into the *lo* society. Wassing (1970) considers them to be a prize for winning a hoeing contest (although other authorities assert that the prizes are wooden figures of flying birds attached to a pole). *Daleu* staffs usually end with a figure of a woman seated on a four-legged stool; two figures, one above the other, as in this case, are a rarity. It is quite possible that a staff with two figures signifies a higher rank in the hierarchy of the society. In the Senufo female figures seated on a four-legged stool, the figures' legs merge into two of the stool legs, often even replacing them, as in this instance. **Height 164.5 cm.**
Náprstek Museum, Prague.

28

Republic of Mali, carving is one of the duties of the caste of smiths, logically so, since the smiths must develop carving skills in order to make wooden handles for the iron implements that are their main products. Among the southern neighbours of the Bambara, the Senufo (Siena) tribe in the northern part of the Ivory Coast, there is a caste of carvers called *kule*, who inhabit separate villages or quarters. The same caste also exists among the Bambara. Its position in the social hierarchy is even lower than that of the caste of smiths, which is itself not particularly high; yet the Bambara smiths are prepared to admit that the members of *kule* are better carvers than themselves. Himmelheber recorded an interesting statement by a Bambara smith, who said that wood came from the bush to the *kule* carvers of its own accord, but never obliged the smiths in such a way.

But if the carver does not occupy a particularly privileged position in African society, his work is nevertheless appreciated and held in esteem. The practice of the craft was never despised, as is demonstrated by cases in which carving was done by leading figures in the community. Among the Bakuba in Zaire, carving is even considered to be the most esteemed of all crafts. A Bakuba king is reported to have compelled his son to learn carving, and King Bobeken himself carved wooden boxes. The paramount chief of the neighbouring Bashilele tribe (belonging to the style area of Bakuba art) carved cups in the form of human heads for the ritual drinking of palm-wine, and was especially famous for making drums decorated with reliefs. According to K. Nicklin, the highest chief of the Bangwa tribe in north-western Cameroon

27 Figure of a *calao* horn-bill. Senufo (Siena), Ivory Coast. Pale wood with traces of brown-grey paint on the surface. Thick patina on the beak, legs and rounded base. The horn-bill is considered a symbol of fertility by the Senufo. The long beak symbolizes the male sexual organ, and the bulbous belly a pregnant woman. Painted figures of this bird, up to 150 cm in height, appeared in European collections in relatively large numbers only in the 1950s, after the iconoclastic *massa* cult had spread among the Senufo, making them hostile to their former practices; until that time the figures stood in sacred groves which the uninitiated were not allowed to enter. **Height 42 cm.**
Náprstek Museum, Prague.

28 *Kpelie* face mask. Senufo (Siena), Ivory Coast. Yellow-white light wood with brown-black stained surface; red-brown pigment stains on the stylized hair. The flat horns of this mask of the *lo* secret society represent the hairstyle of Senufo women, arranged in two plaits. According to Himmelheber's interpretation, the bizarre projections on the perimeter of the mask represent the wings, tail feathers and legs of the sacred calao bird (horn-bill), and the bulging forehead of the mask his chest. **Height 33.8 cm.** Náprstek Museum, Prague.

carved dance masks, personally covering them with skin.

Except in cases where carvers belong to a hereditary caste, practice of the art is open to everybody. In tribes such as the Dogon, all boys had to acquire a rudimentary knowledge of carving in the bush-school, even though carving as a regular craft was the business of the smiths. Where there are no provisions of this sort or caste rules, the craft is usually passed down from father to son. But this is not obligatory, and even a person with no family history of carving may take up the craft. The motivation for such a choice tends to be economic, although there have been cases in which a drive towards artistic self-realization was the decisive factor.

The novice who is born into a family of woodcarvers is generally taught by his father or maternal uncle, because apprenticeships must otherwise be paid for; and, moreover, the family loses a hand if the boy leaves his home. The term of an apprenticeship varies, but the maximum is about three years. The apprentice, whether or not he is a member of the family, does not spend more than half his time learning the craft; he must also work in the fields as a part-payment for his tuition. Sometimes the apprenticeship is divided into a number of separate periods, between each of which the boy may spend a couple of months back at his own home. The master's fee varies according to local custom. As well as payment by work, it may include items such as a goat or a few chickens. And among the Bakuba of Zaire, the payment received by an apprentice for his first independently made carving belongs to the master. But not every carver takes in unrelated apprentices: in some places the craft is practically confined to the carvers' families, who treat it as a hereditary professional secret.

On the other hand, instances of self-taught carves are far from rare, especially where ritual requirements do not compel them to work in seclusion from the rest of the community, so that the procedures of established craftsmen can be freely observed. Such self-taught carvers are found among the Dan on the Ivory Coast, for example; they specialize in making anthropomorphic spoons, because

29 Animal helmet mask. Senufo (Siena), Ivory Coast. Pale wood with surface stained black. The Senufo have a large number of animal masks used for ritual purposes by the *lo* secret society, or, as in this case, the *korubla* society, the aim of which is to combat sorcery. This mask represents a hyena (*kanamto*, according to Holas). Different sources give these animal masks different names, probably depending on the place where the name was recorded.
Height 22.5 cm, length 32 cm.
Náprstek Museum, Prague.

such spoons may be carved in public. Specialization sometimes occurs because the carver has had no opportunity to become acquainted with another genre: Robin Horton questioned eight carvers among the Ijo of Calabar in Nigeria, and discovered that none of them had served a formal apprenticeship or had even seen any other carver at work. Most of them had started carving by trying to copy for themselves a mask owned by an older member of their family for a dance performance. Since the mask they made was liked, they had obtained orders for more, and had later increased their reputations by, for example, making figures for sanctuaries.

The formal apprenticeship involves executing work of progressively greater difficulty. Thus among the Baule of the Ivory Coast, studied in detail by Himmelheber, an apprentice first of all carves spoons, moves on to loom pulleys decorated with little heads of men or animals, and only then starts to make complete human figures. Not all novices prove capable of mastering every genre —

but then, even accomplished masters sometimes prefer to specialize. In the Bakuba style area of Zaire, where cultural tradition required even many utility objects to be carved with great skill, in eight out of twelve tribes the carvers specialized in artifacts of a particular type, which they sold to members of their own and other tribes.

African carvers mostly worked to order, either from individuals or from secret societies. It was exceptional for them to have carvings in stock, although Baule carvers kept stocks of small profane artifacts and individually conceived works that would be given their final form by a gilder, after the object had been purchased.

In Africa the basic material for carving is wood. Less widely used materials include ivory, which was in some places reserved for carvings executed for the royal court; it was employed on a larger scale only in the carvings of the Bakongo in the Lower Congo region and, for initiation purposes among the Balega (Warega) in eastern Zaire. Other materials occasionally used were hippopotamus' teeth, bones, stone (especially steatite, which is relatively easy to work) and reed-pith.

Long museum experience has taught the present writer that Europeans are interested in the kind of wood used for African carving, which they usually suppose to be ebony, probably because so many figures are dark brown or black. In actual fact the traditional carver never employed ebony or similar woods. It is only present-day Africans who use ebony in their work; these include the well-known Makonde carvers of popular modern sculptures in Tanzania and Mozambique, as well as makers of (usually worthless) souvenirs, who have realized that ordinary tourists are not interested in art, but are attracted to a fine wood spiced with an exotic and sometimes also erotic flavour.

A hard wood such as ebony can only be worked with modern imported steel tools, which were not of course available to traditional African wood-carvers. Then what kind of wood was used by African carvers? The answer is: many different kinds. In some places, cultic tradition prescribes a particular kind, whereas elsewhere the type of wood

30 Handle of a loom pulley. Senufo (Siena), Ivory Coast. Pale wood, black-stained, with glossy functional patina. Among the Dogon, the Senufo and the tribes of the eastern half of the Ivory Coast, these pulleys are decorated with small human or animal heads, often representing the spirit under whose protection the weaver and his loom are believed to stand. Here the head has a bird hairstyle typical of Senufo women. **Height 13 cm.**
Private collection, Prague.

varies according to the kind of carving it is to be used for. Generally speaking, however, softer woods are preferred because they are easier to work; harder woods are usually selected only where the object is expected to survive the attentions of white ants for a considerable period of time. Because greater ease of working is important to him, the African carver, unlike his European counterpart, uses the raw timber of recently-felled trees, despite the fact that this may cause lengthwise splitting in the carving, a flaw that often spoils the appearance of some beautiful masks and figures in western collections. We must remember, however, that African carvers work for contemporary ritual purposes, not for the aesthetic satisfaction of future generations of museum visitors. Naturally they must adapt themselves to available resources, sometimes having to use the centuries-old wood of dead trunks preserved in dry sand, as is often the case in the arid areas of Mali.

African carving tools are very simple. The most important is the adze, a slightly curved blade attached crosswise, roughly at right angles, to a longer wooden helve. The carver works sitting on the ground, holding the wooden log in place with one hand or foot, and by means of regular strokes with the adze he liberates the future figure or mask from the log. He creates the basic outlines with a large adze, then works out grosser details with a smaller one. An ordinary knife is used to carve fine details such as the eyes, the mouth, striations representing the hair, and ornamental scars on the trunk and face, thus giving the sculpture its final form. Where tradition requires the surface of the carving to be smooth, showing no trace of tool marks, the artist finishes off with rough-surfaced leaves using them in the same way as a European craftsman might use sand paper or something similar.

The finished sculpture usually then receives its final treatment. It is stained dark with various plant juices or by dipping it in river silt for a couple of days, it is saturated with red palm oil and polished, or coloured with various natural pigments mixed with kaolin, coloured clays or even imported oil-paints. In Cameroon the entire surfaces of some carvings were covered with colourful glass beads; in Gabon, copper or brass sheets were used. The eyes of various figures and masks have been filled with glass beads, the mother-of-pearl buttons of European shirts, or potsherds. Teeth are made of potsherds, metal or reed, and among the Makonde of

31 Stylized female figure. Bijogo, Guinea-Bissao, Bubaque Island, Bijante village. Pale wood with patinated glossy surface. The surface of the hair is highlighted by a coating of vermillion paint. A string of many-coloured glass beads encircles the waist. The figure belonged to the collection of E. Hintz, Berlin, and was published for the first time by E. V. Sydow in his *Handbuch* (1930). Young unmarried women carried these dolls, intended to promote fertility, hitching the forked legs against their sides or backs, much as African women carry their little children. **Height 71.3 cm.** Náprstek Museum, Prague.

32 Figure of a standing woman. Bijogo, Guinea-Bissao. Pale wood without any surface treatment or patina; only the hair and the upper part of the rounded base are painted brown-black. The figure was probably intended to stand on the house altar dedicated to ancestors. The hair, cut straight around the head, is in a typical traditional Bijogo style. The black paint put on the hair imitates the traditional dressing of the hair with mud (cf. the vermillion paint in plate 31).
Height 31.5 cm.
Náprstek Museum, Prague.

Mozambique human hair was inserted into slits on the top of the figure's head. Not all of this work was executed by the carver himself. For instance, among the Ijo of Calabar the colouring of a mask was done by the customer, and in other tribes the owner himself renewed the colouring of a mask he had been using for years. Among the Akan peoples of Ghana and the Ivory Coast, there are craftsmen who specialize in covering with golden foil the symbolic carvings of particular political significance.

With a few exceptions, African sculptures are based on the vertical axis of the tree trunk, and are carved from its middle, in order to make the work easier. This is why we usually find a hole in the middle of the top of the head, between the legs or in the centre of the base, representing the soft heart of the tree. The majority of African carvings are monoxylous, which means that they are carved from a single piece of wood; it is rare to find sculpture in which, for example, the carver has complemented a figure with an arm made from another piece of wood, or modelled a missing part from some plastic material.

A carver who makes figures personifying supernatural beings is operating in an area which is very dangerous to himself and to the entire community. In a culture that believes in the omnipresence of spirits, it is first of all necessary for the carver to propitiate the spirit of the tree he is going to cut down; this is achieved by a preliminary rite, for example by killing a cock. The carving itself must be done in a state of ritual purity, which may involve behaviour such as sexual abstinence for a prescribed period before or during the work. The actual practices differ according to local customs and beliefs. In some places the carver must take care not to insult the spirit whom the sculpture is to personify; elsewhere the work in progress is considered nothing but a lifeless piece of wood until it is finished. Among the Guro in the Ivory Coast, a chicken is sacrificed by the carver while he is working on a mask, or else, later on, by its owner. It is only then that the mask is given life and the spirit may enter it. In some places, tradition requires the carver to work unobserved and in isolation from the community,

either in the bush or the furthest outskirts of the village. In other tribes, people may watch him at his work without infringing any ritual prohibitions. Carvers of the Ekoi (Ejagham) tribe in the Upper Cross region in Eastern Nigeria were allowed to work in public while making the wooden parts of mask headdresses in the form of human heads, but the masks had to be covered with skin in seclusion. All such ritual practices are very varied, differing from tribe to tribe. They appear to have no direct connection with the creative process, but the ritual significance with which they surround the carver's work almost certainly acts as a spur to creation.

HISTORICAL DIMENSIONS OF AFRICAN ART

The standard way of presenting African art tends to create the impression that it is an art without history. A selection of photographs and a set of explanatory captions acquaint the reader with typical specimens of the styles found in various parts of Africa; but in doing so they give the impression that African art is fixed and unchanging. In the case of European art the reader knows better, since he or she has some familiarity with the historical context in which works have been created; but the unfamiliar aspect of African art makes its apparent fixity perfectly plausible. In reality, African sculptures, masks and carved ceremonial implements are also products of historical development, even though our knowledge of this history may be woefully inadequate.

As we have seen, the majority of surviving works of African tribal art were made during the last hundred or hundred and fifty years; but in many areas our knowledge is confined to a much shorter period. The numbers of surviving objects also vary greatly: for some areas, dozens, or even hundreds, of carvings have been acquired over the last two centuries, making it possible to compare and classify them, and to identify chronological and other relationships; whereas elsewhere there may be no more than a handful of examples, acquired over a very short period.

33 Standing male (?) figure. Bijogo, Guinea-Bissao (?). Pale wood with painted surface and no patina. The hair blackened by burning. The style of the unpainted hair and some other traits suggest that this undocumented figure may be assigned to the Bijogo. It is not clear whether this is a male or female figure, since the small projection on the belly may represent

Naturally, the oldest examples are of great interest, since only they can provide us with clues to the earlier history of African art.

Historical records show that from the 15th century, African carvings were included in the collections of curios that had become fashionable among feudal magnates and wealthy merchants. But, because of the contempt felt by Europeans for Africans and their culture from the 17th century, almost none of these artefacts have been preserved. Perhaps the only exception is a wooden plaque, decorated with rich relief carving, of the kind that was used at the Yoruba divination called *ifa*. This divination was taken over from the Nigerian Yoruba by some tribes living farther west. The extant plaque originated in Ardra in the Republic of Benin (formerly Dahomey) and it is impossible to determine the ethnic origin of its author. It formerly belonged to the famous Weickmann Collection, but is now in the City Museum of Ulm in South Germany. The plaque was brought to Europe at the beginning of the 17th century, but in artistic conception it is identical with analogous Yoruba plaques used up to the present day. On the other hand, details of the figures of the relief reveal striking affinities with the figures of the Ewe tribe, collected in what is now Togo at the beginning of the century, as recently demonstrated in a convincing way by Ezio Bassani.

Although we have no exact idea how many African carvings became part of the oldest European collections, or which types they belonged to, there could not have been many of them, for they represented no more than exotic curios with nothing to recommend them to the European taste of that time. However, the European upper classes *were* familiar with African ivory carving, for ivory had been known and admired since antiquity. That is why Portuguese merchants, having reached the West African coast by sea and recognized the skill of local carvers, started to give them commissions for ivory artifacts,

34 Figure of a hippopotamus. Bijogo, Guinea-Bissao, Orango Island. Light-brown wood with faintly patinated and slightly glossy surface. The figure probably served as a fetish. This piece was a part of the collection of E. Hintz, Berlin. **Length 17 cm.**
Náprstek Museum, Prague.

knowing that there would be a demand for them in Europe. These artifacts initially comprised oliphants (hunting horns made of tusks), table utensils, especially spoons and forks, luxurious salt-cellars and pepperboxes decorated with human figures and entire scenes on their high, sometimes openwork bases and convex lids. A horn and a spoon of this kind are reproduced here (plates 1, 2, 3). As well as the general design of salt-cellars, the relief decoration on hunting horns was undoubtedly influenced by European models, most probably woodcut illustrations of books and perhaps also the pictures painted on playing-cards.

These Afro-Portuguese ivory carvings (to use the name given to them by William Fagg) originated in two areas. A relatively small number were made by carvers from the Benin kingdom, but the overwhelming majority were the work of artists of the Sherbro or Bulom tribes (now in Sierra Leone). Though affected by European influences, they are important for our knowledge of African art. This is because the figure decoration of objects made by the Sherbro, especially salt-cellars, shows many characteristics of the local style. Some of the figures are of Africans. The style of these figures corresponds to that of the steatite figures called *nomoli* (plate 5), found buried in Sierra Leone in the territory at one

a navel. As women played a leading role in traditional Bijogo society, however, male figures were rare here. **Height 42 cm.**
Náprstek Museum, Prague.

time inhabited by the Sherbro and Temne tribes. (They were later driven out by the Mandingo.) This stylistic correspondence makes it possible to date the steatite figures to the 16th century.

Because of the unpropitious climate and the activities of termites, it is exceptional for older wood-carvings to be preserved. The oldest is the animal head excavated in central Angola and published at the beginning of the 1970s. According to radiocarbon dating it originated in the 8th century AD. It remains unique, having no stylistic or other affinities with any artifact known in this area from a later period.

The first large surviving group of relatively old wood-carvings consists of figures found in tombs hewn in the rock walls of the Bandiagara Cliffs; these are in the southern part of the Republic of Mali, in the territory now inhabited by the Dogon tribe. The Dogon, themselves makers of very elaborate wood sculpture, attribute these figures to their mythical ancestors, whom they call the Tellem. Radiocarbon dating assigned some of the figures to the 13th—15th centuries. However, this dating, as well as the attribution of the figures to the legendary Tellem, is uncertain. The carbon 14 method is based on the fact that, once an organism has perished, the deposits of radioactive carbon in it decay at a known rate so that a calculation of the amount lost makes it possible to ascertain the approximate date at which the organism ceased to exist. In the case of a wooden sculpture, radiocarbon dating tells us when the tree was felled — not when the figure was made. As William Fagg observed, 'carbon 14 dating refers... to the death of a tree, and not

35 *Banda* anthropo-zoomorphic mask. Nalu, Guinea-Bissao. Pale wood with rich colouring. The mask is connected with the highest grade of the *simo* secret society, and was said to kill an uninitiated person who looked at it. Undocumented pieces such as this one are usually assigned to the Nalu, but the mask was used also by other tribes of this area, especially the Baga and Landuman. William Fagg sees a Portuguese influence in the painting and the carved superstructure. In this example the forehead is surmounted by a carved house of European type. The mask was originally higher, the tips of its horns having disappeared. The toothed muzzle is derived from that of a crocodile or shark. **Height 128 cm.** Náprstek Museum, Prague.

36 *Koni* dance headpiece. Nalu, Guinea-Bissao. Pale wood, painted. The headpiece represents a bird with a snake on its back. At the ceremony concluding the initiation ritual, the dancer wearing a *koni* headpiece accompanies a performer in a large mask in the form of an erect python. Like the *banda* mask (plate 35), this headpiece may be found among the neighbouring tribes, so that its attributed provenance remains hypothetical. **Height 33.5 cm.**
Náprstek Museum, Prague.

37 Mask. Baga, Guinea. Pale wood with surface stained black. Eyes made of convex nail-heads. A necklace of yellow glass beads. This dance mask, in the form of a bust of a nubile young woman, is a lesser known variant of the huge mask representing Nimba, the goddess of fertility. The members of the *simo* secret society perform wearing this mask at harvest-home festivities. The bust rests on the dancer's head, the hole below the breasts making it possible to see. The dancer is completely covered with fringes made of vegetable fibres that hang from the edges of the mask. The dancer controls its movements by means of two legs in front. **Height 71 cm.**
Náprstek Museum, Prague.

to the birth of a sculpture' (*African Tribal Images*, No. 6). The difficulty of dating the figures from the Bandiagara tombs is reinforced by the fact that in this arid area, African carvers sometimes make use of dead trees which may have been preserved in dry, loose soil for an indeterminate length of time. For this reason, the radiocarbon dating of the 'Tellem' figures is reliable only where it can be supported by analogous results obtained by analysing other organic remains found in association with them. The ethnic attribution of the 'Tellem' figures presents another difficulty: both their subjects, drawing from cosmogonic myths, and their style reveal a close affinity with the works of the later Dogon, so that on occasion one may even identify the

simultaneous presence of both Tellem and Dogon features in a single figure. Thus the so-called Tellem carvings probably represent nothing more than an earlier stage of development of Dogon art. Items from this stage might prove to be datable to the 17th or 18th century, or in some cases to an even earlier period. From the point of view of the development of tribal art, the latter eventuality would be of greater interest, representing an altogether unique case in which the development of a tribal style could be followed through artifacts dating over several centuries without any interruption.

Exceptional in all African art, but more problematic as far as its age is concerned, is a group of commemorative figures of Bakuba

39

38 Figure of a standing woman. Baga, Guinea. Wood with black-stained surface, eyes made of iron, necklace woven from raffia fibres. Stylistic features identical with those of plate 37 indicate that this undocumented figure originated among the southern Baga. Nothing is known about its function, but the exaggerated breasts and the bulging belly may mean that it was connected with the fertility cult, perhaps even representing the goddess Nimba. **Height 68.5 cm.** Náprstek Museum, Prague.

Fig. 4 Portrait figure of King Shamba Balongongo. Bushongo, Zaire. **Height 56 cm.** British Museum, London.

nyimi, named Shamba Balongongo (or, according to Cornet, Shyaam Mbula Ngoong), who ruled between 1600 and 1620. He is a kind of Bakuba culture hero to whom tradition ascribes two technological and cultural innovations. One was the introduction of a game now played in most parts of the African continent and known as *mankala*. The other was the custom of carving an idealized commemorative royal portrait figure, the *ndop* (fig. 4), during the lifetime of every Bakuba king. He is always shown as a stout man sitting with crossed legs, with a relatively large head taking up about a third of the height of the sculpture. The figure is 50—70 cm high and usually carries a short sword at its left side. On the front of the base, a symbol is carved that helps to identify which king is represented by the figure. Thus Shamba Balongongo's portrait bears a table for *mankala* on its base, because it was he who introduced the game; King Mikope Mbula (or, according to Cornet, Miko mi Mbul) was famous for social reforms and for marrying a slave girl, which is why the base of his portrait is decorated with a female figure; another *nyimi* was an excellent smith, so a miniature anvil is shown; and so on. A large number of recent replicas of these figures are known, since they have become popular with the tourist market. The originals,

kings from central Zaire. These *ndops* were first collected by a Hungarian, Torday, and an Englishman, Joyce, in 1907. The sculptures are now kept in the British Museum and the Musée Royale d'Afrique Centrale, Tervuren. Torday and Joyce also recorded a genealogy of 124 rulers of the Bakuba kingdom, preserved by oral tradition. The most extraordinary personality in the sequence was the king, or

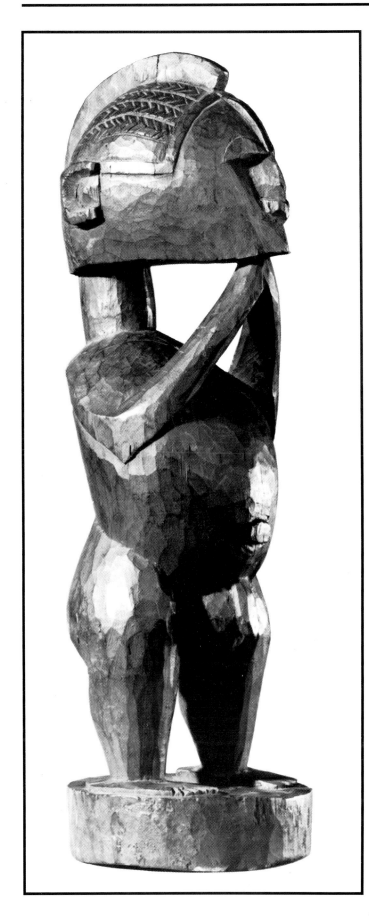

39 Figure of a standing man. Baga, Guinea. Wood with black-stained surface. Figures of this type, in the northern Baga style, identical in the conception of the head with the large masks of the goddess Nimba, are said to have served the *simo* society as symbols of fertility and protectors of maternity. However, male figures such as this one were also placed as guardians on the roads leading to the village. **Height 42 cm.**
Náprstek Museum, Prague.

40 *Anok* cult object. Nalu, Guinea-Bissao (?). Hard dark-brown wood with slightly glossy surface. Eyes made of heads of brass hobnails. This requisite of the *simo* society is used by many tribes. The *anok* is kept in a cylindrical base (lost in the present instance) from which it is taken during the dance. Members of the *simo* society dance round the *anok* at harvest-home festivities. Magical substances are put into the geometric holes in the head. **Length 50.5 cm.**
Náprstek Museum, Prague.

however, collected by Torday and Joyce when the Bakuba were still unaffected by contact with the Europeans, are only five or six in number. Adding further examples from other sources, the total number of historic *ndops* is said to be eighteen. But it is doubtful whether these figures were really made during the lifetime of all the kings they represent. Some appear to have been made by the hand of a single carver, and therefore seem likely to be replicas of older models, created as a kind of genealogical gallery of Bakuba kings. Even this does not seriously challenge the antiquity of the art itself, because there is little doubt that it was introduced by Shamba Balongongo and that its iconography was fixed.

Before becoming the ruler of his tribe, Shamba Balongongo is said to have spent a long time in the west, where the old kingdom

41 *Sowei* (*nöwo*) helmet mask. Mende, Sierra Leone. Yellow-white light wood, stained brown on the surface. The hollow of the mask blackened by burning. These helmet masks are also used by the dignitaries of the *bundu* or *sande* female secret society in some other tribes of Sierra Leone and Liberia, such as the Vai, Gola or Temne. More than half of the lozenge-shaped face is usually taken up by the forehead. The form of the face is almost constant, the elements most frequently altered being the hairstyle and added ornaments and symbols. There are great differences in mastery between the individual carvers. The projections on the back part of the mask's perimeter represent a duiker's horns, which are believed to possess magic powers. The rounded rings on the neck of the mask are usually interpreted as adipose folds which are said to be a symbol of affluence and sign of a woman's mature beauty. But according to Frederick Lamp, who has recently studied these masks among the Temne, the folds represent the abdominal segments of a butterfly chrysalis. **Height 41 cm.** Náprstek Museum, Prague.

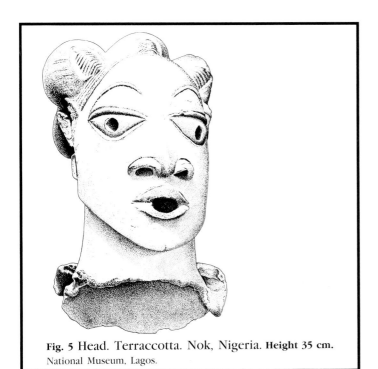

Fig. 5 Head. Terraccotta. Nok, Nigeria. **Height 35 cm.**
National Museum, Lagos.

of Congo was flourishing. His innovations are supposed to have been brought from there, and in fact, likely models for the Bakuba portrait figures do exist in the Lower Congo region. These are wooden figures of both men and women seated in the same posture as the Bakuba portraits, and especially sitting figures, made of steatite and called *ntadi*, which European records suggest were in existence as early as the 15th century. They were used as the tombstones of tribal chiefs and their wives and mothers, and probably also served as symbolic replacements for absent chiefs. These stone figures are found on the southern side of the Lower Congo in Zaire and northern Angola, and the materials for making them were obtained from quarries in the vicinity of the town of Matadi. Of course, not all *ntadi* figures in present-day collections are so old.

42 Standing female figure. Mende, Sierra Leone. Light-brown wood with grey-black stained smooth and glossy surface. The head is conceived in a similar way to the masks of the *sande* society (plate 41). The figures are called *minsereh*, and are used by the members of the *yassi* female society, who deal in divination and healing. There is often an overlapping of function between the *sande* and the *yassi* societies. **Height 62 cm.**
Náprstek Museum, Prague.

45 *Kaogle* anthropo-zoomorphic mask. Dan-Ngere, Ivory Coast (?). Light-brown wood with a thick layer of brown-red crusty patina on both the outside and the inside. This 'cubistic' mask represents a chimpanzee, and expresses a somewhat extroverted trend within this style complex. Masks of this type are also reported from the Liberian side of the frontier. **Height 23.6 cm.** Náprstek Museum, Prague.

43 Anthropomorphic mask. Toma (Loma), Liberia. Pale wood with grey-black stained surface and functional patina. The Toma, who live on the Liberia-Guinea border, make use of masks belonging to the Dan-Ngere style complex, and flat much-stylized masks, whose prototype had been brought by the ancestors of this Mande tribe long before from their original home in the western Sudan. This mask is worn horizontally on the head, a long covering robe being tied to its edge. **Height 51 cm.**
Náprstek Museum, Prague.

44 *Kaogle* monkey mask. Dan, Ivory Coast. Brown wood with dark-brown functional patina. Monkey fur and animal tusks. The wearer of the mask plays the role of a clown. The monkey head is represented in masterly fashion by two geometric masses, a part of a spherical cap and a truncated cone. A similar piece, published by Fischer and Himmelheber (1976), originated in north-eastern Liberia. **Height 23 cm.**
Náprstek Museum, Prague.

Apart from a single example, we have so far considered only works of art going back no further than the Middle Ages, whether preserved in the older European collections or acquired by ethnographers during the present century. However, recent advances in archaeology have provided us with objects at least two thousand years older, although it must be stressed that our knowledge is still very fragmentary; outside Egypt, the soil of Africa has not been excavated as thoroughly as that of other inhabited continents. We shall survey the archaeologists' discoveries chronologic-

ally, in terms of the age of the remains rather than the order in which they were found.

By chance, the majority of discoveries were made, and the oldest objects found, in Nigeria; and therefore it is only in respect of this region that we may, with a certain licence, talk of reconstructing a history of African art. Even here much remains to be uncovered, and material evidence has not yet been found for many chapters of this history. But what has so far been discovered leaves no further room for doubt that African art has a history reaching far back into the past and comparable with that of other continents, and it is an independent art, albeit (like any other art) open to external influences that were shaped to its own purposes.

The first find of the oldest known group of terracotta sculptures in Africa was made by chance in 1928, when a mineowner in north-western Nigeria found a head of a monkey that bore no resemblance to anything known until then in Africa. It was only after a further fifteen years, in 1943, that a clerk at a tin mine near the small village of Nok, about 40 miles from the place where the first find was made, came across a terracotta human head which he took back home, using it as a scarecrow in his fields. A year later it was taken by the manager of the mine to Jos, where it was seen

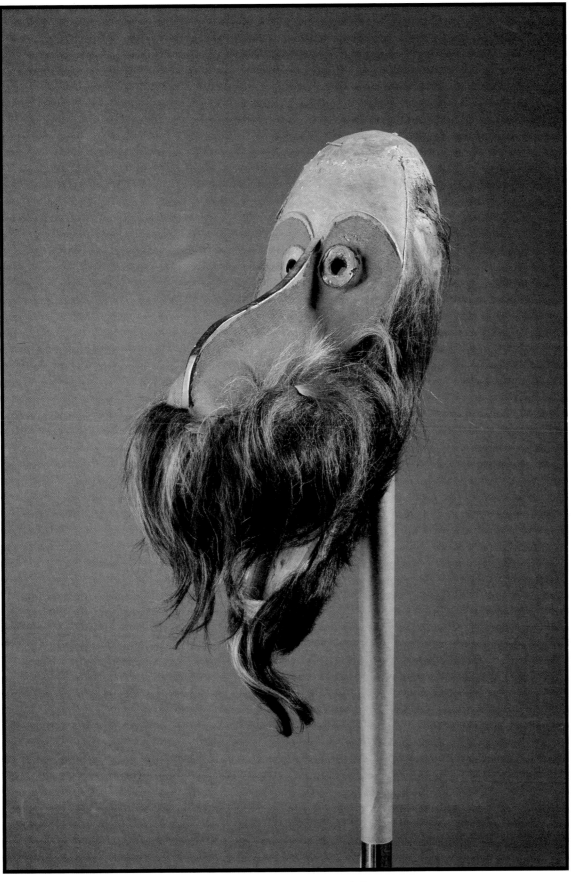

46 *Gägon*
anthropo-zoomor-
phic mask.
Northern Dan, Ivory
Coast. Brown wood
with a functional
patina on the
forehead and inside.
Imported red cloth
glued to the cheeks.
Monkey fur glued
to the perimeter of
the mask and its
movable lower jaw.
The iron peg above
the forehead of the
mask is an
expression of the
belief in the magic
power of iron. The
gägon type masks,
sometimes also
called judge's
masks, are said by
some authors to
have originally been
involved in the
maintenance of
social order. Now
performances with
these masks are no
more than a means
of general
entertainment.
Height 31 cm.
Náprstek Museum,
Prague.

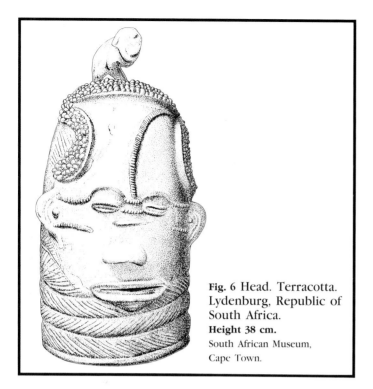

Fig. 6 Head. Terracotta. Lydenburg, Republic of South Africa. **Height 38 cm.** South African Museum, Cape Town.

by the British archaeologist Bernard Fagg, brother of the better-known William Fagg. He realized its affinity with the first and named the newly-discovered culture the Nok culture.

The foregoing is how the discovery is described by Ekpo Eyo, Head of the National Museum of Nigeria, in his introduction to the catalogue of a large exhibition of ancient Nigerian art, 'Treasures of Ancient Nigeria', which toured a number of American and European cities in the early 1980s. Since 1943 about 150 more finds have been made, all of them fragments of terracotta statuary, in a remarkably large area, about 300 miles long and 100 miles wide, between the Kaduna and Benue rivers. Many are human heads (fig. 5), the largest being 35 cm high, and these belonged to full-length figures, many fragments of which have also been found. Two fragments of an arm holding a hoe or an axe demonstrate that the Nok culture was one of farmers, and we are certain that they knew how to smelt iron. The figures are life-sized, and even where the head may have occupied as much as a quarter of the overall height of the figure (as is frequently the case in African art), they are at least 120—130 cm high. From the technical point of view, to fire such large objects,

whether in an open hearth or in a kiln, was a difficult achievement indicating the existence of an advanced culture.

As with almost all remains of ancient African art, the dating of the Nok culture is not easy. The Nok pieces are not found *in situ* (that is, in the place where they had been used and ultimately abandoned before being covered by earth), but in alluvial deposits to which they had probably been carried by flooding rivers. Vegetal remains found with the sculptures and used for carbon 14 dating are not necessarily connected with them and may well be later rather than earlier or contemporary. The radiocarbon dating indicates that the sculptures may have originated between 500 BC and around AD 200, but other estimates go as far back as 900 BC. Objects excavated at a later time suggest that Nok terracotta statuary continued to exist in a decadent form in northern Nigeria throughout the first millennium AD.

Despite common features, several styles can be identified in Nok sculptures, a fact which accords with the long life and wide geographical diffusion of this culture. One common feature is a tendency towards geometrization, the heads of the figures being treated as cylinders, cones or spheres, and the eyes as triangles or segments of a circle, over which is placed another segment forming the upper lid. The pupils of the eyes, the nostrils and the ears are pierced. The stylistic maturity of Nok statuary suggests that it represents the advanced phase of a longer development whose earlier history we may never learn if the material used was perishable wood rather than clay.

Nok statuary is separated by almost a millennium from later Nigerian art. Yet there may have been some continuity between the two, since certain artistic and especially stylistic principles discovered by Nok artists seem to have been preserved down to the Middle Ages or even to the present day. For example, rich jewels shown in relief on the fragments of Nok works resemble the jewels on medieval statues from Ife which will be described later on; and the treatment of the eyes of some 'bronze' sculptures of the Lower Niger region, and especially some Yoruba

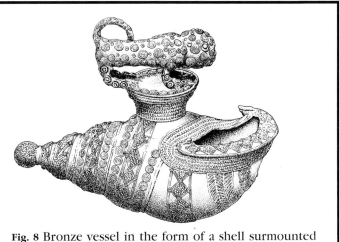

Fig. 8 Bronze vessel in the form of a shell surmounted by a quadruped. Igbo-Ukwu, Nigeria. **Length 20.6 cm.** National Museum, Lagos.

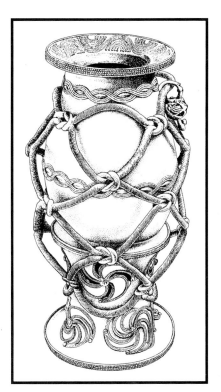

Fig. 7 Pendant in the form of a human head. Bronze. Igbo-Ukwu, Nigeria. **Height 7.6 cm.** National Museum, Lagos.

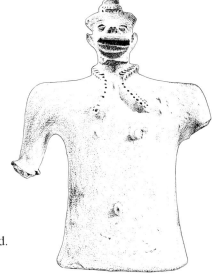

Fig. 9 Bronze vessel. Igbo-Ukwu, Nigeria. **Height 32.3 cm.** National Museum, Lagos.

Fig. 10 Human figure. Terracotta. Sao, Republic of Tchad. **Height 33 cm.** Musée de l'Homme, Paris.

gelede masks, may represent elements in an unbroken tradition coming down from Nok terracottas. Furthermore, the hairstyles of some Nok heads, arranged in a set of ball shapes, closely resemble those of recent wooden figures made by tribes who now live in the ancient Nok territory; but this testifies to the continuity of a fashion in hairdressing rather than a continuity in sculptural stylization.

The second oldest group of terracotta statuary finds was made in the far south of Africa, where fragments of human as well as animal figures have been found during recent decades. Very little is known about these figures. The most remarkable find so far was made in Lydenburg in the eastern Transvaal,

at the beginning of the 1960s. It consists of seven terracotta heads, of which six are human and one belongs to an animal, probably a dog. They have been dated to the 5th century AD. Two of the human heads are larger than the rest: one is 35 cm high (fig. 6); the original height of the other cannot be established exactly because of its fragmentary state. The size of the remaining five heads varies between 20 and 24 cm. They are all made in a single style. They are conceived as hollow cylinders, rounded at the upper end, the facial features being modelled with added pieces of clay: the nose with a concave ridge, the eyes in the form of cowries, the mouth with parallel lips and round corners (in the large figures cut as slits, like the eyes), the hairline indicated by granules, and the forehead marked by horizontal scarification. On both of the larger heads the neck is formed by a couple of convex rings; each head carries a small figure of an unidentifiable animal on the top. Each of the small heads has two holes in its neck, indicating that they were attached to a pole, or rather, like head-dress masks, to the top of a mask dress, in much the same fashion as some dance head-dresses from the Cross River area in eastern Nigeria. Both the larger

Fig. 11 *Oni* of Ife in
a coronation costume.
Bronze.
Ita Yemo, Nigeria.
Height 48 cm.
Museum of Ife Antiquities, Ife.

47 *Deangle* face mask. Dan, Ivory Coast. Dark-brown wood with brown-black glossy functional patina. A stuffed roll of tough home-made cloth is attached above the forehead. Though worn by men, the mask represents a female face. Metal pins of the kind formerly used for traditional local hairstyles were stuck in the stuffed roller, or else cowries were sewn on to it. According to Himmelheber, this is the mask worn by a dignitary charged with maintaining contact between the village and the initiation camp of boys; for example he begs food for them from the village women. According to other authors, judgements are issued through this mask to resolve quarrels. **Height 25 cm.**
Náprstek Museum, Prague.

heads are big enough to serve as helmet masks. This function also seems to be indicated by the slits in their eyes and mouths. When looking at them one cannot help being reminded of the wooden helmet masks of the female secret society, *bundu*, of some tribes in Liberia and Sierra Leone. The similarity, including the rings on the neck, is really astonishing, although the separation between them in time and space makes any direct connection improbable. The high quality of these South African heads makes them of such importance that they demand to be mentioned, although nothing is so far known about the people who made them or the diffusion of this art.

To study the next archaeological find, we must return to Nigeria. The discovery was again made by chance, this time in 1938, when a man was digging a cistern for storing rainwater behind his house in the village of Igbo Ukwu in the eastern part of the country. About 60 cm below the ground he uncovered a number of bronze objects, mostly vessels. Not knowing their significance, he and his neighbours kept them for luck as well as for use. A few months later the place was visited by a British colonial official who bought some of the objects from the finder and, after publishing a report about them, presented them

48 Face mask. Wobe, Ivory Coast. Vegetable fibre plaiting, reed pulp, and fur cuttings. This rare basketwork mask imitates the shape and style of Ngere wooden masks (the tube-shaped eyes, the wooden arch above the forehead). Short reed-pulp pegs, tied to the lower part of the mask, replace the discharged cartridges often used to decorate wooden masks of this type. This is the third known Wobe basketwork mask, the others being a mask in the Ratton collection in Paris, and a mask in the collection of the Abijan Museum. Holas (1966) offers two possible interpretations of these masks: they are reserved either for minors, or for the families who are for some reason forbidden the use of wooden masks. **Height 26 cm.** Náprstek Museum, Prague.

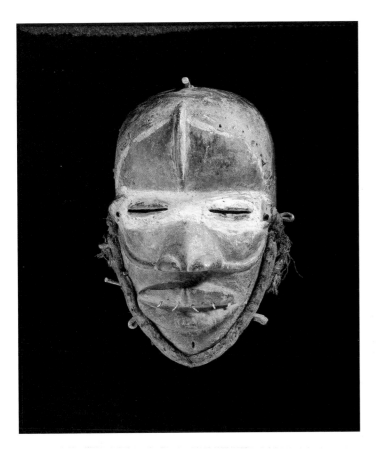

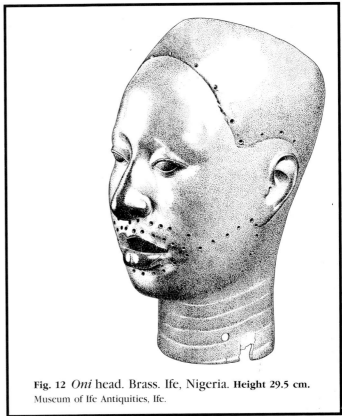

Fig. 12 *Oni* head. Brass. Ife, Nigeria. **Height 29.5 cm.**
Museum of Ife Antiquities, Ife.

50 Face mask. Ngere, Ivory Coast. Light-brown wood with surface stained grey-brown or black-brown with glossy functional patina. Teeth made of aluminium wire. The source of this mask is uncertain. A Ngere provenance is suggested by the 'castanet' eyes and the characteristic facial scarification forming a long curve from the nostrils to the temples. The vertical scarification on the forehead (sometimes erroneously assigned only to masks representing women) appears in the masks and figures of many tribes in this area, its ethnic origin being unknown. The horizontal strip of white across the eyes imitates the initiation painting of the face. Instead of magical iron nails on the perimeter of the mask, a modern material, aluminium wire, has been used. **Height 25 cm.**
Náprstek Museum, Prague.

49 Free-standing male figure. Dan, Ivory Coast. Pale wood with grey-black stained and faintly glossy surface. Teeth made of iron sheeting. The human figures called *lü mä* are relatively rare, especially male ones. These are portraits of living people, or commemorative portraits of the dead, not part of the ancestor cult. They are said to emphasize individual features of the living models, for example a large nose or distinctively shaped breasts, enabling them to be identified by contemporaries. It is not difficult to guess what the model for this portrait was noted for. **Height 66 cm.**
Náprstek Museum, Prague.

to the Federal Department of Antiquities. Later another official obtained the rest of the find and sent it to the competent office in Lagos. From the very beginning its importance was clear to all participants except the villagers, yet a further twenty years had to pass before Bernard Fagg (the man who identified the Nok culture) invited the British archaeologist Thurstan Shaw to start excavating in Igbo Ukwu. These excavations were carried out during the 1959—60 season and again in 1964, at first on the site of the original find and then in the compounds of two brothers of the first finder. The original site brought in the richest harvest of bronzes. A small hut, either a shrine or a storehouse for ritual objects, had originally stood there, with the objects placed on a four-sided floor. When the hut collapsed, its ruins buried the objects and the site was gradually covered with soil.

The other site made it possible to gain at least a glimpse of the way of life of this unique culture. It was the burial chamber of an important tribal dignitary. His body was seated on his stool, there was a crown on his head and a breastplate on his breast, there were bracelets on his arms, and he was holding a fan and a fly-whisk in his hands. Apart from some other objects, a ritual staff with a bronze head in the form of a leopard skull was put beside the body. As well as bronze objects, the excavations uncovered more than 130,000 glass beads with which various objects, notably the dress of the buried dignitary, were decorated. The beads were not of local origin: they must have been imported, probably from some Islamic society, or perhaps even from southern Europe.

The bronzes are also evidence of trade relations with the outside world. The main raw material used in their manufacture, namely copper, is found nowhere in the area; and the second component of bronze, tin, is only found in the north-eastern part of the country in the territory of the former Nok culture. Since the style and subjects of these bronzes have no analogue anywhere else in Africa, and there is no evidence of bronze-casting in the area, it is possible that the bronzes were imported as finished casts. In this connection the date of the burial of these objects is of great importance. Four tests by the carbon 14 method gave the same answer: the 9th century, long before the Nigerian coast was reached by the Portuguese ships which might otherwise have been put forward as the possible suppliers of the bronze.

In fact, the bronze objects made by the cire-perdue (lost-wax) method of casting were undoubtedly the work of African artists. This is indicated by the way in which human and animal figures are represented, which is characteristically African. There is, for example, a small figure of a rider decorating the

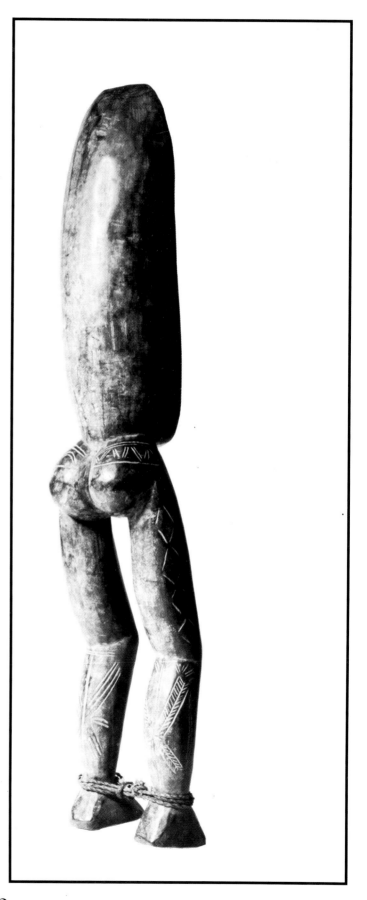

51 *Wunkirmian* spoon with a figure handle. Dan, Ivory Coast. Pale wood with brown-black stained surface. These large spoons (which it might be better to call ladles) have a handle in the form of the lower part of a woman's body, or a female or ram head. They are the insignia of social distinction — that of being the most hospitable housewife of the village or quarter. They are used at a ritual distribution of food on festive occasions. The loop with which the feet of the figure are tied was used for hanging up the spoon.
Height 55.5 cm.
Private collection, Prague.

end of the handle of a ceremonial fly-whisk, and a pendant representing a human head (fig. 7). The cheeks and foreheads of both bronzes are covered with oblique parallel scarification marks. Moreover, the style of two pendants representing a ram's head and an elephant's head is reminiscent of the way in which animal heads were stylized in later Nigerian art.

The most significant bronzes from Igbo Ukwu are the vessels. One of the most remarkable is a pot on an openwork stand, more than 32 cm high and made to look as if it had been enmeshed in a net of bronze strings (fig. 9). The manufacture of this vessel required a very complicated casting technique. Equally unique in the African context are two vessels, each in the form of a shell, probably a Triton; they are approximately 30 and 20 cm long, and their surfaces are decorated with tiny granules arranged in geometrical patterns and rhythmically repeated crickets and flies; the smaller vessel also carries a figure of a quadruped, perhaps a leopard (fig. 8). In spite of the undoubtedly African provenance of these and other bronzes from Igbo Ukwu, they are comparable with the achievements of the most advanced cultures in the exquisite quality of their workmanship, sophisticated design (for example the pendant in the form of a bird lying on top of two eggs), and precise execution of detail.

Probably only a few centuries later, another independent culture began to develop in central Chad and the northernmost fringe of Cameroon — that is not very far from the eastern frontier of Nigeria. This culture, discovered by the French archaeologist Jean Lebeuf and known as Sao, flourished down to the 16th — 18th century (estimates of the date of its demise vary widely). Its remains include terracotta figures from the mouth of the Chari River south of Lake Chad; they probably represent ancestors (fig. 10), and mostly consist only of heads and broad trunks found in burial urns alongside small terracotta heads and bronze ornaments. Some of these figures may represent masked dancers, but according to William Fagg they are more likely to be part-human and part-animal, a common African conception. Any more precise identification

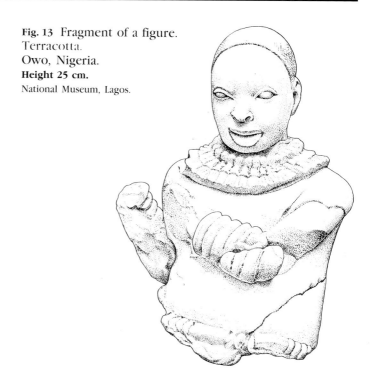

Fig. 13 Fragment of a figure. Terracotta. Owo, Nigeria. **Height 25 cm.** National Museum, Lagos.

of such highly conventionalized objects must necessarily be speculative.

But let us return to Nigeria. Ife in the south-west has been, since the European Middle Ages, the seat of a city-kingdom and a centre of the religious life of the large Yoruba nation. The Ife culture may have started to develop as early as the 9th century and from the 11th to 15th centuries produced an art in no way inferior to the antique art of the Mediterranean in realism and technique. It became known in the West shortly before the First World War. In 1910, Ife was visited by a famous German Africanist, Leo Frobenius, whose discoveries included a bronze head that probably represented Olokun, the god of the sea; the original of the head is now lost. Frobenius also brought to Europe eight terracotta heads which are now in the Museum für Völkerkunde, Berlin. Another important find — eighteen bronze sculptures — was made in 1938, while the foundations of a house were being dug in a compound that had formed part of the palace of the king (*oni*) of Ife, until the 19th century. Some sculptures have since been discovered by accident, but between 1949 and the early 1970s a number of proper archaeological excavations were carried out in various parts of Ife and its environs

52 Detail of plate 53.

53 Standing male figure. Bete, Ivory Coast. Pale hard wood with glossy surface, stained dark brown. Hair made of black monkey hair. Eye slits filled with white paint, grooves under the eyes with red. A necklace of red glass beads. The figure was collected at the beginning of the 1930s. It originated in the south-eastern part of the Bete tribal territory. Altogether about fifteen figures are known, mostly undocumented. Characteristic of the style of this Bete tribal group's figures are the small egg-shaped head, the neck, and the trunk, the excessive height of which may have resulted from the need to cram the complicated scarification on to it; also the position of the arms, the hands with palms turned upwards, and the way the buttocks are joined to the trunk. The function of the figure is not known; it may represent a clan ancestor. **Height 87.5 cm.**

Náprstek Museum, Prague.

54

54 Loom pulley. Bete, Ivory Coast, Gagnoa subdivision. Pale wood with dull surface, stained grey-black. This object appeared at the beginning of the 1930s. It has obviously never served its purpose, since no holes for fastening the pulley have been drilled into the fork. It may have been made for the neighbouring Guro, because as far as is known the Bete were not themselves weavers. During the last ten years at least two further pulleys, undoubtedly made by a Bete carver although less 'classical' in style, have been recorded. **Height 30.7 cm.** Náprstek Museum, Prague.

by (among others) Bernard and William Fagg, Frank Willett and Ekpo Eyo.

The main subjects of Ife art were the king (fig. 11), the queen, and others who were probably court dignitaries; some of this last group were outsiders (that is, Yoruba from areas beyond Ife), as we can tell from the realistically executed scarification marks on their faces. Animal motifs also appear, for example a hippopotamus head and an elephant head which served as lids, perhaps of burial urns, and ritual implements with figure decoration. In all, about thirty cast metal sculptures have been found so far. Ife metalwork is usually called bronze, but in fact it is an alloy of copper, zinc and lead — that is, it is brass. Interesting exceptions are seven items — five heads, a mask and a sitting human figure — found far from Ife. They were cast from almost pure copper, a remarkable technological feat that must have resulted from considerable experience on the part of the founders. In Ife, as in Igbo Ukwu, metal and glass beads had to be imported from North Africa, the Middle East and perhaps Europe. From the 16th century, when the 'post-classical' period of Ife began, all the known sculptures are made of terracotta; they are more stylized than works of the preceding period, and are beginning to display features characteristic of Yoruba tribal art as we know it from the 19th and 20th centuries. This change was undoubtedly connected with a decline in

the political importance of Ife and an inability to go on importing expensive raw materials.

From what has been said, it can be concluded that Ife art served the needs of the state and the prestige of the ruler. Cast heads (fig. 12) were used in the secondary burial ceremony, after which they were placed in the king's palace. Some of them are arranged in such a way that the crown of the dead king can be put on them. The terracotta heads are either broken off from full figures, or were originally made separately so that they could be placed on an altar or perhaps attached to a wooden body (as was done with some cast heads). The treatment of some of the heads, especially the cast ones, is so lifelike that one cannot help feeling that they must be true portraits, albeit somewhat idealized.

The most strikingly stylized feature of Ife art is the upper eyelid. In both corners of the eye it overlaps the lower lid, and a groove in it runs parallel with its edge. Other features are the downturned mouth and the distinct, protruding edges of the full lips. The stylization of the toenails, which are shaped as triangles or wedges, may represent an artistic legacy of the Nok culture which Ife then transmitted to the Yoruba city-state of Owo, with which Ife was connected by historical and cultural ties.

Owo is about 120 km south-east of Ife, roughly halfway between Ife and Benin. Archaeological excavations were carried out here in the early 1970s by Ekpo Eyo. Carbon 14 dating of the finds indicated that Owo culture was at its height in the 15th century, that is, at the end of Ife's 'classical' period and when the political power of Benin was reaching its greatest extent. The terracotta sculptures which have been excavated here display many affinities with Ife art, but make a much more vivid impression (fig. 13). At the same time, a tendency towards Yoruba stylization may be observed in them (bulging eyes, protruding lips, highly stylized ears). The Yoruba character of Owo art is much more conspicuous in works of applied art, especially the ivory carvings known from Benin, where Owo craftsmen probably worked and to which Owo was also, from time to time, politically linked. The influence exercised by this kingdom is

56 Face mask. Bete, Ivory Coast. Pale wood, painted. The mask was collected among the Badie clan (*tribu*) in the Gagnoa subdivision. An influence from the neighbouring Guro is noticeable, both in style and in the way the dancer holds the mask, using his teeth to grip a bar placed in the hollow back. The realistically conceived head of the superstructure and the abstractly conceived mask demonstrate the tribal carver's ability to master two different styles. Here two styles were used either because the small head was intended to represent a member of a foreign tribe, or because the mask proper personified a supernatural being. **Height 70 cm.** Náprstek Museum, Prague.

55 Face mask. Bete, Ivory Coast, Doudonkou village in the Gabnoa subdivision. Pale wood with surface stained grey-brown and artificial glossy patina. This mask belonging to the Pacolo clan (*tribu*) was collected at the beginning of the 1930s. A stylistic trait of masks from the south-eastern part of the Bete territory is the carving of the upper eyelids in a rounded low relief. The horns on this mask probably imitate the two-plaited traditional hairstyle of the neighbouring Gagu. **Height 44.5 cm.** Náprstek Museum, Prague.

shown in Owo art by some typical motifs, such as a mudfish, a leopard, or a human face with two snakes issuing from its nostrils. However, this last motif, the significance of which is unknown, may have originated elsewhere and been taken over both by Benin and Owo. A peculiarity of Owo art is the frequency with which offerings are shown: a hen, a woman carrying a cock as a sacrifice, even a basket full of severed human heads. The figure of a leopard sitting with a human leg in his mouth may also represent a sacrificial occasion.

The most famous of Africa's ancient arts is the art of the Benin kingdom. It owes popularity not only to its undeniable quality, but also to the dramatic fashion in which it became generally known. This occurred in 1897, when a British Vice-Consul announced his visit to the *oba*, the king of Benin. The *oba* refused to receive him, since the proposed visit clashed with the most important ceremony of the year, during which the king was considered to be a divine personage and was not allowed to receive foreigners. The self-confident official nevertheless set out on his journey — a decision for which he and his retinue, including the porters, were to pay a high price. The entire party, only excepting two Europeans and about 40 porters, were killed. Although the *oba* was not in fact responsible, a punitive expedition was mounted, the city was conquered, the king's palace was plundered and the *oba* was sent into exile. Countless events of this kind took place during the colonial era; they are typical of encounters between mutually uncomprehending cultures, immensely destructive in their effects where the more powerful side is lacking tolerance or respect for others.

The spoils from the royal palace amounted to more than two thousand artifacts, including bronzes and ivories as well as carvings in wood. These were sent to England, where they created a sensation — so much so that over the next three years two substantial books about Benin art were published. This was because, for the first time in western history, Black Africa was seen to have an ancient and rich cultural tradition and art of its own, comparable with those of other con-

57 Anthropo-zoomorphic *zamle* mask. Guro, Ivory Coast. Pale wood with black-stained and painted glossy surface. Masks of the *zamle* type, combining elements from the human face with antelope horns and the muzzle of a beast, are also popular among the neighbouring Baule. To judge from some documented analogous masks, this one originated in the area between Bouaflé and Zuénoula. The characteristic outline of the forehead with two inverted U-shaped projections also appears in some rare human figures of the Guro. The mask is held in front of the face by the teeth, which grip on a stick inserted in the sides. **Height 46.6 cm.** Náprstek Museum, Prague.

Fig. 14 Plaque with a figure of a Portuguese. Bronze. Benin, Nigeria. Museum of Mankind, London.

tinents. In 1919 Felix von Luschan, the well-known German ethnographer and Director of the Museum für Völkerkunde in Berlin (itself one of the largest ethnographic museums in the world), gave his frequently quoted verdict on the Benin bronzes: 'Benvenuto Cellini could not have cast them better, and nobody else either before or since Cellini.'

After they had been brought to England, some of the spoils were acquired by the British Museum. Much the greater part was sold in order to recover some of the costs of the punitive expedition. Hence, there are now collections of Benin art not only in London's Museum of Mankind, but also in Berlin, Leiden, Vienna, Leningrad and Dresden,

58 Face mask. Guro/Bete, Ivory Coast. Brown wood with black-stained surface. Coloured with local clay pigment. Hair, beard and eye-lashes (now moulted) made of monkey fur. Functional patina on the outside as well as inside. Before the Second World War this mask belonged to the collection of the modern Czech painter Emil Filla. This is one of the few known masks of this type, usually assigned to the Guro. The mask was obviously made in a mixed milieu where the Bete and the Guro were living side by side. The Bete stylistic elements are clearly predominant, the Guro style accounting for the choice and sobriety of the colours and the bar in the hollow of the mask, used to hold it in place. **Height 29.5 cm.** Náprstek Museum, Prague.

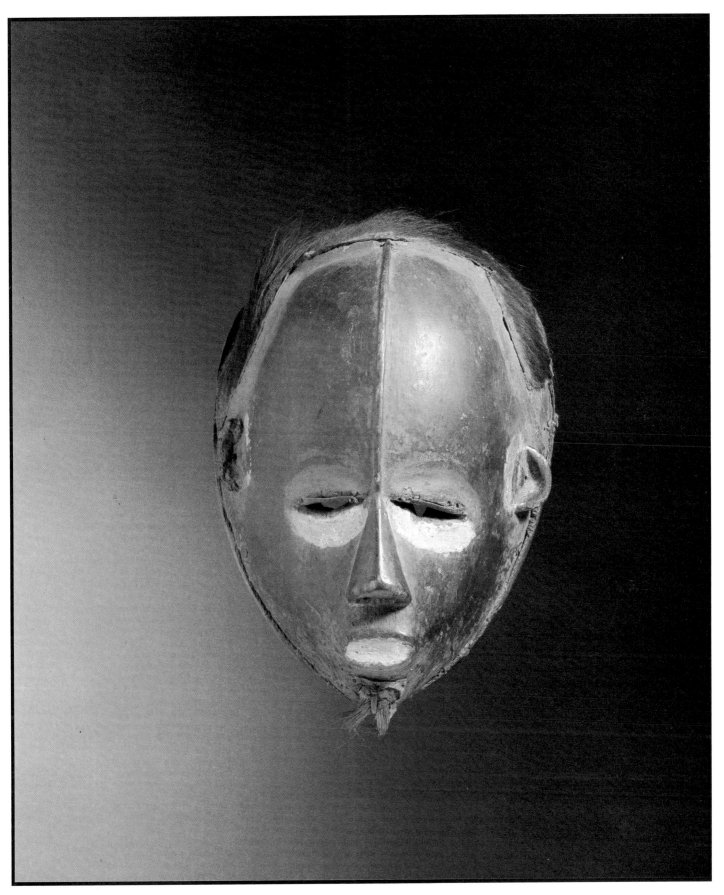

Fig. 15 Head of the Queen Mother.
Bronze.
Benin, Nigeria.
Height 51 cm.
National Museum, Lagos.

as well as in private hands all over the world. Only a small part of the Benin legacy has remained in Nigeria or has been recovered by purchases on the world art market.

Another consequence of the punitive expedition was a break in the five-hundred-year tradition of Benin art, although it had obviously passed its zenith by the late 19th century. Bronze casting was a royal monopoly in Benin. Bronzesmiths, like ivory carvers, were organized in a special guild which worked exclusively for the king; with his departure, the guild lost its patron. After a new *oba* ascended the throne in 1914, the renewal of court ceremonial caused an artistic revival, but on a much lower level. Eventually, the tourist was to become the main customer, with predictable consequences.

Unlike the mainly archaeological remains we have examined so far, the corpus of Benin art has never fallen into oblivion among the people who created it, and until the fatal punitive expedition it formed part of a living cultural tradition. This is why Benin works cannot be dated by the usual archaeological methods. However, thanks to the unbroken Benin tradition and the narrative quality of Benin art, a rough outline of its history has always been available. The oral court tradition of Benin has been particularly valu-

able in preserving a history of the state, including a list of rulers. This comprises thirty-nine *oba*, going back to the 12th or 13th century, at which time a foreign ruler, the first member of the dynasty, is said to have been invited to Benin. He was a prince, a son of Oduduwa, the founder of the kingdom of Ife. This explains why a number of Benin's cultural and politico-religious traditions had their roots in Ife. Bronze casting is accounted for in the same way. At some time towards the end of the 14th century, the sixth *oba*, named Oguola, is said to have asked for an Ife bronze-smith to be sent to Benin. Tradition names the man who was sent Igueghae, and he is supposed to have taught local craftsmen his craft, thus ending Benin's dependence on Ife for ready-made bronzes. In Benin, wood-carving and perhaps also ivory carving probably existed prior to this event, for the oldest known Benin bronzes are different in style from those of Ife. This would not be the case if there had been no local tradition to which the new bronze casting technique could be adapted. On the other hand, the discovery of an imported bronze statue representing an *oni* of Ife in ceremonial costume confirms the accuracy of tradition as regards the sending of bronzes from Ife to Benin. According to Frank Willett, the composition of the alloys in some of the oldest Benin bronzes corresponds approximately with that of the Ife alloy; so we may surmise that smelted Ife bronzes were used in making them.

In 1485 — about a hundred years after the introduction of bronze casting to Benin — the city was visited by the Portuguese who established diplomatic and trade relations. The Portuguese acquired pepper, ivory and, to a lesser extent, slaves. In exchange, they supplied the much sought-after bronze in the form of open horseshoe-shaped bracelets called *manila*. It is certainly not a coincidence that the greatest efflorescence of Benin bronze casting took place in the 16th and 17th centuries, when imported raw materials were abundant. The Portuguese, clad in typical early 16th century costumes, frequently appeared in Benin artifacts; this was especially true of bronzes (fig. 14), although they may also be seen in ivory carvings. Such

60

59 Bronze plaque. Benin, Nigeria. A gate of the *oba*'s palace is shown in relief, with two armed watchmen and their servants.
A bronze python is hanging head down from the roof of the gate, figure reliefs being attached to the side pillars.
Two trained panthers are standing inside the gate.
Height 53 cm, width 35.5 cm. Museum of Mankind, London.

61

Fig. 16 Hunter with an antelope.
Bronze.
Lower Niger region, Nigeria.
Height 36 cm.
British Museum, London.

representations indicate the age of Benin art and help with its dating, but they are not always reliable since the 16th century appearance of the Portuguese later became a convention of Benin art, reproduced long after it had ceased to correspond to reality.

For richness of subject-matter, the royal Benin art is unrivalled in Africa. The oldest subject is a stylized head of the *oba*, obviously connected with the custom of separating the head of a deceased *oba* from his body and sending it to be buried at Ife, a custom that was part of the royal burial ceremony in the early period of the kingdom. At Ife a bronze head was then made and sent back to Benin, where it occupied a permanent place on an altar of the deceased monarch in the royal palace. (Of couse, all of the *oba* heads now known are the work of Benin artists.) Around

60 Free-standing female figure. Guro, Ivory Coast. Pale wood with surface stained black. This rare figure was in Czechoslovakia before the Second World War (probably from the 1920s and perhaps even earlier). The zig-zag line on the forehead is one of many variations on the traditional shaved hairline, to be found on figures and masks in this tribal style. The scarification, in the form of three pip-shaped bumps on the forehead, is an identification mark of the Guro. **Height 49.3 cm.**
Opočno Castle, Czechoslovakia.

61 Handle of a loom pulley. Guro, Ivory Coast. Brown wood with black-stained dull surface. Traces of red paint on the muzzle. This piece, which has probably never been used, is decorated with a stylized bat's head. **Height 17 cm.** Náprstek Museum, Prague.

62 Loom pulley. Guro, Ivory Coast. Brown wood with black-stained surface and a crust of functional patina. **Height 17 cm.** Private collection, Prague.

63 Loom pulley. Guro, Ivory Coast. Brown wood with black-stained surface and glossy functional patina. **Height 25 cm.** Private collection, Prague.

The loom pulleys of the Guro, decorated with small human or animal heads, are without doubt the most beautiful representatives of this particular genre of carving, spread among many tribes. Both of these examples reproduce the traditional female hairstyle of the Guro, and the second also illustrates the custom or tribal fashion of passing a tress of hair through a perforated cube made of wood or ivory. This fashion is also often depicted in the masks of this tribe. The string on which the pulley was suspended over the loom passed through holes drilled through both heads.

the middle of the 16th century, when the title of Queen Mother (*iyoba*) was introduced, the ceremonial was extended to include her head, shown with a characteristic conic coiffure (fig. 15). In the course of time, the appearance of the *oba*'s head changed in accordance with the stylistic development of Benin art as well as changing royal fashions. The final form of the head, with a crown composed of corals and with two little wings raised on both sides, as worn by the contemporary Benin *oba* on ceremonial occasions, originated as late as the first half of the 19th century.

Unique in African art are the Benin cast bronze plaques, oblong or almost square in shape and on average about 50 cm long. They had holes in the corners by which they were nailed to columns supporting the roof of the royal palace. The plaques are decorated with relief figures of Africans, the *oba* himself often represented as unnaturally large (in order to emphasize his importance), accompanied or supported by smaller figures of attendants. There are scenes of life at court as well as historical events, and individual courtiers and warriors as well as figures of Portuguese traders and soldiers; in some of them crocodile masks or fish are modelled; and so on. The total number of surviving plaques is about nine hundred, the overwhelming

63

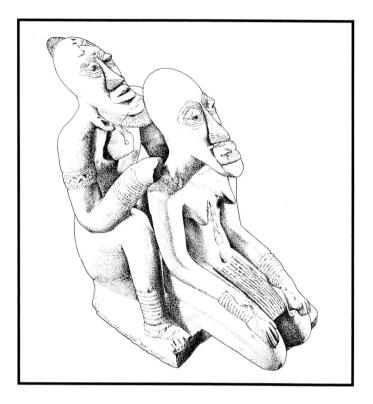

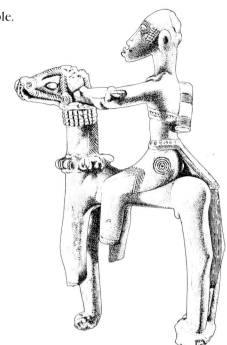

Fig. 17 Human couple. Terracotta. Djenné, Mali. **Height 24 cm.** Entwistle Collection. London.

Fig. 18 Rider on horseback. Terracotta. Djenné, Mali. **Height 64 cm.** Entwistle Collection, London.

majority made during the 16th and 17th centuries, which William Fagg has called the middle period of Benin art. They are an indispensable source of information about Benin's art, history, customs, court life and religious ideas.

There were also other architectonic elements made of bronze. Large figures of ibises decorated the ridges of palace roofs, and heads and bodies of large pythons, composed of cast links, were fixed head-down to the sheer roof slopes of palace towers. Evidence for the original placing of these items is provided by the accounts of European visitors to Benin and also by the details of a Benin bronze box, cast in the form of the *oba*'s palace, and two of the relief plaques featuring a palace gate with a tower (plate 59).

Among other works that deserve to be mentioned briefly are freestanding figures of the *oba*, courtiers and even the Portuguese, and figures of leopards. All of them were meant to be placed on palace altars. There are also various appendages of the *oba*, courtiers and royal messengers, including human and animal masks carried at the waist of ceremonial costumes as insignia of rank, breastplates, the broad openwork bracelets ornamented with

figures which were a part of these costumes, and a few helmet masks.

As in the case of Ife bronzes, Westerners at first sought for the origin of Benin bronzes outside Africa, everywhere from the ancient Mediterranean to India. Now there is no doubt that they were made by African artists. Only the Benin relief plaques, because of their size (unparalleled in Africa), are with some justification thought to have been inspired by Portuguese book illustrations or woodcuts. This hypothesis is supported by the inclusion of vegetal motifs, otherwise rare in Africa, which are strikingly reminiscent in their stylization of similar motifs in some Afro-Portuguese ivory carvings, where the influence of European models (see the illustration of a hunting horn) is beyond doubt.

Of Benin ivory carving, mention must first be made of entire tusks, the surfaces of which are covered with relief carvings of the usual Benin figurative motifs. In comparison with Benin sculptures, their style is more rustic. These tusks were placed on altars, inserted by their broad ends into holes on the top of commemorative bronze heads. Other very well-known carvings in ivory include two leopard figures, now in the Museum of Mankind,

64

London, and a few human masks, notably two in the collections of the Museum of Mankind, London, and the Metropolitan Museum of Art, New York. These masks, insignia of royalty, which hung by a string from the breast of the *oba*, are among the finest works of Benin art.

Benin carvings in wood are relatively unknown, because most of them were burned during the conflagration that engulfed the city at the time of the punitive expedition. Apart from a few motifs that would have been better executed in bronze, the majority are stools carved with relief decoration reminiscent in style of the decoration of the tusks placed on altars. Some of the carvings are more related in style to the tribal art of the Bini, who form the ethnic nucleus of the present-day population of Benin.

Benin art is a typical court art, serving to glorify the ruler and his ancestors, to perpetuate the memory of his deeds and to commemorate important events. The ruler is not presented realistically, but as an idealized stereotype, differentiated from courtiers and warriors not by his face but by his insignia and costume. The principle that clothes make the man is almost without exception true of Benin art. On the other hand, Benin sculptors were perfectly capable of capturing a human likeness, as is shown by the bronze figures of two dwarfs in the Museum für Völkerkunde, Vienna. The dwarfs probably played a similar role as jesters in Benin as they did at the courts of medieval Europe.

Works from Benin are by no means the only examples of Nigerian art to have survived. A number of other artifacts, including bronzes, originated in various unknown centres. It is often possible to identify their style and to link new discoveries with works already unearthed; but we know practically nothing about their origin and history. And there is no doubt that further research and archaeological excavations will bring to light more new works in hitherto unknown styles. Let us hope that they will at least partly elucidate the origin of those works which we already have.

Among the bronze sculptures, one of the mysteries is a group, heterogeneous in style, for which the term Lower Niger Industries was coined by William Fagg because they were found in the area between the confluence of the Niger and Benue River in the north and the mouth of the Niger in the south. Some of these sculptures were seized in Benin by the punitive expedition of 1897. The most representative piece is the figure of a hunter carrying a dead antelope on his shoulder (fig. 16). The entire group is sometimes labelled as being in 'the hunter style', after this particular figure. Many of the bronzes reveal a thematic dependence on Benin court art, but they are quite different in style. They do not have the rigidity of the Benin works, since their creators evidently strove for an artistic treatment of the whole figure rather than a detailed rendering of hierarchical symbols.

Another important group consists of bronze figures from the island of Jebba and the nearby village of Tada on the Niger River, in the northern part of the country. Especially notable among these are three bronze figures, the largest ever found in Africa, namely a warrior, a bowman and a woman with a fan (this last figure has been missing since the beginning of the 1970s). Some of the stylistic traits of these figures suggest an affinity with Ife art, perhaps mediated by Owo, whereas other elements point rather to Benin. According to tradition these bronzes came to the area from the south-east. They are said to have been brought from the city of Idah on the Lower Niger, at some time in the 16th century, by Tsoede, the founder of the Nupe kingdom, to which Jebba and Tada belonged. Hence the figures are known as the Tsoede bronzes.

Nigeria was not, of course, the only West African country in which the visual arts flourished centuries ago. In 1940 two terracotta figures were discovered in the southern part of what is now the Republic of Mali, in the interior Niger Delta. Thanks to subsequent finds, by the 1970s there were about twenty documented figures (that is, figures of whom it was known where they had been found). They all came from an area bounded by the cities Djenné on the Bani, Ke Macina on the Niger, and Mopti on the confluence of the Bani and Niger. But it is only since 1977 that scientifically conducted excavations have been carried out. As far as the terracottas were concerned, the most important excavations were undertaken in 1977 at Djenné-jeno by Roderick and Susan McIntosh. At one time a fortified city, with hundreds of houses made of dried bricks, was situated here. It was settled for about a millennium without interruption, and then abandoned around 1500. Another terracotta figure was unearthed in the foundations of the city, and the existence of a precise archaeological context for it made possible its stratigraphic dating by the carbon 14 method. According to this, the figure probably originated in the mid-12th century. All the other figures could be dated only by a purely physical method, thermoluminescence, based on measuring the changes in the structure of the electrons in a ceramic object since the time of its firing. According to this method, which cannot give precise results, these terracottas of southern Mali originated at various times between 1250 and 1700. There are certainly considerable differences in style, indicating a long period of development and/or their manufacture in a large number of workshops.

The most important and artistically most remarkable group of Mali terracotas belong to what Bernard de Grunne called 'the style of multiple eyelids' (fig. 17). The stylization of the eyes in these figures is really very striking, and important for their classification. Typical of these terracottas is the shape of the head. It is elongated, and cylindrical in its upper half, the top being egg-shaped and the lower part somewhat flattened. It is attached to the body at an angle of approximately 45°, giving the impression that it is tilted back. The eyes protrude in relief from the surface of the face; they are almond-shaped and usually slitted horizontally in the middle. They are often framed with a few parallel lines, which prompted de Grunne to name them as he did. The lids are not actually multiple, as is proved by the similarly multiplied quarter of a bow by which nostrils are traced on the triangular nose. The thick-lipped mouth protrudes from the face in line with the tip of the nose.

The iconography of these terracottas is unusually varied. The figures are most often kneeling (fig. 17) or squatting, with hands placed on the knees or the head, or with arms crossed on the breast and hands placed on the shoulders (as is the case with the piece uncovered in Djenné-jeno by Roderick and Susan McIntosh). However, figures of riders (fig. 18) are also known, as are recumbent figures and couples sitting one behind the other or face to face.

Their height varies from 20 cm to about 65 cm. No reliable information exists concerning the function, or functions, they served. They may have been connected with ancestor worship, as the fact that some of them were found in burial urns seems to indicate. But, although the circumstances of the find in Djenné-jeno do not exclude this possibility, the placing of figures in the foundations of a house may also suggest that they played some magic protective role. The squatting figures, especially those with their hands placed on their shoulders, may be invoking a supernatural being, or may just represent an expression of humility and respect in the face of secular authority. Some figures seem to have come straight out of everyday life; their asymmetrical poses, even half-sitting and half-lying, or comfortably resting with an elbow touching the ground as at an ancient Roman feast, are unlikely to have had anything to do with religion. On the other hand, the larger group of terracotta figures whose bodies are covered by rolling snakes must surely have had a cultic significance. In this context, Bernard de Grunne draws attention to the role played by snakes in the cosmogony of the present-day local inhabitants. And although it is true that we know nothing about the ethnic origins of the people who made the terracottas, it seems likely that they belonged to the Mande group, like the present-day tribes. As for the time of their origin, the terracottas made in the 'multiple eyelids' style belong to

64 Elephant mask. Baule-Yaure, Ivory Coast. Pale wood with surface stained grey-black, and traces of colours. The mask carries some fire-marks. In this animal mask surmounted by the figure of a bird, the attributes of the elephant (trunk, tusks and large ears) form only miniaturized distinguishing marks added to the schematized face. The saw-like belt on the perimeter of the mask is a favourite decorative element in this style. **Height 44.5 cm.**
Náprstek Museum, Prague.

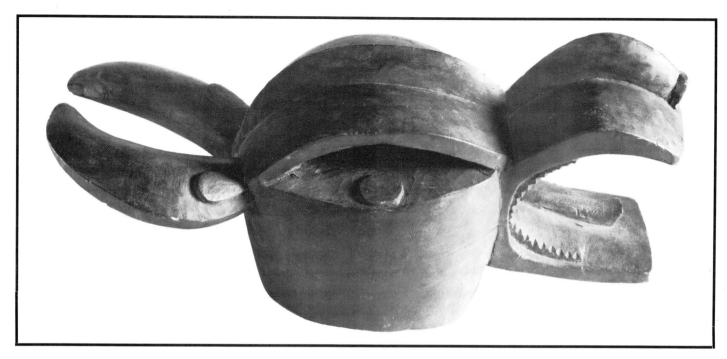

65 *Goli-goulin* buffalo-demon mask. Baule, Ivory Coast. Pale wood with surface stained grey-brown.
The mask is attached horizontally to the head of the dancer, whose body is hidden by raffia fringes.
Height 41.5 cm. Náprstek Museum, Prague.

a period when this area was part of the medieval Mali empire. De Grunne even hints at a possible connection between the iconography of the figures and the members of the royal family, but so far this remains pure speculation.

Several dozens, perhaps even hundreds, of Mali terracottas are now known. Unfortunately, when new works appear on the art market — frequently displaying previously unknown treatments and sometimes of outstanding quality — their scholarly value is considerably impaired because their provenance is inadequately documented. Most of them come from illegal excavations, or rather from the treasure-hunts conducted by local people eager to earn a little extra money. Naturally they have no idea of the sky-high prices commanded by their treasures when they eventually reach the world market.

THE UPPER NIGER REGION

The earliest of the great cultures arose in the basins of large rivers, and Black Africa was no exception in this respect. This advance was made possible by the discovery and development of agriculture, which was most favoured by conditions in large river basins. Until the 5th millennium BC the inhabitants of all of Africa were hunters and food-gatherers, nowadays found only in extreme conditions, in parts of the Congo rain-forest and the Kalahari Desert.

The transition to the new neolithic (that is, agricultural) way of life was nowhere sudden and did not take place over entire continents. In fact there were only four main centres in the whole world from which agriculture gradually spread to other areas; and one of them was in Africa. This was the Upper Niger basin, the region of southern Mali through which the Niger River flows in a roughly north-easterly direction from the frontier of Guinea, before turning southwards in a large bend. The Niger is fed here by the waters of large tributaries; it ramifies into numerous branches and forms an inner delta which, from time to time, floods when there is heavy rainfall in the south, at the source of the river. This essentially steppe-like region, situated between the southern border of the Sahara and the northern boundary of the tropical rain-forest, became the cradle of African agriculture. Many plants were cultivated here for

68

the first time in Africa and subsequently spread over the greater part of the continent.

Geographically, this part of Africa is called the western Sudan. It is the only region of Africa whose previous history is mentioned by Arab sources as early as the 11th century; even its name was given to it by the Arabs, who called it Bilād as Sūdān, or 'Land of the Black'. Great trade routes had passed through the western Sudan since ancient times, connecting the Mediterranean with the gold and ivory-rich lands on the Gulf of Guinea. Along these trade routes arose market towns such as Djenné, where so much terracotta statuary was discovered. At some time in the second half of the first millennium AD, repeated attempts began to be made to carve out large states or even to unify the western Sudan; such attempts were still taking place when the colonial powers arrived on the scene in the 19th century. The most famous examples of state expansion were the empires of Ghana and Mali, whose names have since been taken by two modern African states. The state-makers were various tribes belonging to the Mande language group who now constitute the local population, especially the tribes of the Soninke (kingdom of Ghana), the Malinke (kingdom of Mali) and the Bambara (the states of Segou and Kaarta). From the 11th century onwards the western Sudan was subject to strong Islamization, and some of its cities — notably Timbuktu and Gao — became renowned centres of Islamic culture.

Although the states of the western Sudan were typical African despotisms, no court art like that of Benin ever developed there. This was undoubtedly due to the anti-iconic tradition of Islam, to which the ruling strata in particular adhered. By contrast, changing state forms and frontiers had no radical impact on the basic structure of the tribal population, and even Islam could not altogether suppress traditional cosmogonic concepts and ancestor cults, which represent the main sources of inspiration of local tribal art. In spite of ever more intense Islamization, a number of reports indicate that tribal art continues to flourish in places where it had long ago been supposed extinct — that masked dancers still dance in some Islamic com-

munities, even during the great Muslim festivals, and that traditional carvers, now Muslims by religion, still make masks and figures for their pagan co-tribesmen, or at any rate for the European tourist.

The eastern part of the region borders on the territory where the Mande tribes settled and is closely linked with them in culture. This area is situated within the great bend of the Niger River, which continues on to the Black and White Voltas in Ghana. It is here that the discoveries of African farmers, ascribed to the ancestors of the Mande tribes, became intensively diffused; and even today groups of Mande are found among the members of the Voltaic language group. This also explains the cultural affinities between this area and the Niger basin. Because some parts of the region were relatively inaccessible, Islamic penetration was limited; and this is also why local tribe art has survived intact. Supertribal state organizations did develop in the northern part of this area, but they never succeeded in overcoming the centrifugal tendencies represented by tribal differences and reinforced by the greatly varied landscape.

The traditional tribal art of this cultural province reflects this situation. Certain common traits can be identified, works by the western Mande being more uniform in style, whereas the eastern part, Volta, produces greater stylistic variety in accordance with its ethnic variety. The main representation of the Mande tradition is the large, agricultural tribe of the Bambara, or Bamana, settled around Bamako. Their headpiece repertory of carvings includes human and animal masks, dance headpieces in the form of stylized antelopes, figures of ancestors as well as relatively little-known figures connected with the cult of deceased twins, marionettes, locks treated in the form of human figures, and stools with human caryatids. Considering the numbers of the tribe and the extent of its territory, it is hardly surprising to discover that there are many regional and personal styles. The other Mande tribes succumbed more completely to Islamization, which is why their art is of far smaller significance. Although their artifacts do reveal certain idiosyncratic features that make them easy to recognize, they may be considered a sort of local 'vernacular' version of the basic Bambara style. This is especially true of the face masks made by the Marka tribal group who live scattered all over the area and belong to the Soninke tribe, as well as of the masks and rare figures carved by the Islamized Malinke. Somewhat more independent in style are the painted animal masks of the Bozo, a tribe of fishermen who live on the banks of the Niger and the Bani, especially around their confluence near the city of Mopti.

In terms of traditional carving, the Voltaic tribes fall into two groups. The first consists of the tribes who settled south of the Bani and the Niger, in the territory of the Republic of Mali near the frontier of Burkina Faso (formerly Upper Volta), along with the tribes of northern and central Burkina Faso. The second group comprises the tribes living in the northern part of the Ivory Coast and the adjacent territorial belt running along southern Mali, the south-west of Burkina Faso and an area near the western border of Ghana.

The best-known and most prolific carvers in the first group belong to the Dogon tribe. The Dogon culture gives us what is probably the most comprehensive picture of how the culture of the entire province looked before Islamization. Its character has been preserved relatively unaltered because of the inaccessibility of the Dogon settlements at the foot of the Bandiagara Cliffs. The villages of the Dogon farmers are perched like swallows' nests high above little stony fields under steep rock walls. We owe our knowledge of Dogon art and of the entire culture, to French scholars who worked in the area during the 1930s, under the guidance of the famous Marcel Griaule. After the Second World War there was renewed interest in the Dogon, thanks to Dutch expeditions that studied the Dogon tombs high in the cliffs, supposedly hewn out by the mythical predecessors of the Dogon, the Tellem. Interest in the Dogon was also aroused by the activities of film producers, who were attracted by the spectacular natural environment as well as by the picturesque dance festivals in masks.

Dogon carving is very rich and varied, its traditions evidently reaching back to the dis-

66 Detail of plate 67.

67 Two-faced human head (Janus head). Baule-Yaure, Ivory Coast. Pale wood, faces stained slightly red, boat-shaped ears and base left natural hair and strip under the neck stained red-brown. A cult object of undocumented purpose, carved in the characteristic style of this sub-tribe (polished surface and oval, convex, stylized face with typical hair outline). Cult objects of this type occur in the western part of the Ivory Coast. This is probably the furthest east they have been found.
Height 21.5 cm.
Náprstek Museum, Prague.

tant past. Whether the wood carvings found in rock tombs were really made by the Tellem, as the Dogon believe, or by the tribes' own ancestors, all the carvings originating in the Dogon area belong to a single line of development. In some instances the figures undoubtedly represent mythical ancestors, a frequent subject being the primordial male and female. The significance of many figures, especially the older ones which may be called Tellem because of their style, can only be inferred rather than stated with certainty. For example, the figures with upraised arms called *nommo*, sometimes carved with one hand opened and the other clenched, seem to represent mythical ancestors and culture heroes, but are sometimes interpreted as rainmakers. Other figures, such as a rider or a woman husking corn, are strikingly reminiscent of terracottas from the inner delta of the Niger River; which is why some scholars consider the terracotta-makers to have been ancestors of the Dogon. A well-known type of Dogon carving are granary doors covered with figure reliefs. The latter are either horizontal rows of stylized female figures, or figures of crocodiles. These creatures occupy a special position in Dogon mythology: a crocodile is said to have helped the Dogon to cross a river which had stood in the way on their journey to their present homeland. Dogon drums and ritual vessels are decorated with

70

similar reliefs. And here too we find locks carved as figures.

Dogon masks deserve special attention. Thanks to a comprehensive monograph by Griaule, they were, until recently, the most thoroughly documented of African masks. The mask proper, covering the face, is not remarkable in any way. It consists of a flat, vertical oblong, divided by two broad vertical grooves in which triangular or rectangular eyes are placed. Sometimes the mouth is indicated by a horizontal incision under a central vertical bar, or a dart-shaped nose is carved on to this bar, in low relief. The structure of the face is so strictly geometrical that it suggested to William Fagg that it had been derived from the architecture of Sudanese mosques with a similar layout.

In spite of their simplicity, the iconography of Dogon masks is very varied. The defining iconographic elements consist of attributes added to the basic form. For example, a mask with a rounded top represents a black monkey, a pair of small horns an antelope and larger fork-shaped horns a buffalo. Some masks are surmounted by a figure of a standing or sitting woman with outstretched arms; a mask with a stylized figure of a sitting monkey represents a white monkey; and so on. However, the best-known masks are those called *kanaga*. This type has a high, flat superstructure crossed by two shorter horizontal boards; each of these has a short projection attached to the end at a right angle. These boards, reminiscent of a Lorraine cross, represent a crocodile. To complete the picture, mention must be made of the 'Large Mask' whose flat and geometrically curved superstructure of which is sometimes as much as six metres high. This is the largest known African mask.

69 Drum decorated with carvings in relief. Baule, Ivory Coast. Light-brown wood with surface stained black. Leather membrane stretched by means of five pegs. The body of the drum is decorated with five almost identical masks with different hairstyles, carved in relief and supplemented by figures of a serpent and a lizard. The drum probably accompanied a dance performed by dancers wearing the masks carved on it. **Height 41.5 cm.**
Náprstek Museum, Prague.

The flat superstructures of the Dogon mask represent a tendency characteristic of the art of both groups of Voltaic tribes, although it is much more pronounced in the eastern group. This is a tendency, not met anywhere else in Africa, towards a flat expression of the conceptual content of the mask by means of its superstructures. The meanings of these masks are conveyed through the outlines of the superstructures, geometrical and figure designs carved into their surfaces, and the single- or multi-coloured painted decorations.

The next most important tribe of this group are the Bobo, who live in the area between the cities of Djenné and Bobo Diulasso. They

are often referred to as the Bobo-Fing or the Black Bobo. The style of their helmet masks, which are often multi-coloured, is akin to the geometric treatment of the human face by the Bambara; the tops of some masks are decorated with a high and flat geometric superstructure. By contrast, animal masks reveal a tendency towards realism, which is rather surprising in western Sudanese art. The closely related Bwa, also called the Bobo-Ule or the Red Bobo, are settled in the bend of the Black Volta River. They have a large repertory of animal masks (crocodile, chameleon, bull, owl), in which the tendency towards a flat representation of the subject is taken to the limit. The common feature of these masks is an anthropomorphic face in the form of a flat disc with the eyes represented by concentric circles. Only the rounded or lozenge-shaped mouth protrudes from the surface. The majority of these masks are provided with either a single vertical flat superstructure (fig. 20), or two horizontal ones sticking out on the sides like wings (owl, butterfly). There are also masks whose tops are decorated with human figures. Again the entire mask is multi-coloured; its superstructures carry multi-coloured geometric decorations, with white predominating. The Bwa also use animal helmet masks without superstructures; these mostly represent buffaloes, whose eyes are treated as concentric circles, while the mouth is stylized as a triangle.

Masks with high and flat superstructures may also be found among the eastern neighbours of the Bwa, the Gurunsi, in the area between the Black and Red Volta Rivers. They are sometimes difficult to distinguish from the masks of the Bwa; some authors (for example, Delange) even assert that they were taken over from the Gurunsi by the Bwa. Figure sculpture too seems to have been made by the Gurunsi, although only rarely.

70 Figure of a seated man. Baule, Ivory Coast. Pale wood with slightly glossy surface, stained grey-black. To judge by an analoguous example published by Himmelheber (1935), the figure may be a posthumous portrait of a chief. It shows clearly the Baule convention of a flat treatment of the human face, best seen from the front, whereas in Guro figures the emphasis is laid on the side view. **Height 49 cm.**
Náprstek Museum, Prague.

According to recent research, the cult of deceased twins, seen among the Yoruba of Nigeria in the most developed form, also played a part in Gurunsi sculpture.

Between the 10th and 15th centuries another tribe, the Mossi, formed three states in the north-eastern part of modern Burkina Faso. Works made by the subject peoples of these states — peoples of different ethnic origins, although they are now known under the common name of the Kurumba — have sometimes been wrongly ascribed to the Mossi. We owe our knowledge of the Kurumba to the Austrian scholar Annemarie Schweeger-Hefel, whose 1980 monograph on Kurumba masks is one of the most comprehensive books of its kind. She distinguishes at least five sub-styles among the richly varied masks of the area, assigning them to various communities. Although the existence of two parallel styles in a single African tribe is in no way exceptional, the different sub-styles of the Kurumba seem more likely to represent a continuation of the styles of various original ethnic elements among the subjects of the Mossi, who were probably ignorant of the art of carving at the time of their conquest.

The masks collected by Leo Frobenius in the Yatenga area became known in the outside world at the beginning of this century. The masks made in this sub-style are usually ascribed to the Mossi, and even though they originally developed among the Kurumba group of the Nioniosi (fig. 19), some of the carvings in this sub-style do seem to have been made by the Mossi. In these masks, the face is reduced to a vertical ellipse, centrally divided by a saw-like vertical partition, with an eye-hole on each side. The forehead is usually surmounted by a pair of fork-shaped horns or a standing human figure. A flat superstructure towers above the top of the mask; it is sometimes more than two metres in height, geometrically cut through and painted in several colours, very much on the lines of the superstructures of the Bwa, Gurunsi and some Dogon masks. The form of these superstructures inspired the name given to all these masks: blade masks.

The masks made in the second sub-style have also been known since Frobenius's day.

They are in fact dance headpieces in the form of recumbent antelopes with bow-shaped horns. They are attached to rounded basket-work caps with long fringes hanging down from the sides and covering the head of the dancer. The figure of the antelope is flattened, so that it can only be identified when seen in profile. Both in its subject and the way it is attached to the head of the dancer, this dance headpiece, called *sa-saidu*, is reminiscent of the Bambara *chi-wara* headpiece. According to Schweeger-Hefel, these are masks of the Kurumba smiths.

The dance headpieces called *numtiri*, which represent the third sub-style of the Kurumba, have become very popular among collectors since the 1960s. A mask of this type takes the form of a roan antelope's head on a high neck (plate 19), the whole surface being covered with coloured decoration in the form of equilateral triangles, which is a cosmogonic symbol. Such a mask is attached to the head of the dancer in a similar way to the *sa-saidu* headpiece. The headpieces cut from the forks of large branches of kapok trees originate in the north-eastern part of the Kurumba region.

Since the 1970s stylistically different masks mostly assigned to the Mossi have appeared, both in written accounts and on the art market. According to Schweeger-Hefel, however, they are the work of the Sikomse social group of the Kurumba. This type of mask consists of a low wooden helmet carved in the form of a highly stylized antelope's head, with bow-

71 Standing female figure. Baule, Ivory Coast, Daloa City area. Light-brown wood with black-stained, dull surface. The figure seems to be a portrait of a living young woman, made because of her physical beauty. This is indicated by the overall conception of the figure, which is designed to be viewed from all sides. Whereas the treatment of the face and trunk presupposes a frontal view, the profile of the figure, especially the stylization of the buttocks to balance the volume of the belly, was obviously composed with a side view in mind. **Height 46.5 cm.** Náprstek Museum, Prague.

72 Standing female figure. Baule, Ivory Coast. Pale wood with glossy surface, stained brown-black, and crusty patina in incisions. Here the carver concentrated on elaborating surface details rather than organizing the volumes and making them interdependent. The head takes up a third of the overall height of the figure and seems to have absorbed all of the carver's creative powers. **Height 45 cm.**
Náprstek Museum, Prague.

shaped horns and a narrow mouth somewhat reminiscent of a bird's beak. When seen in profile, the entire mask looks like a bird's head rather than an antelope's, since together the bent horns and beak-like mouth suggest a crest of feathers.

The fifth Kurumba sub-style is represented by the masks originating in the vicinity of Mengao. They are mainly known from the writings of Schweeger-Hefel and the exhibition of her collection in the Museum für Völkerkunde, Vienna. This type is a helmet mask with a strongly schematized human face, a pair of stylized horns above the forehead and a blade-shaped headpiece, usually forked in the upper part, on the top. According to Schweeger-Hefel, the outlines of these headpieces correspond in detail to the outlines of Kurumba tombstones. These masks are said to be made in memory of the deceased, replacing them in the bereaved families.

We have described Kurumba art in terms of sub-styles and not styles in deference to their common ethnic origin. However, the differences must not be minimized; for example, the *numtiri* antelope heads differ in style from the dance headpieces of the Kurumba smiths much more than many carvings made by altogether different tribes who live far apart from one another.

The art of the second group of Voltaic tribes, which we might call south-western, is somewhat hybrid in style. Its most important creators are the Siena tribe, generally known as the Senufo. A majority of the tribe inhabits the northern part of the Ivory Coast, but smaller groups are found in Mali and Burkina Faso. Despite its unmistakable western Sudanese character, Senufo art also has affinities with the art of tribes much further to the southwest, on the coast of the Gulf of Guinea. The other tribes of this Voltaic group display on the one hand, a more or less obvious dependence on Senufo face masks and, on the other,

73 Stylized figure of a baboon (*mbotumbo*). Baule, Ivory Coast. Light-brown wood with the encrusted blood of sacrificed chickens. A loin-cloth made of African cloth. This ritual sculpture is used at the great festival of the first yam harvest. Offerings are placed in the bowl held by the baboon. **Height 64 cm.** Náprstek Museum, Prague.

74 Standing female figure. Baule, Ivory Coast. Pale wood with surface stained brown-black and grey-brown to black patina, glossy here and there. Clad in a string of bone beads and a shred of African cloth. Plates 71—75 give some sort of indication of the possibilities of individual expression within the framework of a single traditional canon of style. The maker of this small and undoubtedly old figure was indifferent to details, but certainly not because he lacked the skill to execute them. This is proved by the way in which he has endowed the tiny face with an admirably vivid expression. The flat treatment of the back is equally deliberate in its utilization of the play of the light on the geometric surfaces. The large head is balanced by massive leg muscles, the length of which correspond with the height of the head. **Height 26 cm.**
Private collection, Prague.

75 Rear view of plate 74.

preserve the Voltaic tradition of a flat treatment. This last tradition is most obvious in the masks of the Nafana (perhaps a sub-tribe of the Senufo), who dwell near the frontier of the Ivory Coast and Ghana, in the region around Bondoukou. In these, the face comprises a sort of flat shield with three small holes forming an inverted triangle. The holes represent the eyes and the mouth, or perhaps the nose. From the top of the face shield protrude two or three little upright columns carrying a flat symbolic superstructure (plate 23). According to Holas, masks of this type are also used among the Kulango in the north-eastern part of the Ivory Coast, as well as some other tribes in Burkina Faso and Ghana (the Abron).

Among the most expressive examples of a flat geometric treatment are the little-known animal masks of the small tribe of the Tussian, in the south-western part of Burkina Faso.

They were recently given much publicity by the New York exhibition 'Primitivism in 20th Century Art', where a Tussian mask (plate 215) was juxtaposed with a similarly treated bronze sculpture by Max Ernst. A Tussian mask consists of an oblong, almost square board, diagonally divided into four triangles. The upper triangle contains two rounded eye-holes. Fringes are attached to the sides and the bottom edge, and there is a small symbol of the animal which the mask is to represent (for example, a buffalo's horns) in the centre of the upper edge. This flat treatment of an animal's head also occurs on three-dimensional sculptures of animals, as in the bronze pendant in the form of a buffalo (plate 20). A buffalo with such a flat, square head also appears above the crown of very rare low Tussian helmet dance headpieces. It is symptomatic of the complicated mutual in-

fluences in this area, that dance headpieces, almost identical in their layout, are also found among the Senufo, although their design is naturally influenced by local traditions.

The carvings of the Lobi comprise an isolated artistic enclave, apparently unrelated in form and content to the other Voltaic groups influenced by Senufo art. The Lobi mainly live close to the south-western frontier of Burkina Faso, although some of them are found in the Ivory Coast and Ghana. Their artistic isolation may be explained by the fact that the Lobi only came to their present home from Ghana in the late 18th century. (In fact this tribe has no permanent abode, because when the soil they farm has been exhausted, Lobi families simply move on.) Furthermore not all of the carvings ascribed to the Lobi were actually made by them, since the Lobi are mixed in with other small tribes. Between the two World Wars a few rare Lobi carvings in wood had been included in European collections; and it was only in the 1960s that they started appearing on the art market in larger numbers. Our present knowledge of Lobi art is the work of Piet Meyer, who published the results of his field research in the catalogue of the 1981 exhibition of Lobi art organized by the Rietberg Museum in Zurich.

Many male and female Lobi figures are fetishes with unemphatic sexual differentiation; they serve magical purposes such as hindering the evil influence of a witch, protecting the owner against diseases or helping him in lawsuits. Also magical is the role of a rather frequent subject of Lobi art, namely a copulating couple; its purpose is to help the owner find a partner. Other figures seem to re-

76 Loom pulley. Baule, Ivory Coast. Pale wood with glossy surface stained brown-black. Raffia suspension cord. The face of the head is flatly carved to be viewed from the front. With refined deliberation, the carver made use of the frayed end of the raffia suspension cord to indicate the male beard, which is often carved in wood in Baule male figures. **Height 15.5 cm.** Private collection, Prague.

77 Ceremonial fly-whisk. Baule, Ivory Coast. Pale wood with brown-stained, glossy surface. Vegetable fibres. The handle is carved in the form of pincers. On both sides of the jaws there is a small figure of a tortoise, and at the upper end a pair of miniature face masks. The sitting panther at the end of the handle symbolizes a chief's authority.
Length of the handle 24.6 cm. Náprstek Museum, Prague.

present dead ancestors, but only ancestors of the last two generations, that is, the owner's parents and their parents. There was probably no difference in form between the figures serving magical purposes and those of ancestors.

Lobi carvers also make dance staffs, decorated with figures, which are carried attached to the shoulder, and three-legged stools, decorated at one end with a small human head. Men are said to have carried these about with them everywhere, and also to have used them in emergencies as weapons.

The figure carvings of the Lobi reveal some common traits, such as the mostly natural anatomical proportions, the absence of emphatic sex distinctions (women, for example, are given flat triangular breasts), and the accurately reproduced hairstyles. But there are, nevertheless, considerable differences in

style and great variations in skill among them. The reason is that Lobi carvers are self-taught craftsmen who have not served any kind of apprenticeship. The outstanding artistic quality of some figures is therefore attributable to the extraordinary gifts of some individuals (plate 22). From the point of view of the magic effectiveness of a figure, of course, its artistic quality is irrelevant.

Let us return to the Senufo, a people who are the most prolific carvers in the entire western Sudan, and who have greatly influenced the art of the neighbouring ethnic groups. Since the time when people started collecting African art, there has probably not been a single collection without an example of Senufo carving; and for many non-specialists Senufo carving became emblematic of the art of the entire Black Continent. Probably because of the existence of a professional caste of carvers among them, Senufo craftsmen adjusted to the modern world more satisfactorily than those of any other African tribe, making the transition from craft production for traditional tribal institutions and individuals to large-scale production for a wider market. Although derived from traditional Senufo works, these modern and mostly worthless objects, produced in large series, now disfigure thousands of European and American living-rooms.

However, even putting aside this modern hyper-production, Senufo traditional carving has always been prolific and Senufo masks and figures have never been a rarity. The territory of the Senufo has long been relatively accessible, and in the 20th century it has been visited by a number of investigators who observed Senufo artists at work and studied the role of art in religious and social life. That is why we possess so much concrete information on the subject. Nevertheless, the information is fragmentary and often contradictory, and there is still no comprehensive monograph to critically evaluate and systematically classify what is known. Seemingly reliable authorities sometimes disagree, and contradictions sometimes occur in the writings of a single author. There is, for instance, no agreement as to which ethnic groups are independent Voltaic tribes whose art was in-

81

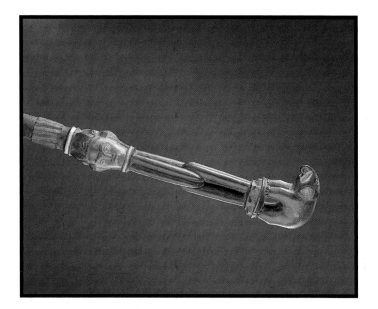

78 Ceremonial fly-whisk handle. Baule, Ivory Coast. Pale wood with stained surface and paint. This handle, like that of plate 77, was probably meant for the fly-whisk of a chief or court dignitary, since it ends with a figure of an elephant, which also symbolizes high political authority. The stem of the handle is carved in the form of two large, double chain links. Above the thorn to which the fly-whisk was tied are masks, their ears forming two figures of birds sitting on eggs. According to Himmelheber, these fly-whisks were sometimes used only as private objects of luxury, valuable enough to be offered as bail by a defendant to his accuser before the beginning of a law-suit. **Length 33 cm.**
Private collection, Prague.

79 Detail of plate 78.

fluenced by Senufo art, and which are sub-tribes, their arts being only local variants of Senufo art. One of the most blatant contradictions occurs in discussions of Senufo masks. It is always stated that these serve the ritual purposes of a secret society called *lo,* similar to the African *poro* society, and that only Senufo farmers and the caste of smiths belong to the *lo* society. But immediately afterwards we can learn from the same author that the best-known Senufo mask, called *kpelie* and used by the *lo* society, is of a type reserved to the caste of weavers — who supposedly have no *lo* society at all. The society is generally known to be divided by age into grades, the transition from a lower grade to a higher one being accompanied by a ritual in which masks are used which correspond to the appropriate age and grade. But the question of which type of mask belongs to which grade is

either not mentioned at all or answered differently by various writers. It is also generally understood that a female *lo* society exists among the Senufo, but little is known about it and even less about the use of wood-carvings in its rituals. This female society makes use of animal sculptures as visual means of instruction (figures such as a guinea-hen sitting on eggs, or a wart-hog boar because of his virility), but no more exact information is available.

Senufo art is a complex of local as well as personal styles, frequently very original in treatment, with unusually rich subjects drawn from mythology and serving a complicated system of rites. But we are able to locate these styles only occasionally and in a rough and ready fashion; and even the most original work is lost in the universal anonym-

80 Mask with a miniature bird head. Tussian, Burkina Faso. Wood with fringes made of strings tied together. The outline of the eyes and the diagonals dividing the mask into four triangles are done with abrus seeds. **Height 67 cm.**
Musée Barbier-Müller, Geneva.

82

81 Beater of a *dawle* iron gong. Baule, Ivory Coast. Pale wood with surface stained brown-black and patinated. Cotton cushion. The sounds of a goblet-shaped *dawle* iron gong accompany performances with the buffalo demon mask. A miniature of this mask is carved at the end of the beater.
Height 25 cm.
Náprstek Museum, Prague.

82 Ceremonial fly-whisk handle. Baule, Ivory Coast. Pale brown-stained wood with glossy patinated surface. This object (like that in plate 81) accompanies performances with the buffalo demon mask. In Africa the fly-whisk is a symbol of nobility and authority, features very much in evidence here. The double loop carved in the handle the 'knot of wisdom', is a symbol of authority among the Akan tribes. Two crabs are carved in low relief above the thorn to which the whisk is tied, and there are two lizards below the buffalo mask.
Length 30.8 cm.
Náprstek Museum, Prague.

ity. Most of our information about Senufo art is related to the centre of the Senufo population, the region around the city of Korhogo. Other large areas, especially those of sub-tribes such as the Kulango, remain more or less unknown, except for single documented carvings, although it is probably these areas which have been least affected by the impact of the modern world. Senufo art still awaits its William Fagg or Annemarie Schweeger-Hefel. The question is whether such an investigator will come while there is anything left to study, apart from the economics of present-day production and the ecological consequences for the growth of trees.

Let us briefly survey the repertory of Senufo carving. There is, first of all, a large variety of ritual masks: the *kpelie* face masks (sometimes doubled) with bizarre protrusions on their edges; animal helmet masks representing long-horned antelopes, hyenas or fantastic animals composed of parts of various real creatures; rare pot masks with a square hole for the eyes, above which rises a small column with saw-shaped contours, ending with a miniature head (perhaps a centipede); and dance headpieces in the form of a large oblong openwork board decorated with figures and diagonally attached to a small basketwork cap. In these headpieces, which are used as masks at the rituals of the *lo* society, it is probably correct to see a continuity with the above-mentioned Voltaic tendency towards a flat artistic treatment. Some of the animal masks, especially those which are made in the form of a pair of heads looking in opposite directions, do not represent real animals but supernatural beings.

The main subject of Senufo sculpture is a young, sexually mature woman, ready to fulfil her reproductive function; she may appear standing or seated. A variation of this subject is the nursing mother seated on a four-legged stool. Other common subjects include mythological figures, either in the form of the first parents or as various supernatural beings composed of human bodies and fantastic zoomorphic heads.

To this must be added insignia staffs topped with figures; chiefs' stools with legs in the form of figures; vessels for various cosmetics

84 Miniature *dawle* gong and beater. Baule-Atutu, Ivory Coast. Pale wood with brown-stained surface. Miniature wooden replicas of utilitarian objects are rare examples of 'art for art's sake' in Africa. Although they undoubtedly served to enhance the social prestige of their owner, their primary significance seems to be aesthetic.
Heights 16 cm and 17.6 cm. Private collection, Prague.

83 Ceremonial fly-whisk handle. Baule-Atutu, Ivory Coast. Light-brown wood. Some Akan insignia of authority are covered with a golden foil pressed into the finely carved and ornamentally arranged grooves on the surface, which are filled up with resin. Among the Baule this technique was used only by the Atutu sub-tribe (although it reached its peak among the related Asante), and this handle would have been gilded in the normal course of events, after being purchased by a local customer. It is decorated with masks and stylized cowries. **Length 27 cm.**
Private collection, Prague.

and ritual ointments with lids ornamented with figures; figures of flying birds said to be given as a reward for the swiftest labourer during hoeing contests; standing figures of the hornbill (worshipped for his mythological role as well as the sexual symbolism of his body); large drums decorated in relief, each on a caryatid in the form of a woman seated on a stool; and, last but not least, symbolic carvings in relief decorating the doors of shrines and probably also those of the dwellings of dignitaries belonging to cult organizations.

THE WEST GUINEA COAST

A clear-cut division of the African continent into individual art provinces is extremely difficult. For centuries, entire ethnic groups moved and intermingled, a process involving a similar interpenetration of ideas and techniques. This resulted in the development of art provinces, of which the artifacts were characterized by certain common basic traits and were made for similar purposes. But the dynamic of ideas and techniques constantly tends to pass across 'provincial' boundaries, which are, of course, no more than theoretical constructs, convenient for classification and study.

In no other art province of Africa are the limitations of the concept so manifest as in the western half of the coast of the Gulf of Guinea and the broad belt of the former rain forest (now to a large extent cultivated and turned into plantations) connected with it and gradually changing into a region of moist savannahs. In terms of political geography, this area covers Guinea-Bissau in the west, continuing through the Republic of Guinea, Sierra Leone, Liberia, the Ivory Coast, Ghana and Togo, and extending into part of the territory of the Republic of Benin in the east. In the north, it borders on the western Sudan province along the whole length of this geographical belt. But the frontier is in no way absolute. On both sides of this imaginary line of demarcation we may meet elements that have been taken over from the neighbouring province; and that is why it will remain doubtful just where this line should be placed. Eberhard Fischer has recently (1981) studied the theoretical demarcation of the West Guinea province and its internal divisions. For good reasons he included, as an independent area, the art of the Senufo; whereas the present book — for *its* good reasons — considers it as a part of the province of the western Sudan. This is not to deny the possibility that, for example, the concept of face masks was probably taken over from the south by the Senufo, or that the subject of these Senufo masks (that is, a stylized form of a bird's body) was taken over by their southern neighbours as an element of decoration for some of their face masks. Furthermore the distortion of the natural proportions of the human body, as seen in the Senufo rider's figure, represents a tendency characteristic of the West Guinea province. Against such arguments must be set the fact that the whole rich repertory of Senufo animal masks and the perhaps residual tendency towards flatness of treatment clearly point to the western Sudan.

The West Guinea province was originally settled by a large number of tribes and subtribes belonging to three language groups of the large family of Nigritic languages. At one time, before the rise of the medieval western Sudanese empire of Mali, a number of tribes belonging to a fourth language group, that of the Mande, began to penetrate the area from the western Sudan, causing an advance in agriculture in the Niger basin. But this ethnolinguistic mosaic is not reflected in the art of

85 Two knives in a single sheath. Baule-Atutu, Ivory Coast. Brown wood with natural patina. Another example of a Baule miniature which would normally have been gilded. The knife-handles end with a cone in traditional Baule fashion, and the sheath too is an accurate copy of a Baule warrior's equipment. The convex shield is a stylization of a certain kind of red sea shell, and the horseshoe-shaped object below represents a war trophy, the lower jaw of a killed enemy.- **Height 19.2 cm.** Private collection. Prague.

86 Standing male figure. Attie, Ivory Coast (?). Light-brown wood with glossy surface, stained black-brown. Eyes made of inset light-blue glass beads, necklace of beads of the same colour. The ethnic source of this figure is hypothetical. The origin of the figure in a minor Akan tribe settled between the Baule and the coast is indicated by the rigid posture of the figure, creating an impression of angularity in spite of the roundness of all anatomical elements, the way in which the buttocks are connected to the trunk, and the enlargement of the lower legs so that they look as though they are thrust into high boots. An Akan origin is also indicated by the stylization of the face. **Height 64 cm.** Náprstek Museum, Prague.

this province in any direct fashion. Of course, there are even more art styles than ethnic units here, but the borders of the larger style areas are not defined by ethnic or linguistic boundaries, but rather by the prevalent type of economy, geographical conditions, reli-

gious and cultural ties between various ethnic units, and political institutions. These factors imbued the province's art style with a considerable degree of homogeneity in spite of its ethnic and linguistic diversity.

In terms of tribal political institutions, this art province can be divided into western and eastern halves. This is worth mentioning, since the political differences led to corresponding artistic differences, in subjects and to some extent in style, choice of materials and techniques. The dividing line between the western and eastern areas runs roughly north-south along the watershed of the Bandama and Nzi Rivers in the Ivory Coast. However, in terms of the arts this line is even more permeable than the demarcation line between two art provinces.

Among the western tribes, political authority is usually restricted to the single village, which forms a closed administrative unit. This authority rests with a council of elders, or a chief whose powers are very limited. Some functions of a higher social authority, on a tribal or even supra-tribal level, are taken over by secret societies in which the religious life of the people is concentrated. And, as we have seen, the secret societies also exercise a form of social control and function as courts of law. Not unexpectedly, then, the most important carved works are made for various specialized ritual purposes within the secret society, and for its various dignitaries and officials.

This western half of the art province can be further divided into three main areas. The westernmost includes the tribes settled in Guinea-Bissau and the adjacent coast of the Republic of Guinea, namely the Bijogo, the Nalu, the Landuman, and the Baga. The artifacts of the Bulom and Sherbro, encountered by the first Portuguese visitors to this part of Africa, also belong here. Among the relatively large masks, animal masks predominate. They are executed in a broad range of styles, from the realistic masks of the insular Bijogo, made in the form of cows' and sharks' heads and devil-fish, through the stylized dance headpieces in the form of birds (Nalu; plate 36) and upright cobras (Baga), to the Nalu and Landuman *numbe* masks, schematic in an abstract

87 Standing figure of indeterminate sex. Ebrie, Ivory Coast. Almost white grey-brown stained wood with crusty patina. A stylistic parallel published by Holas makes it possible to assign this figure to the minor tribe of the Ebrie, dwelling in the lagoon area of the Ivory Coast. Common to both figures are rounded, bulging eyes, the hairstyle and the rings on the neck. This figure seems analogous to the supernatural being called *mmoatia* by the Asante, a forest goblin with its feet turned backwards. In this case, unfortunately, the feet are lost, so it is impossible to be certain; but such an interpretation is supported by what look like elongated 'heels', and by the shape of the legs, with the calves indicated at the front. However, the Asante *mmoatia* figures published by Rattray in 1927 have monstrous faces. Moreover, a belief in supernatural beings with a human appearance and reversed feet was also found among the Bete.
Height 30.7 cm. Náprstek Museum, Prague.

tive and inventive, figure sculpture played a part in the decoration of spoon handles and pot lids. The carvers of this tribe were also skilled at creating group scenes.

The second area includes a large number of tribes in Sierra Leone, Liberia, the south-eastern part of Guinea and the western territory of the Ivory Coast, roughly as far as the Sassandra River. This is an area known for face masks connected with the *poro* secret society; however, face masks are also made in the area by tribes which have no secret society of this type. The predominant style is that of the Dan-Ngere complex, which displays two tendencies: one, which might be called idealized realism, is ascribed to the Dan (plate 39), while the other, fantastic or even surreal, is connected with the Ngere (plate 45). The focus of this style complex is the borderland between the Ivory Coast and Liberia. The second main style of this area is centred on the opposite, western range in Sierra Leone. This is a relatively realistic style, mostly employed for helmet masks of the *bundu* female secret society (plate 41) and usually associated with the Mende.

The masks of both these style centres, modified by local traditions, also appear in a number of tribes in their immediate vicinity and in more distant areas situated between the centres. The area in which face masks of the Dan-Ngere complex occur is, of course, much larger in extent. Eberhard Fischer may well be right in considering *bundu* helmet masks to be only variants of the face masks which developed from the originally carved face masks attached to a bell-shaped wickerwork construction.

The third style focus of this area is to be found in the borderland between Guinea in the north and Sierra Leone and Liberia in the south. Its typical subject is a mask representing a highly stylized human face, usually flat and often rather elongated, with variously shaped horns on its low top. These masks are carried on the head in a slanting position. A typical example, illustrated in this book, is a Toma mask (or Loma; plate 43), but such masks may also be found, in modified forms, among certain other tribes (the Kpelle, the Kono).

The third art area in the western half of this

88 Human head. Terracotta. Anyi, Ivory Coast. Fragment of a figure, of a kind placed on graves in the territory of the old Krinjabo kingdom. Some of these figures may be two or more centuries old. Their schematic bodies are cylindrical, hollow and mostly legless, the arms being short. They are reminiscent of some Asante grave terracottas. Among the southwestern Asante, oral tradition has it that the local terracotta grave figures were made by Anyi women potters. These terracottas display stylistic links with Asante sculpture through the rings on the neck, the box-shaped line of the eyebrows, and the tilted-back head. **Height 15 cm.** Private collection, Prague.

fashion and featuring the horned heads of animals, perhaps antelopes. These mostly very large masks also include the Nalu *banda* initiation mask, syncretic in iconography (plate 35), and the famous mask of the Baga, in the form of a stately female bust representing Nimba, the goddess of fertility. Figure sculpture — standing and seated human figures, half-figures and animal figures — plays its most important role in the art of the Bijogo, who carve figures of ancestors, fetishes, and dolls intended to ensure women's fertility. In this tribe, which was at one time very produc-

89 Stool with a human caryatid. Fante, Ghana. Pale wood, the stool stained blue-black, dark patches on the figure (hair, eyes, rings round the neck, nipples and genitals) blackened with some resinous material. William Fagg wrote of a somewhat smaller stool with two caryatids in the British Museum, that its extraordinary size suggested that it was the stool of a Fante chief or king, and served as a receptacle for part of his soul. The same may be said of this example, collected at the beginning of the century. Judging by the blackening of the stool proper, its owner was already dead when it was acquired, and the stool had become a cult object and receptacle of his soul. Fante art was inspired by their great northern neighbours, the Asante, and represents a 'rustic' version of Asante art. The Fante style is more abstract, with a tendency to geometrize its forms, as often occurs on the periphery of great African style centres. **Overall height 86 cm; figure 57 cm.**

Náprstek Museum, Prague.

90

province takes in the Bete and Guro. This is a kind of transitional zone. Its art has a certain original quality of its own, but also shows signs of influences from all the neighbouring areas. In the west, the stylistic influence of the Dan-Ngere complex is so noticeable that William Fagg even included the Bete in this complex, although only the western section of the tribe is affected. The influence of Senu-fo works penetrated from the north, affecting some Guro masks. And from the south-east the Akan tribes, especially the prolific Baule, exercised their influence. Moreover the Guro and the Bete had an influence on each other.

Of all the tribal styles in the province, that of the Bete is the least known. It was at the beginning of the 1960s that William Fagg published the first Bete human figure. Field research undertaken among the Bete was not — with a single, episodic but valuable exception — concerned with artistic questions; it was also confined to the north-western part of the tribe's territory around the city of Daloa, the area most influenced by the Dan-Ngere style complex, especially in its fantastic aspect. The overwhelming majority of the Bete masks published during the last two decades originated here. But many other works demand to be considered. Figure sculptures, rare and extremely pure in style (plate 53), and masks in the form of human heads with a high bulbous forehead and introverted facial expressions, originated around the city of Gagnoa, in the south-eastern part of the tribe's territory. In the north-east a mixed style arose, in which the stylistic and constructional influences of Guro masks can be traced. No exact information is available concerning the purpose of Bete carvings, with the exception of a single American monograph on masked dance performances in the Daloa region and a few, mutually contradictory notes by Denis Paulme and Bohumil Holas.

Our information about Guro carvings is considerably more comprehensive. This is largely thanks to the work in the 1930s of Himmelheber, who devoted his pioneer field research to this tribe and their Baule neighbours; this was in fact the very first field research in Africa to be specifically concerned with traditional tribal art. The most frequent-

90 Comb. Asante, Ghana, Kumasi. Pale wood. Two crosses, made on the ridge with slings to be attached to a necklace, indicate that this comb as probably made within the area of influence of some Christian mission. The little head between the crosses represents a miniaturized *akuaba*, at once a toy and a magical doll for securing the fertility of Asante girls. These openwork combs, sometimes decorated with entire figures, were ornaments rather than objects intended for use. Another example, undoubtedly made by the hand of the same carver, was acquired by the Berlin Museum für Völkerkunde in 1905.
Height 27.5 cm.
Náprstek Museum, Prague.

ly found works are masks featuring a somewhat idealized human face, highly stylized buffalo masks whose style reveals the western Sudanese origin of the tribe, and popular *zamle* masks (plate 57) with short antelope horns twisted in a spiral and the mouth of a beast of prey. The significance of Guro figure sculpture is purely conjectural. As recently as 1960, Himmelheber denied their existence. Free-standing figures are certainly rare and very heterogeneous in style. Only a few of them (plate 60) are in the clean-cut Guro style, known from masks and finely carved girls' heads that ornament loom pulleys (plates 61, 62). Characteristic features of this tribe's style are soft outlines, S-shaped facial profiles, and smooth surfaces stained in black and often combined with red and white clay. More recent masks are usually painted. Some face masks are surmounted by a carved pair of standing human figures, in the same heterogeneous style as the free-standing figures. Apart from their style, their Guro provenance is usually indicated only by a characteristic peripheral hairline above the forehead.

In the eastern half of this art province, the decisive factor is the existence of despotic

91 Standing figure of a young woman. Asante, Ghana. Pale wood. The hairstyle, rounded base, outline of the eyes, tattoo, nipples and genitals are blackened. The flattened head and the rings round the neck of this undocumented figure (collected before the First World War) indicate that this is the work of an Asante carver. The vertical holes drilled through the fingers of both hands suggest that the figure was originally holding some object attached by means of pegs in front. The varied types of glass bead strung round the neck, waist and ankles — even including rosary beads with crosses in relief — may have come from the goods of a Czech company, on sale in Accra. The figure was formerly a part of the collection of A. Sachse, the owner of the company. **Height 45.5 cm.** Náprstek Museum, Prague.

states ruled by autocratic kings surrounded by court dignitaries. The king's authority is underpinned by a hierarchy of local chiefs, who function as governors on his behalf. The centres of religious life are the state cults endowed with professional performers of rites.

Among the Baule sub-tribes of the Ivory Coast, ancestor worship is restricted to deceased persons belonging to the immediately preceding generation. The figure carvings of them are an expression not so much of regard as of fear; the soul of the deceased, which has nowhere to go after the loss of its earthly body, is dangerous unless offered a figure in which to dwell. Of the same character are the relatively rare figures made by the Akan tribes, and some tribes related to them, in the area of lagoons and the adjacent interior of the Ivory Coast near the frontier of Ghana. Such tribes include the Attie (plate 86), the Adioukrou, the Alagya, and the Ebrie (plate 87). The art of the last-mentioned tribes is relatively little known. Besides original local elements, echoes of the art of the neighbouring Bete and Baule tribes can be discerned.

The Baule sub-tribes in the eastern part of the Ivory Coast are the most prolific carvers in the entire area, in terms of quantity and also variety of genres. This is without doubt due to the borderland position of the tribe's territory, which is linked to the very differently motivated western half of the province and is at the same time connected with the western Sudanese province in the north. Because of this, a variety of cultural influences can be seen among the Baule sub-tribes. It is certainly no coincidence that, whereas in the entire eastern half of the art province of the West Guinea Coast, masks do not exist (disregarding a few insignificant exceptions); among the Baule sub-tribes there is a rich repertory of mask types which generally deviate from the distinctive style canon of the Baule. Nowadays the style of these masks is considered to be an integral part of the Baule style, but if we compare them with the masks of their western and northern neighbours we must conclude that the prototypes must have come from there. The Akan Baule arrived in their present Ivory Coast territories from what is

92 Headrest. Asante, Ghana (?). Hard brown wood with a thick layer of greasy functional patina on the upper surface. As with plate 91, this object belonged to the collection of A. Sachse. This is probably one of the two African headrests which the collector bought from the Amsterdam firm of J. P. Oppers around 1900. The provenance of undocumented realistic tribal carvings is singularly difficult to establish, since there are no stylistic criteria to rely on. However, this particular caryatid in the form of a sitting hen appears to have been made by an Asante master, evidently a specialist in prestige objects. **Height 17 cm.**
Náprstek Museum, Prague.

now Ghana as late as the 18th century; they may have taken over some elements of their style from the original inhabitants, and others as a result of inter-tribal contacts. The contrast between the Baule style, with its naïve realism and rounded forms, and the angular abstract rigour of the western Sudanese styles, is most conspicuous in the flat disc-shaped Baule masks, known as *kple-kple*, which represent forest demons; they look like rounded versions of the tetragonal flat animal masks of the Tussian from Burkina Faso. This is not to say, of course, that there is any direct connection between the two.

We have already mentioned Baule figure carving. Apart from figures intended to serve the cult of ancestors, many of the numerous human statues made by Baule carvers represent fetishes, while others are simply idealized portraits of living contemporaries or dolls to be played with. There are no differences of form between these categories.

93 Akan gold weight with abstract decoration.
1.9 cm × 1.4 cm. Private collection, Prague.

94 Akan gold weight with abstract decoration. **3 cm × 2.3 cm.**
Private collection, Prague.

95 Akan gold weight with geometric decoration, brought
to the required weight by the addition of wire. **1.6 cm × 1.5 cm.**
Náprstek Museum, Prague.

96 Akan gold weight in the form of an axe. **Length 6.2 cm.**
Private collection, Prague.

97 Akan gold weight in the form of an ornamental knife.
Baule, Ivory Coast. **Length 4.8 cm.** Private collection, Prague.

98 Akan gold weight representing a signalling horn made
from an elephant's tusk, with attached lower jaws of slain
enemies. **Length 6.3 cm.** Náprstek Museum, Prague.

99 Akan gold weight in the form of a cock. **Height 3.2 cm.**
Private collection, Prague.

100 Akan gold weight in the form of a panther and a cock,
proverbial in significance. **Length 6 cm.**
Náprstek Museum, Prague.

101 Akan gold weight in the form af an antelope.
Length 5.6 cm. Private collection, Prague.

102 Akan gold weight in the form of a ceremonial shield.
4.2 cm × 3.4 cm.
Private collection, Prague.

103 Akan gold weight in the form of a stool. **Length 3.1 cm.**
Náprstek Museum, Prague.

104 Akan gold weight in the form a 'knot of widsom'.
Length 3.8 cm. Náprstek Museum, Prague.

105 Akan gold weight in the form of a basketwork ceremonial shield. **3.5 cm × 2.5 cm.** Private collection, Prague.

106 Akan gold weight in the form of a chief with a ceremonial sword and shield, seated on an *asipim* chair for dignitaries. **Height 6.2 cm.** Náprstek Museum, Prague.

107 Akan gold weight in the form of a dignitary on horseback and two drummers. **Height 7 cm, length 10.1 cm.** Náprstek Museum, Prague.

The weights for weighing gold dust (*mrammo*, singular: *abrammo*) are usually ascribed to the Asante, but were in fact used and manufactured by other Akan tribes, especially the Baule in the Ivory Coast. To determine their tribal origin is very difficult and in most cases impossible. This secular art dates back to the 15th century. T. F. Garrard estimates that by 1900 about three million Akan weights had been cast, involving the consumption of about thirty tons of metal (brass alloy acquired from European trade).

A genre of Baule carving, and one that links it with the west and north, is the loom pulley. Baule pulleys, like those of the Guro, are decorated with small human heads, but unlike the latter they are mostly heads of men (plate 76), figures of birds and miniature replicas of Baule animal masks. Generally speaking, Baule pulleys are not executed with the mastery characteristic of their Guro equivalents; this is probably because, according to Himmelheber, this work is left to the apprentices, some of whom never attain sufficient skill to carry out work regarded as more exacting. The wooden doors of house and shrines, decorated with relief carving of animals, fish, or scenes from everyday life, are strikingly reminiscent of Senufo doors. The Baule perhaps became acquainted with this genre, too, after arriving in their present homeland.

The other Baule arts are mainly based on Akan sources. These are representational and are carved adjuncts of social prestige, mostly secular in character. Typical examples are fly-whisk handles (plates 77, 78), which are carved with a great deal of inventiveness of subject

The oldest weights were geometric in shape, often with an abstract decoration with a symbolic meaning. From the 17th century, when the Asante kingdom arose, weights began to be made in the form of a great variety of creatures found in West Africa, including fish, reptiles, birds, quadrupeds, and even insects; they also took the form of flowers, seeds and fruits, tools, weapons, musical instruments, and so on. Commonly occurring subjects are the paraphernalia of court life. The weights of a higher nominal value are in the form of figures and scenes from everyday life. Some natural objects, such as hard seeds, crab claws and the bodies of beetles, might be cast from the actual originals. The endless variety and ingenuity of Akan weights are reminiscent of another object favoured by European collectors, the Japanese *netsuke*. Unlike the examples still manufactured for the tourist trade, the older weights are characterized by the obliteration, through long use, of surface details.

and design, unfettered by any religious iconographic requirements. They are outward signs of social position, in a few cases symbolizing the holding of a ritual office, but often also (again according to Himmelheber) valued simply as personal luxuries. This is proved by the existence of handles which were obviously never intended to serve their supposed function. The Baule delight in beautiful objects, which give their owner

108 Pipe bowl in the form of a quadruped devouring a fish or some small animal. Collected in what was then the Gold Coast in 1885-9. Terracotta. **Height 6 cm.**
Náprstek Museum, Prague.

109 Pipe bowl in the form of a chameleon. Terracotta. **Height 7.5 cm.**
Náprstek Museum, Prague.

110 Pipe bowl against which a standing male figure leans with his hands placed on his stomach. Terracotta. **Height 9.2 cm.**
Náprstek Museum, Prague.

111 Pipe bowl against which a seated male figure is leaning. Terracotta. **Height 7 cm.**
Náprstek Museum, Prague.

The pipes in plates 109—111 were collected during the first decade of the present century. The pipe in plate 111 was probably made in the same workshop as the pipes published by Rattray in his classic *Religion and Art in Ashanti*. Rattray studied Asante terracottas in the potters' village of Taffo, but it is not known whether the pipes published by him originated in the village. The grey-black tint was achieved by smoking the object after it had been fired.

social prestige and, without a doubt, also satisfy his aesthetic tastes, is demonstrated by the precise carving of miniature copies of functional objects, comprising African analogues of European bibelots (plates 84, 85).

This kind of art in the service of social prestige culminates in the gilding of some Baule objects, especially the insignia of dignitaries, with a golden foil which is pressed into fine grooves in the surface of a wood-carving. However, there were many more occasions for using this technique on the very varied apparatus of court dignitaries and chiefs of the Asante kingdom in neighbouring Ghana, from which the Baule broke away in the 18th century.

The art of the Asante, previously known as Ashanti, is mainly a court art. Gilded objects include staffs decorated with figures, as well as mountings of umbrellas with scenes of everyday life, which served as the insignia of men of various ranks; umbrellas play a similar role, as symbols of political authority, as they did in the ancient East.

The development of gilding technique was not an accident. The land of the Asante is rich in gold. This is why it was once the terminus for trans-Saharan trade routes along which many cities of the western Sudan flourished. It is also here that 'Guinean' gold originated; English pounds were coined from it, for which reason they were called 'guineas'. Gold dust became a form of currency among the Asante, and this gave rise to an artistic genre which is quite unique in Africa — the brass weights used for weighing gold dust, and the brass vessels known as *kuduo*, with lids decorated with figures and scenes of everyday life, for holding it. (These vessels are sometimes erroneously considered to be funerary objects because they — and other personal possessions — were put into the graves of the dead.)

The weights are miniature sculptures cast in brass by the lost-wax method. If African art is, in general, relatively poor and stereotyped in subjects, this is certainly not true of these Akan brass miniatures. Their wealth of motifs is almost inexhaustible: simple geometric forms, often with almost graphically codified symbols on the surface, tools, weapons, the fruits of plants, the most varied fauna of the Asante country, single human figures, and scenes of everyday life (plates 93—127).

112 Figure of a standing woman. Ewe, Togo. Pale wood. Hair painted with blue pigment, black glossy paint in the scarification incisions on the neck and abdomen. A triple string, plaited from raffia fibres and coated with resin, encircles the waist. This is one of the five known figures in this style. The arms terminate in wedge-shaped projections, to which hands holding a bowl were probably attached. The other known figures in this style carry a bowl on the head. These figures served the *abiku* cult connected with the death of a twin. Alms were put into the bowl held by the figure. The tilted-back head and the unbroken bow-shaped line of the eyebrows are probably the easternmost signs of an Akan influence. The relatively rare figure carving of the Ewe is otherwise mostly influenced by Yoruba art. Enzio Bassani detects an affinity with the abdominal scarification marks on the relief figures of the famous 16th century divination plate from Ardra (Wieckmann Collection, Ulmer Museum, Ulm).
Height 55.5 cm.
Náprstek Museum, Prague.

113 Figure of a seated woman with two children. Yoruba, Nigeria. Pale wood with slightly glossy surface, blue pigment in the grooves carved to indicate hair. The figure may represent the Mother Goddess, or only a Yoruba woman who is the mother of twins and a worshipper of Shango, the god of thunder. The latter interpretation is supported by the hairstyle which is reminiscent of a butterfly's wings but is in fact derived from the double axe, Shango's thunderbolt symbol. In the Oyo region, Shango is considered a guardian of *ibeji* (deceased twins). This figure probably stood in one of Shango's shrines.
Height 53 cm.
Náprstek Museum, Prague.

114 Sculpture of a hunter with a gun, taking aim at a lion. Fon, Republic of Benin. The figures were cast separately and riveted to a base made of brass-sheeting. Brass cast by the lost-wax technique. This miniature sculpture was probably collected before the First World War. It represents an early souvenir piece by the bronze-casters who worked exclusively for the Fon court. Out of such pieces developed the well-known figures with long thin limbs, made for the tourist trade up to the present. Here the lion figure is still modelled in the old court style used for animal sculpture.
Height 11.4 cm.
Náprstek Museum, Prague.

Many of these subjects are explicitly or implicitly linked with various genres of Asante carving. The Asante language is very rich in proverbs, and many weights and carvings have common subjects — a scorpion, for example — that also arouse in the user a number of secondary ideas inspired by proverbs in which this creature appears. When choosing their subjects, Asante carvers take these secondary associations into account. This communicative character of Asante art may explain their liking for a variety of scenes, whether in weights, *kuduo* lids, mountings of umbrellas, or the handles of ladles for the ritual offering of crushed yams. They are not scenes of everyday life in our sense, but illustrations of generally known proverbs which are a living part of the Asante language and the expression of an essentially metaphorical Asante way of thinking.

Another specifically Akan genre of carving is the manufacture of stools. Like most other Akan objects, these are made by specialized craftsmen. Their production was formerly concentrated in the village of Afwia, near Kumasi, the seat of the Asante king (*asantehene*). These stools carved from a single piece of wood are of a special type. The oblong base is connected with the curved oblong seat by a carved openwork leg in the form of a complicated geometric design of symbolic significance, a kind of three-dimensional ornament of a human or animal caryatid. In some cases, these legs too are illustrations of well-known proverbs. Besides standard designs which are distinguished by name and were formerly by tradition reserved for certain individuals (the king, the chief, a certain court dignitary, the Queen Mother), new forms arise, either as modifications of old designs or combinations of old and new. The great variety and social significance of Akan stools is in many respects reminiscent of Javanese batiks.

Almost every Asante, whether man, woman or child, has his or her own stool, and usually more than one. As an object intimately connected with the personality of its owner, and sometimes accompanying him throughout his life, the Akan stool also serves a ritual or religious purpose. As soon as a man becomes a king or chief, he is turned into a sacred person, and part of his soul enters his stool. The stool therefore becomes a symbol

99

115 *Ere ibeji* figures of deceased twins. Yoruba, Nigeria. Brown wood with glossy patina and crusts of red cosmetic powder. Eye-pupils made of aluminium wire. To judge from analogous examples published by M. and G. Stool, this pair originated in Ibadan. **Height 23.5 cm.** Private collection, Prague.

of political sovereignty, much as a European throne does, but imbued with far greater spiritual force. After the death of a dignitary of whom the whole family is proud, and whose name must not be allowed to fall into oblivion, one of his stools is chosen to become the permanent seat of his soul. Usually it is either the one on which he sat while carrying out his duties, or the one that he used while washing; this might be chosen because the stool had absorbed a part of his personality that had been washed off by the water. The stool is blackened and deposited in a special shrine in the dwelling of the head of the family, to which offerings and oblations are brought.

116 *Ere ibeji* figures of deceased twins. Yoruba, Nigeria. Brown wood with glossy patinated surface. The hair and head covering painted with indigo. Crusts of red cosmetic powder in incisions. Judging by the hairstyle of the female figure and the tribal marks on the cheeks of the male, this couple came from Ilorin region. **Height 25.5 cm.** Náprstek Museum, Prague.

The shrine of a distinguished family comes to constitute a kind of ancestral gallery.

This distinctive form of ancestor worship is met with not only among the Asante, but also among other Akan tribes such as the Baule, the Abron and the Fante (plate 93).

Relatively little attention has been paid to Asante figure carving in wood. The best known type is a small, highly stylized doll

117 *Ere ibeji* female figure clad in a miniature version of the costume worn by a priest of the god Shango. Yoruba, Nigeria. Brown patinated wood with vestiges of red cosmetic powder. Eye-pupils made of driven-in nails, costume of several layers of cloth sewn with cowries and glass beads. A similar example published by R. F. Thompson indicates that this piece was made by the carver Amos Lafia in Ibadan. The glass-bead ornamentation of the costume symbolizes the double axe of the god Shango (see caption to plate 113). **Overall height 27 cm; costume 17 cm.**
Náprstek Museum, Prague.

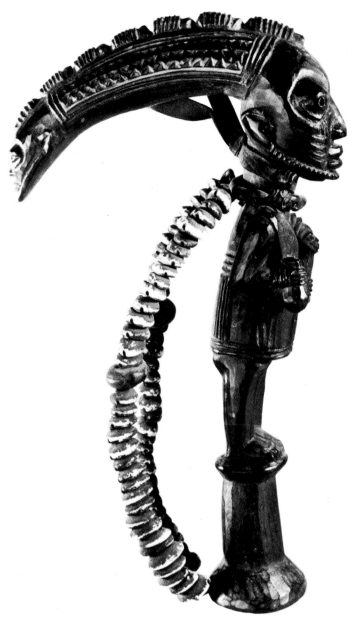

118 *Ogo elegba* dance staff. Yoruba, Nigeria. Light wood with dark-stained surface, straps strung with cowries. The staff serves the cult of the god Eshu (Elegba). The god is indicated by a head-dress with phallic symbols. While dancing, the dancer carries the staff on his right shoulder by the hook-shaped head-dress. **Height 36 cm.**
Náprstek Museum, Prague.

magical means of ensuring the fertility of the future woman. There were similar dolls among the costal Akan tribe of the Fante, but their heads were shaped as high, narrow oblongs.

Other wooden figure sculptures of the Asante are realistic, but even they reveal the fundamental Asante style tendency towards flattening the head and tilting it slightly back. Very little is known of their function, except that some of the figures representing young women were toys. Some figures, for example, that of a hangman holding a human head in his hand, may have been intended as elements in Asante insignia — in the case of the hangman, the insignia of a formerly indispensable office of the Asante despotism.

Funerary clay statuary is considered, with every justification, the most important genre of Asante sculpture. Almost life-sized idealized portrait heads or full human figures were placed on the graves of important people, along with their insignia. This practice, extant until the early 20th century, has been traced back to the 18th century, and we may expect continuing archaeological excavations to uncover earlier examples. As with African ceramics in general, systematic attention has been paid to Asante terracottas only in very recent times. There are relatively few documented archaeological finds; the majority of Asante terracotta heads on the art market come from African middlemen who have acquired them as a result of unscientific diggings. The stylistic variety of these heads indicates that there were formerly a number of ceramic workshops, sometimes functioning in close proximity in a small area. Some of these heads show the influence of Asante wood-carving. According to the recorded testimony of some contemporaries, this funerary statuary was made by women, which is rather surprising, since the manufacture of pipe-heads treated as figures (plates 108—111), which was still flourishing at the beginning of the present century, was strictly reserved for men. On the other hand, women were allowed to make simple undecorated pipes; and this means that is was not the manufacture of pipes as such that was taboo, but only the anthropomorphic and zoomorphic forms.

called *akuaba* (plural *akuamma*), with a flat head slightly tilted back on its neck, which is attached to a cylindrical body with short stumpy protrusions representing outstretched arms. Girls carried these dolls thrust into the backs of their waistcloths, in much the same way as Asante mothers carry their small children. The *akuaba* was a toy, but also a

103

The fact that women *were* allowed to make funerary wares might be explained by McLeod's theory that the taboo did not apply to women after the menopause — except that it is hard to see how a woman who spent her life making only utilitarian wares could suddenly create works of supreme skill. Obviously we need to know far more about this subject.

Although there has been detailed research on Asante culture since the early 20th century, it is again attracting the attention of investigators — and rightly so, in view of the many problems still unsolved. Even more needs to be done in the case of the art of lesser Akan tribes, both on the coast and in the interior. It would be particularly interesting to learn more of the Abron, the northern neighbours of the Asante, whose settlements extend into the Ivory Coast. According to one of William Fagg's theories this tribe transmitted a number of cultural impulses to the Asante. But we know practically nothing of its art besides a few bronze masks in peculiar style, said to have been uncovered during undocumented excavations.

THE EAST GUINEA COAST

This province of traditional African art includes the modern Republic of Benin, Nigeria south of about latitude 10° S., and the north-western part of Cameroon up to the Sanaga River. Of all the art provinces of Africa, this is the most varied in linguistic and ethnic composition. Tribes of the language sub-family Twi (Ewe, Fon) extend into the western part of Benin, while the eastern part and south-western Nigeria are inhabited by tribes belonging to several independent branches of the Kwa language sub-family. In south-eastern Nigeria, the large tribe of the Ibo, along with numerous sub-tribes, also belong to this sub-family. However, the various languages of the sub-family are very different from one another, even within a single branch. The Ijo, who at one time inhabited the Niger Delta, form an independent sub-family of the large family of Nigritic languages, which the other language sub-families of West Africa also belong to. The tribes settled in the Cross River basin, along with those inhabiting the Grasslands of Cameroon on the eastern edge of this province, belong to the Bantoid language sub-family, forming a linguistic transition to the

119 *Ogo elegba* dance equipment. Yoruba, Nigeria. Male and female figures made of pale wood with black-stained glossy surface, sewn in a leather bag covered with cowries. The worshippers of the god Eshu, trickster and messenger of the gods, carry this object hanging from the left shoulder at an annual ceremony. **Height 29.5 cm (without pendant).** Náprstek Museum, Prague.

Bantu inhabitants of central and southern Africa. Also members of the same Bantoid sub-family are some tribes dwelling on both banks of the Benue River (the Jukun, Tiv, Kantana, Jaba, Mambila). Tribes of two further language groups, some of them renowned for their carving, extend into the Benue

River basin; among Chadic tribes there are the Goemai and the Wurkun, and among eastern Nigerian tribes the Chamba, the Mumuye and the Namchi.

This linguistic and ethnic admixture has its counterpart in an extremely rich variety of styles and subjects. However, the latter do not always respect linguistic or ethnic frontiers. Their extent has been determined by factors such as political dependence on given centres of authority, or cultural dependence often resulting from nothing more than proximity. It is this complex of historical, political and cultural dependencies that makes this vast area a single art province. In the almost inexhaustible variety of the province's styles, from the highly realistic to the most abstract, we can almost always find some aspect of form, subject or function that links a particular ethnic style with the apparently unrelated work of some other tribe.

The art province of the East Guinea coast is divided into four main style areas whose distinctive features intermingle along the borders; and certain correspondences may sometimes be found even between very distant

120 *Agere ifa* palm-nut bowl. Yoruba, Nigeria or the Republic of Benin. Pale, heavy wood, painted. Bowls with caryatids are used at the daily *ifa* divination. The course of a divination is shown in the scene on the base. The caryatid of the bowl is the *babalawo* (the priest performing the divination), the other figures representing the members of the family for whom the divination is performed. During the proceedings the *babalawo* throws up sixteen palm-nuts with his right hand, catching them with the left. **Height 36 cm.** Náprstek Museum, Prague.

105

121 *Opon ifa* tray. Yoruba, Nigeria. Wood with brown-black stained surface. On the tray *babalawo* records the results of the throws (see caption to plate 120); that is, whether he has caught an even or an odd number of palm-nuts. The throw is repeated several times. The future course of events is deduced from the recorded results by means of complicated calculations in which an important role is played by multiples of four and sixteen. The border of the tray is decorated with an intricate carving in relief, and especially with one to four faces, among which one always represents the god Eshu. **Diameter 29 cm.** Náprstek Museum, Prague.

parts of the province. Lack of historical information sometimes makes it difficult to decide whether this is a case of influence or of a parallel evolution. This is particularly so with regard to the similarities of subject found in the three centres of court art in the province.

THE REPUBLIC OF BENIN AND WESTERN NIGERIA

Undoubtedly the most important area is the south-western part of Nigeria and the adjacent territory of the Republic of Benin in the west; the boundary of the area is formed by the Niger River in the north and east. The decisive element here is the Yoruba style tradition. As we saw in an earlier chapter, the first traces of this tradition appear in Nok art, which flourished beyond the north-eastern boundary of this area more than two thousand years ago. After some ten centuries, as yet

not documented by archaeology, the Yoruba tradition attained one of its high points in the court art of the kingdom of Ife, later passing to neighbouring Benin. The state was the creation of the Bini, who were not Yoruba but belonged to another language group (Edo); hence the Yoruba art tradition grew into a large but grafted branch, exclusively serving the requirements of the court. At the same time, the Yoruba tribes preserved traditions of their own, which were little affected by the style of Benin's official art. However, because of Benin's political importance, its art did influence that of the Yoruba Kingdom of Owo, which to some extent took over the leading political role in the Yoruba world from Ife during the 15th century. Ife, however,

122 Hare mask of the *egungun* society. Yoruba, Nigeria. Light-brown wood, painted. This mask was made by the well-known Adugbologe family of carvers in the town of Abeokuta. The object between the long ears of the hare represents the Yoruba talking drum (*gangan*). **Height 50 cm.** Náprstek Museum, Prague.

still remained the most important Yoruba religious centre. Second in respect of religious significance was the city-state of Oyo, which became important during the 13th or 14th century, but was sacked by the Muslim Fulbe coming down from the north in the early 19th century. Its royal city, Oyo-Ile ('Old Oyo'), was later abandoned and a New Oyo built further south. Many other Yoruba city-states derived from Ife or Oyo.

In many respects the Yoruba occupy an exceptional position in Africa. Their productivity as carvers is unrivalled and so probably is the variety of their artistic achievements. As well as carving in wood, Yoruba bronze casting, wrought-iron sculpture, ceramics and glass beadwork all reached a very high level. This was the result of Yoruba cultural traditions and also of their social organization. However, we must bear in mind that although the present-day Yoruba constitute a nation of more than ten million people, with a written language and literature, the nation developed from a number of tribes whose cultural traditions partly retain their local or regional significance and have partly become the common cultural property of the entire Yoruba nation. The process of integrating many local tribal traditions was strengthened by pressure from Muslim tribes from the north. This upset the political equilibrium between the Yoruba states, resulting in many wars and consequent population movements.

One of the peculiar features of the Yoruba is their tendency to create urban societies and cultures. The Yoruba are the only people in Africa who reached the stage of creating a large-scale urban culture in its pre-literate period. Every Yoruba state had a capital where the ruler resided. There were also a number of small towns, each with its own palace and ruler, who was properly speaking a governor, usually a blood relation of the ruler of the capital. The ruler (*oba*) of every state or town bore a traditional title; the ruler of Ife, for example, was called *oni*, the ruler of the city-state of Owo was addressed as *olowo*, the king of Oyo as *alafin*, the ruler of the city of Ede as *timi*.

There were considerable restrictions on the ruler's power, and a rival centre of author-

123 *Ikin ifa* miniature human head. Yoruba, Nigeria. Carving in bone. The head represents the god Eshu who, according to Yoruba mythology, taught the men how to carry out an *ifa* divination (see plates 120, 121). This head is placed besides the *opon ifa* tray so that Eshu can control the divination. **Height 7.2 cm.** Náprstek Museum, Prague.

ity existed in the *ogboni* secret society. The elders of this society were charged with maintaining the social order and traditional principles, functioning as a criminal court and intervening in political matters. This dualism of power was manifested in Yoruba art. Some works served to glorify the ruler. They consisted of elements of palace architecture such as the figure columns of verandahs and doors covered with relief carvings of palace life and sometimes of historical events. Among other genres connected with the ruler, we may find artifacts made of glass beads, such as diadems with figure headpieces, sheaths of ceremonial swords and other regalia. The needs of the *ogboni* secret society were met primarily by Yoruba bronze casting, which supplied the symbolic impedimenta used by the society, notably pairs of human figures called *edan* (plate 133). Carvers made their contribution by supplying ceremonial drums decorated in relief.

However, the indirect significance of Yoruba dualism for traditional art appears to have been still greater. It was probably because of this dualism that religion was not entirely bound up with the state (as it was among the Asante and some other Akan tribes), but extended into all the strata of society, along with the art that served it. That is why most Yoruba art is of a religious or ritual character.

124 Mask of the *gelede* society. Yoruba, Nigeria, or the Republic of Benin. Pale wood, painted. *Gelede* masks in the form of two identical human heads originated in the south-western part of Yorubaland. Their precise iconographical significance is not known. According to Drewal, they are called 'mothers of many children'. This piece was collected before the First World War. **Height 37 cm, width 27 cm.** Náprstek Museum, Prague.

125 *Ilari* dance head-dress of the *egungun* society. Yoruba, Nigeria. Pale wood, painted. This head-dress, made in the north-western part of Yorubaland, is formed by a human head with two faces, placed on opposite sides from each other, and two monkey heads on a round base. The human faces represent the ancestors of the clan of the royal messengers. **Height 26 cm.** Náprstek Museum, Prague.

126 Mask of the *gelede* society. Yoruba, Republic of Benin. Pale wood, painted. The figural superstructures of some *gelede* masks are obviously caricatures, such as this representation of a tourist seated in a lounging chair. A counterpart of this piece, from the Meko area in the western part of Yorubaland, is in the Musée de l'Homme in Paris. **Height 48 cm.** Náprstek Museum, Prague.

Yoruba masks are among the best known works of traditional African art. Let us first look at their use in the *gelede* secret society of the western Yoruba, who inhabit the borderland on both sides of the frontier between Nigeria and the Republic of Benin, and in

south-western Nigeria (plates 124, 126, 128). The dances of this society are connected with important events in the annual cycle of work on the land such as sowing and harvesting, their purpose being to secure a good crop. Similar masks, and also very heterogeneous dance head-dresses, are connected with the *egungun* cult dedicated to the memory of ancestors (plates 122, 125). The yearly *egungun* dance festivals are aimed at securing the assistance and protection of the ancestors against diseases, poor crops and other calamities which might befall the family. This cult, which developed in Oyo-Ile in the north towards the end of the 16th century, spread to southern Yoruba areas (Ibadan, Ijebu) as the centre of power in the old Kingdom of Oyo shifted southwards in the 19th century. A role similar to that of the *gelede* dances is played in the north-eastern areas of Ekiti and Igbomina by the *epa* (or *elefon*) dance festivities, featuring helmet masks with high figure superstructures.

Secret societies and dance associations are to be found in many African tribes. One of the peculiarities of Yoruba culture is the fact that, besides these societies, it has also given rise to a crowded pantheon of gods called *orisha*, not unlike those of ancient Greece and Rome. This is usually said to comprise about four hundred deities, but the actual number is probably much larger, since it includes many deities of purely local significance. Among the most important gods are Ifa (or Orunmila), the god of divination, Olokun, the god of the sea, Shango, the god of thunder, and Ogun, the god of iron and war. These are deities with strictly defined functions recognized by all the Yoruba, although they probably originated as local or tribal deities, eventually acquiring nation-wide significance as particular aspects of their powers came to be emphasized — again, just like the classical Greek pantheon. This is proved by Yoruba religious practice. Every Yoruba professing the traditional tribal religion (only about 20 per cent of the Yoruba now do so) worships a single *orisha*, not only revering the function he performs within the Yoruba pantheon, but also expecting the god to fulfil all his wishes, including those which are properly within the competence of his divine colleagues.

127 Box in the form of a duck. Yoruba, Nigeria. Pale wood, painted. Boxes in the form of animals, mostly used to hold presents given to important guests, are frequently found among Yoruba carvers. **Length 36 cm, height 19 cm.** Náprstek Museum, Prague.

Unlike the members of most pantheons, the Yoruba deities have only seldom become the subject of sculpture. On the other hand their worshippers are often portrayed, marked with a symbol indicating the appropriate deity; for example a double-axe signifying a thunderbolt, is a symbol of Shango, the god of thunder. The only god who is a frequent sculptural subject is Eshu (also known as Elegba), who acts as a messenger between people, gods and demons and is a magician able to change his appearance at will and forestall the negative activities of demons. He also keeps an eye on ritual observance. Eshu is the only deity for whom Yoruba art has created distinguishing iconographic features, namely a phallic hair-style and a flute symbolizing his role as messenger of the gods.

Yoruba carving was inspired to the highest degree by Ifa, the god of divination, but in an indirect way. The deity never appears, but the numerous ritual items used at a divination and bearing his name have presented Yoruba carvers with extensive opportunities for creative work. This is especially true of the caryatid dishes used to hold palm nuts; these dishes, called *agere ifa* (plate 120) and used at

128 Mask of the *gelede* society. Yoruba, Republic of Benin, Meko area. Pale wood, painted. **Height 32.5 cm.**
Náprstek Museum, Prague.

divinations, compete with the mask head-dresses of the *gelede* society in sheer variety of subjects and designs.

The most numerous Yoruba figure carvings are the male and female figures called *ere ibeji* (plates 115—117), approximately 25—30 cm in height. Because of their quantity and relative availability, they are also among the best-known works of African art, found in almost every

collection. They are connected with the cult of deceased twins, which is most highly developed among the Yoruba. This is not an accident, since the highest percentage of births of twins in the entire world occurs among this people.

The repertory of Yoruba carving is far from being exhausted by this account. It also includes genres known from other places, such as seats with caryatids, tables for the popular African game known under the Arabic name of *mankala*, cult dance sceptres (plate 118), insignia (plate 119), and mirror cases (plate 130).

The cultic integration of the Yoruba tribes has resulted not only in the creation of the Yoruba pantheon, but also in fixed principles of stylization in Yoruba art; this is especially true of carving, whether in wood or in ivory. Pronounced differences of style occur only in bronze casting and, most evidently wrought-iron sculpture (plate 131) which are reminiscent of similar works by Bambara or Senufo smiths from the western Sudan. However, these similarities are not the result of any blood relationship, but arose of necessity from the nature of the materials used and the technological possibilities they offered.

The fundamental feature of Yoruba carving is a naïve naturalism somewhat akin to certain forms of European folk art. This impression is reinforced by the colourful decoration favoured especially in western Yorubaland. A predilection for rounded forms and spherical shapes is also conspicuous. Even Yoruba masks are very rarely mere facial surfaces; in the overwhelming majority of cases they take the form of slightly tapering globular heads with a bulging face dominated by a high forehead. The eyes are mostly cast down under bulging upper lids, wide open and goggling. The nose is broad and flat, with pronounced nostrils. The lips are full, parallel, mostly straight and often without corners. In figures, the head is between a fifth and a third of the overall height, the legs being, in general, disproportionately short. The hair is usually an accurate reproduction of living models, and the same is true of the characteristic scarification marks on the faces and foreheads of both figures and masks. The breasts of female figures are full and heavy, in accord with the Yoruba predilection for rounded forms as well as the importance of maternity.

The existence of these common features of Yoruba carving does not produce a uniform art. The framework they create is large enough to permit the development of local

129 Door carved in low relief, made from a hewn board. Yoruba, Nigeria, Ilorin (?). Doors decorated in relief may be found among many tribes of West Africa. The figure of a rider on horseback is a frequent motif, especially among the northern Yoruba. The figure of a pregnant woman at the bottom, the pregnant mare beside her, and various other symbols suggest that the door belonged to a shrine involved in securing fertility. **Height 130 cm, width 65 cm.**
Náprstek Museum, Prague.

130 Mirror case with a lid. Yoruba, Nigeria. Pale wood with brown-stained surface, considerably patinated by long use. The works of the Yoruba, undoubtedly the most prolific African carvers, serve not only religious and representative purposes, but also entirely secular, aesthetic tastes. The stylized antelope in relief on the lid is a frequent West African motif. **Height 31.5 cm, width 15.5 cm.**
Náprstek Museum, Prague.

and personal styles (plate 122). This art is one of the most thoroughly studied and best known of African arts, thanks to such scholars as Fagg, Bascom, Beier, M. T. and H. J. Drewal, Thompson and Pemberton.

On the western edge of the Yoruba style area, in what is now Benin, the Fon created a despotic state in the 17th century; it perished in 1894, after a French military intervention and the subsequent deportation of the last king, Gbehanzin. The main traditional enemies of this kingdom, which prospered through the slave-trade, were the Yoruba. Nevertheless Fon art is an offshoot of Yoruba art. It is possible to speak of an independent Fon style, with some reservations, only in connection with the prestigious art of the Abomey king's court.

Almost all known works of Fon court were part of the spoils seized from Gbehanzin's palace by the French. Unlike the spoils from Benin, they do not encapsulate the history of the culture, but consist of various metal sculptures and wooden statues serving to glorify the ruler and having little in common in respect of style. Most of these are now in the Musée de l'Homme in Paris. Among wooden sculptures, there are two monstrous figures, symbolic portraits of the last two Abomey rulers, Gbehanzin and his immediate predecessor Glele. Since they were probably made by the same hand, they must date from between 1889 and 1894, that is, between the ascension and the dethronement of Gbehanzin. His portrait is a standing figure with the lower half of the body in human form; the upper half consists of the torso of a fish (a shark) with human hands. The upper half of the figure of Glele is the torso of a lion (fig. 21). These symbolic portraits are vainglorious visual metaphors representing the despots' view of themselves. If we did not know better we should be tempted to assign these highly distinctive works to the folk art of some Indian village, believing them to portray avatars of the god Vishnu. The most famous pieces from the Abomey palace are two metal sculptures, one made of iron and the other consisting of brass sheets riveted together. Both of them represent Gu, the god of war and iron, an analogue of the Yoruba god Ogun. These

statues are probably allegorical, ascribing the power and strength of the fearful god to the autocrat of Abomey. Both of them — each quite unlike the other — are unparalleled in African art. We do not know of any earlier stages in their development; like two supernovas, they suddenly flash and disappear, leaving no trace of their existence in the style of Fon blacksmiths and bronze-casters.

A homogeneous style can be found in the rare Fon animal sculptures, whether made of metal and put together from riveted parts or made of wood and covered with a silver foil (guineafowl, elephant, lion, buffalo). This is also true of the symbolic high reliefs that fill square niches on the mud walls of the royal palace in Abomey. Like the two wooden sculptures just discussed, they represent allegorical pictographs based on statements made by Abomey kings, recording events of key importance in the history of the state. Although the style of the palace reliefs is without doubt of local origin, it is possible that the very idea of decorating the palace walls with propagandist reliefs was inspired by the Benin palace. If so, the present Abomey palace must have had a predecessor, since the bronze reliefs in Benin were removed towards the end of the 17th century and deposited in the palace storeroom.

The eastern outpost of the Yoruba style area is the region inhabited by tribes belonging to the Edo language branch. Its most important representatives are the Bini, who created the Benin state, and its court art. The Benin rulers' cult of ancestors, manifested in the placing of bronze human heads on altars in the palace, had its equivalents in the residences of the chiefs of villages and the smaller Edo tribes living under Benin sovereignty. On the altars of the male ancestors the Benin bronze human heads were replaced by wooden heads of rams and antelopes; and only from the mid-19th century were local dignitaries allowed to use heads made of wood in style resembling a kind of folk form of the court style. Similarly, instead of the bronze figure standing on the altar of the Queen Mother in Benin, a wooden figure of a cock was placed on the altar of the chief's mother. The original tribal style of the Bini is probably represented by the face masks of the *ekpo* cult society (plate 134).

A few rare wooden masks of this tribe, forming a part of the spoils of the punitive expedition, are known. They originated from a single place, the Benin port of Ughoton, where they were seized by the expedition and where, according to William Fagg, replicas were later made. In style as well as type they are foreign both to Benin court art and to Bini tribal art. Their prototypes obviously originated in the Niger Delta, and the masks used in the local cult came to the Bini via the southern Yoruba. The cubistic angular style of the coastal tribes also influenced the independent style of another Edo tribe, the Urhobo, who are the southern neighbours of the Bini. Little known and seldom represented in collections are their human figures made of wood, which give the impression of being monumental statues hewn out of rock, so robust are they in style.

Fig. 21 King Glele. Symbolic portrait figure. Fon, Republic of Benin. **Height 170 cm.** Musée de l'Homme, Paris.

131 *Opa osanyin* altar consecrated to Osanyin, god of healing and the life force. Yoruba, Nigeria. Forged iron. Figures of stylized birds are either connected with the Yoruba myth of the creation of the world, or based on the concept that birds are carriers of the magic, which Osanyin guards against. The number of the birds — sixteen — is not accidental, that being the basic number of the Yoruba numerical system. **Height 85.5 cm.** Náprstek Museum, Prague.

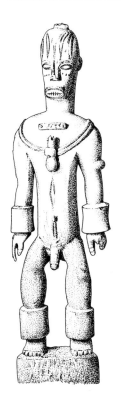

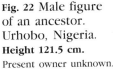

Fig. 22 Male figure
of an ancestor.
Urhobo, Nigeria.
Height 121.5 cm.
Present owner unknown.

133 *Ogboni edan* pair of
figures cast by the lost-wax
method. Yoruba, Nigeria. Brass
on iron rods, by means of
which the figures are stuck
into the earth. These figures of
a man and woman, usually
linked together by a chain, are
symbols of the *ogboni* secret
society executing justice in the
traditional Yoruba community.
Height 20 cm.
Náprstek Museum, Prague.

We possess detailed information about Urhobo art, thanks to Perkins Foss, who studied
it *in situ* at the beginning of the 1970s. The
Urhobo make male and female figures, up to
150 cm in height, which personify various
spirits or ancestors. They are associated with
the military traditions of the tribe, notably
those of its ancestors, who conquered the
tribal territory it now occupies and founded
the present villages and towns. These traditions may have determined some typical features of the Urhobo style, including the
swords, lances and other warlike objects held
by the male figures. On each of these, the head
and neck are formed by a stout column, unbroken at the back and sides, while the face
has an energetic chin protruding in the front

(fig. 22). The high and slightly arched forehead is
decorated with four vertical broad grooves of
scarification; a narrow fifth groove runs down
the middle to the ridge of the nose. This
scarification enhances the impression made
by the monumental figures, which appear to
tower over the viewer in a menacing way. In
female figures the broad vertical grooves are
sometimes replaced by four little squares divided into nine small segments by vertical and
horizontal incisions. The shoulders of the figures are broad, the trunk is erect and the
upper part of the breast bulges out as though
the figure were filling its lungs with air. In
silhouette these figures are somewhat reminiscent of American football players, swollen
with protective clothing. The figures are half-
standing and half-sitting, an attitude which
emphasizes the impression of strength and
inner tension that they convey. The artistically more significant masks of this tribe are
reminiscent in style of the large figure sculptures. They represent water spirits and, ac-

132 Figure of a seated man with a tropical helmet and an
opened book (?). Yoruba, Nigeria. Figures of Africans wearing European clothes, and sometimes Europeans themselves,
have been made by Yoruba carvers since the early 20th century. This piece was probably collected in the 1920s.
Height 85.5 cm. Opočno Castle, Czechoslovakia.

119

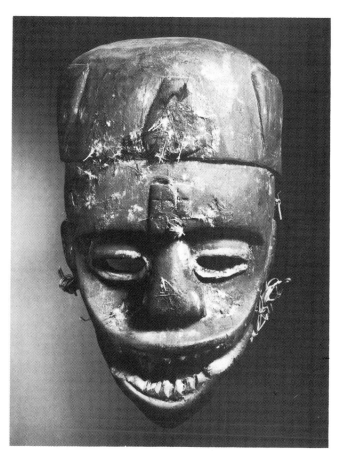

135 Face mask with a movable lower jaw, used by the *ekpo* secret society. Ibibio, Nigeria. Pale wood with black-stained surface, spots of a pink pigment. A flap cut from an inner tube fastened in the mouth. At the level of the upper jaw, there is a bar which the performer holds by the teeth in order to keep the mask in place. Remnants of the feathers of a sacrificed chicken. The mask became part of a collection in the 1970s.
Height 33 cm, width 20.8 cm.
Náprstek Museum, Prague.

Fig. 23 Mask of a water spirit. Ijo, Nigeria.
Height 35.5 cm.
Webster Plass Collection.
Museum of Mankind, London.

cording to tradition, were brought here from the territory of the Urhobo's southern neighbours, the Ijo. This tradition is yet another proof of the evident influence of the cubistic Ijo style on the Urhobo.

Among the Edo tribes living on the periphery of the Benin kingdom's sphere of influence, mention should be made of the Ishan, the north-eastern neighbours of the Bini. The carving of this tribe is independent in both its style and its subjects. The best-known Ishan creations are face masks, the originals of the type taken over by the Yoruba for their *egungun* performance. They have eyeholes which are not situated under the eyes (as is the case with the tribal masks of the Bini) but replace them. Also characteristic is the slant of the eyeholes with the inner corners placed high-

er up, as in the tragic masks of ancient Greek and Roman drama. The open mouth of the Ishan masks, displaying grinning teeth, occupies the entire width of the face; the beard is indicated by an incision in the chin.

The art of certain minor northern Edo tribes, known under the pejorative common name of Kukuruku, has not yet been systematically studied. The published examples reveal only a mixture of foreign models and influences, taken over from neighbouring tribes settled all around the Kukuruku, a situation typical of a people living at the point of intersection of three large style areas.

SOUTH-EASTERN NIGERIA

The second large style area of this art province is situated in south-eastern Nigeria. The limits of its territory are marked off in the west by the Lower Niger (the style area including the delta) and in the north by the Benue River, an eastern tributary of the Niger. In the east, its boundaries roughly correspond to the state frontier between Nigeria

134 Face mask. Bini, Nigeria. Pale wood, painted. The mask probably represents a policeman, one of the seven characters performing in a masked dance of the *ekpo* secret society; the aim of this dance is to protect the community against illness and other calamities. **Height 27 cm.**
Náprstek Museum, Prague.

Fig. 24 Face mask.
Grebo, Ivory Coast.
Height 28 cm.
Musée de l'Homme, Paris.

Fig. 25 *Ejiri* altar.
Ijo, Nigeria.
Height 63.5 cm.
Metropolitan Museum, New York.

and Cameroon. As with the other large style provinces and areas, none of these boundaries are hermetically sealed.

South-eastern Nigeria is divided into four original style centres. The first is to be found in the Niger Delta, the second in the Cross River basin up to the frontier of Cameroon, the third between the Lower Cross River and the Delta, and the fourth in the north, in the triangle formed by the Niger and Benue Rivers. The ethnic political and artistic situation is not unlike that of the Ivory Coast, Liberia and the adjacent area of Guinea, where the dominant factor is the Dan-Ngere com-

136 Head-dress of the *ekpe* secret society. Ekoi (Ejagham), Nigeria, Cross River region. Wood covered with antelope skin. Although collected before the First World War, the mask was probably made for sale to foreigners. This is proved by the fact that several museums possess almost identical pieces, never used ritually and obviously made in a series by a single carver. **Height 61 cm.**
Náprstek Museum, Prague.

plex. In south-eastern Nigeria, however, the situation is more complicated. Instead of two antagonistic style tendencies represented by two tribes, here there are four, based on the above-mentioned four style centres. In some places, especially the area between the Lower Cross River and the Delta, the styles of all four centres may make themselves felt at the same time. South-eastern Nigeria has yet another trait in common with the West African region, namely the lack of high-level political authorities. Political control usually operates here at village level and except among the Ibibio, there is no secret society of the *poro* type to play a unifying cultural role. Secret societies did exist among the Ibo, but even in the 19th century their political influence was severely restricted by the colonial administration. Because of this situation, the local arts are very varied in style.

The coastal belt of the Niger Delta, the first style centre, is inhabited by the linguistically isolated Ijo tribes, and, in the east, by the related Kalabari. Their way of life was determined by the environment — small patches of dry land overgrown by mangroves and crossed by numerous water-courses. Fishing was the basis of economy. A part of the catch was exchanged for other necessary goods with tribes higher upstream on the local river. Their coastal position led to early contacts with European ships, so that the local inhabitants became intermediaries in trade with the interior; the commodities most in demand were slaves and, later on, palm-oil.

These facts have influenced the traditional art of the area. Dependence upon water led to belief in powerful water spirits, whose will determined men's fate. Masks representing the spirits were prerequisites of the festivities of the *sekiapu* secret society and the *ekine* semi-secret dance association. These masks feature stylized heads of water animals, fish, or monsters, made by combining elements from various water animals (fig. 23). Insofar as the human face is shown, it is narrow, elongated and curved like a boat. All of these masks were worn horizontally on the top of the head, with the body hidden under costume. In some festivals, the dancers in masks used to come out from the water, which may

123

account for the horizontal position of the masks. Figure sculptures made for the shrines standing on the banks of water-courses also represent spirits, or mythical heroes of the tribe and the village.

A distinctive artifact, taken over by the Urhobo, is a kind of altar called *ejiri* (fig. 25). This is a figure of a fantastic animal, allegedly an elephant (albeit trunkless), but displaying obvious traits characteristic of the beast of prey. The head is surmounted by a seated figure of the head of the family, sometimes with a companion on each side of him. This monster represents the protecting spirit of the family. His task is to control the life force and to aim it in the desired direction, for example, at success in a war.

The style of carving of the Niger Delta region may reasonably be called cubistic. The faces, heads or bodies of men and animals are first broken down into their anatomical components, geometrized, and then resynthesized into new organic units, but others — cones, pyramids, hemispheres — are also found. Robert Horton, studying this art among the Kalabari in the 1960s, noticed that the carvers do not give the sculpture its basic form with an adze, as is usual in Africa, but with a matchet, which is better suited to cutting flat surfaces and angular joins. Horton wondered whether the development of the style might not have been partly a result of using this tool; but he concluded, probably rightly, that it was rather the traditional cubistic tendency which had brought about the use of the matchet.

It is appropriate to note here that a similarly angular style exists among the Kru, a coastal tribe, and the Grebo (fig. 24), who dwell around the estuary of the Cavally River, near the frontier between the Ivory Coast and Liberia. Masks, based in subject-matter and themes on the monstrous masks of the Dan-Ngere complex, are carved there in a cubistic style. Since the Kru were often hired to man ships along the West African coast, the transfer of this style in one direction or the other is within the realms of possibility.

We have already mentioned that the local style was one of the formative factors in the style of the Urhobo, an Edo tribe settled in the north-west. However, the influence of the style was much more strongly felt among the neighbouring peoples of the north-east. It was practically taken over by the southern Ibo of the Ekpahia group, and it strongly influenced the traditional art of the Ibibio who lived around the Cross River estuary. In the latter case, influence was exerted in both directions. The dance headpieces in the form of human heads placed on a base, which are one of two fundamental types of mask among the Cross River tribes, obviously served long ago as models for similar headpieces adopted by the coastal Ijo. As Horton has noted, for their *ekine* dance associations the contemporary Kalabari take over ready-made masks of the Ibibio of the Anang group, made by carvers from Ikot Ekpene.

Before leaving this coastal area, let us mention yet another local genre of carving — the funerary panels called *duen fobara*. These were made in memory of traders in the Kalabari cities (plate 137), which grew rich through their commerce with European ocean-going ships. These rare objects are now perhaps found only in museum collections. They are oblong wooden frames, horizontally filled with reeds, which form the background for mounted figures carved in the local cubistic style. The arms and legs are made separately and attached to the figures in such a way that they stand out, creating a sort of false high relief. The central figure, representing the dead man, is individualized by an *ekine* headpiece of the type which he used during his lifetime. Beside the central figure there are usually two other figures; they are much smaller, indicating their lesser importance, as in Benin bronze plaques. This fact, together with the size of the panels and certain similarities in the design details, make it virtually certain that the Kalabari were familiar with Benin court art. On the other hand the technique of putting the panels and figures together by mounting the individual parts, unique in African art, is attributed to the local carvers' contacts with European ships' carpenters.

The antithesis of Niger Delta 'cubism' is found in the production of the second style centre, on the Upper Cross River. Some of the local head-dresses in the form of human heads

137 *Duen fobara* funeral panel. Kalabari Ijo, Nigeria.
Painted wood, background formed by a wooden
framework filled with reed.
Height 97 cm.
Museum of Mankind, London.

attached to rounded basketwork bases probably exhibit the highest degree of realism ever achieved in African art. This is especially true of the dance head-dresses of the Anyang, who live on the northern bank of the Cross River in Cameroon. The best examples dating from before the First World War, are now in German museums. However, the realistic masks of the Anyang, which give the impression of being true portaits, represent only one aspect of this style centre. Most carvings of the entire group of local interrelated Bantoid tribes display a greater or lesser degree of stylization which, however contradictory it may sound, sometimes reaches cubistic extremes while retaining the same general characteristics. This is true of the masks and of some rare figure carvings to be seen in the older German collections. For example, the masks of the Widekum, who are the immediate northern neighbours of the Anyang, reveal a high degree of stylization and a strong geometrizing tendency. Here, within a relatively small area, we encounter the stylistic multiplicity typical of all south-eastern Nigeria.

The Ekoi (Ejagham), who live north of the Cross River, are considered the most representative carvers in this style centre. Usually assigned to them are various undocumented carvings, especially masks, which in fact originated in some of the many neighbouring related tribes. Besides the tribes mentioned above, there are, for example, the minor tribe of the Keaka on the southern bank of the Cross River, east of the Ekoi, and the Bokyi, living north of the Ekoi, between the Cross River and the territory of the Tiv; these tribes are also Bantoid, but their art is not influenced by the local style. Some typical elements of the Cross River style centre are found in local stylistic variants in the east among the Bangwa, who properly belong to the culturally different area of the Cameroon grasslands and in the west in some groups of the Ibo and Ibibio. This diffusion in two directions was obviously the doing of the Ekoi, whose territory was crossed by a trade route connecting the Grasslands with the Kalabar coast.

The most important and the best-known products of local carving are masks of two types. The first is represented by the previous-

ly mentioned head-dresses in the form of human heads on basketwork bases, adapted in order to be bound to the top of the dancer's head. They are often female heads with conspicuous hairstyles in the form of high spiral tresses (plate 136). Among the Bokyi, these head-dresses have two faces, one beside the other. They mostly maintain the natural size of the human head, but some are miniaturized. Also known are head-dresses in the form of the head of a fantastic animal with a wide flat beak-like mouth, perhaps representing a monkey. The second type consists of helmet masks. These are cylindrical or bell-shaped, and rest on the shoulders of the dancer. Their surfaces are usually carved with two faces turned in opposite directions (the Janus head), although sometimes there are three or four. The face with eyeholes — the male one — is black, the bright female faces being 'blind'. Bird feathers or porcupine spikes are sometimes inserted into holes on the top of these helmets, and one or two miniature human heads are carved on some of them. Various types of masks and some of the iconographic details correspond to various grades in the hierarchy of the *ekkpe* society.

The realistic appearance of these masks is enhanced by a covering made of ochre-brown antelope skin, which is stretched and fastened with wooden pegs. This technique is unparalleled anywhere in Africa and probably in the entire world. It is often stated that human skin was formerly used for this purpose, but this appears to be unsupported by evidence. It may have been suggested by the former custom of dancing with the head of an enemy bound to the top of the dancer's head. Such trophies have been in German museum collections since the period of German colonial rule in Cameroon.

Some of the Ekoi dance head-dresses take the form of small seated human figures

138 Tailor working at a Singer sewing machine. Ibibio, Nigeria, Ikot Ekpene. Pale wood coloured with modern imported paints. This 'modern' carving from the 1960s may have been meant as the amusing superstructure of a profane mask, designed purely to amuse spectators. An asymmetrical European hairstyle appeared in the masks of this tribe from about 1920s. **Height 45 cm.**
Náprstek Museum, Prague.

attached to a basketwork cap. These figures are also covered with skin; their peculiarity is that they are provided with movable arms.

The third style centre of south-eastern Nigeria is situated between the Lower Cross River and the Niger Delta. This region is inhabited by groups of the large tribe of the Ibibio, whose art displays considerable independence in style, and the related Kana, who are better known under the Ibo name of Ogoni. Two influences are noticeable here — on the one hand, the influence of the cubistic style of the Delta, and, on the other, that of the Upper Cross River style. For example, the famous wooden tomb figures of the ancestors of the Oron clan of the Ibibio from the Kalabar Coast (now mostly in the Oron Museum) are carved in the unique and unambiguous local style based on cubistic principles. The same is also true of some bizarre dance headpieces consisting of a couple of spherical human heads, as well as human figures showing, besides a cubistic tendency, such a basically non-African technique as the use of separately carved components. (The movable arms of Ekoi dance headpieces may have their source here). This technique, as in the case of the *duen fobara* panels, obviously originated in the Delta coastal area. Influence from this nearby area, in which early contacts were made with Europeans, is also obvious in some of the Ibibio figures, including the assuredly older ones, carved with a hat, a coat, or other elements of European dress.

Two outside and stylistically antithetical influences — the direct use of foreign models along with local ones, and an obvious predilection for iconographic innovations — greatly obscure the autochthonous characteristics of this style centre. We may justifiably suppose that they are most clearly

139 Free-standing female figure. Wurkun (?), Nigeria. Hard brown wood with glossy surface stained black-grey. The figure was purchased by the former owner in Paris in 1932; its place of origin was said to be the then Belgian Congo. The column-shaped neck placed on the flat shoulders, and the arms carved in relief on the cylindrical trunk, suggest an origin among one of the tribes in the area north of the Benue River. The hairstyle comprising five globular protrusions is reminiscent of the famous terracotta head from Nok (fig. 5). **Height 39.8 cm.** Náprstek Museum, Prague.

128

revealed by the masks of the *ekpo* secret society (plate 135), thanks to the conservative traditionalism of institutions of this kind. Their extensive iconographic repertory includes masks, simply given the form of a human face, which are particularly revealing. The often reproduced example from the collection of the Linden Museum in Stuttgart (plate 144) will be discussed here, although pieces of the same quality can also be found in other older collections such as London's Horniman Museum. Like most masks of the Ibibio and Kana (Ogoni), this one is provided with a movable lower jaw. The impression of squareness is emphasized by three horizontals which are the main stylistic feature here. The first horizontal is formed by the lower edge of the nose and the edge of cheeks, and the third by the edge of the upper lip, which extends right across the face. Counterpointing these horizontals, a vertical gradually emerges from the bulging forehead as the sharp ridge of the nose, continuing below as a groove in the skin under the nose, and ending in an apex in the middle of the upper lip carved into two elegant wavy lines. The straight lines seen from the front are contrasted in profile with the curves of the bulging forehead, eyelids, cheeks, nose and upper lip. Of course, these curves are not just formalistic contrasts to the linear aspect of the full face, but use the light to model the mask and bring it to life.

We have spent some time on a formal analysis of this one mask because the stylistic elements found here in a crystallized, classic form may be seen in most Ibibio carvings. The local sub-styles are defined by the extent to which they deviate in style from this classic norm, or enrich it one way or another. When looking at Ibibio art from this point of view, we can discern the stylistic links between, say, on the one hand, the figures of the southern Ibibio showing an obvious predilection for contrasting black and white planes and occasional foreign techniques, and, on the other, the black dance head-dresses used during the *ogbom* festival of the yam harvest in the north, between the cities of Umuahia and Ikot Ekpene.

We have already stated that the masks of the *ekpo* secret society are very varied in their iconography. Besides normal human faces, masks are frequently made in the form of faces deformed by the locally widespread disease of *gangosa* (rhinopharyngitis), which assails the nose gristle; others probably represent in stylized form an advanced stage of leprosy. Above the forehead of some masks, a miniature human skull is carved.

The masks of the Anang sub-tribe of Ikot-Ekpene are more realistic. There is little stylization, but they do display a tendency towards idealization in the faces of boys and girls. The male masks are adorned with a carefully carved European hairstyle with a parting on one side, while the tresses of the female masks probably imitate the fashionable coiffures of British ladies during Victorian times. The masks from Ikot-Ekpene are provided with movable lower jaws. During recent decades, these masks have been painted in gay colours with imported oil-colours and synthetic paints; they are therefore glossy, in contrast to the matt surfaces traditionally favoured. The work of the Ikot-Ekpene carvers is based on the principle of co-operative manufacture, and thanks to their productivity and spirit of commercial enterprise, these masks are nowadays used even in distant parts of Nigeria. In the domestic milieu of the Ibibio, the masks are used by uninitiated boys.

The masks of the Kana (Ogoni) are partly miniaturized versions of the basic types of Ibibio masks with movable lower jaws. In terms of proportions they are usually narrower, while the teeth are enlarged. Their faces are white and the hair is brown-black. Besides these masks, probably not autochthonous, the tribe also has masks of its own, namely highly stylized, or even schematized, animal masks (elephant, boar, antelope), which are used in the acrobatic *karikpo* dances during harvest games.

The last centre of traditional art in south-eastern Nigeria is substantially different in character from the other three centres. No unifying stylistic tendency can be discerned in its rich carving. The fundamental ethnic element is the Ibo, now the second most numerous of Nigeria's peoples and divided into dozens of sub-tribes. Although the Ibo are well-known for their intelligence and

129

140 Pipe bowl in the form of a seated man wearing an elephant mask. Bali (?), Cameroon. Fired clay, brown-grey. **Height 17.4 cm.** Náprstek Museum Prague.

141 Anthropomorphic pipe bowls. Bali (?), Cameroon. Brown-grey clay, the second piece with a brick-red slip. Both objects were collected before 1890. **Height 12 cm and 9.4 cm.** Náprstek Museum, Prague.

industry, in the pre-colonial period they had not got beyond village level in their political and religious organization. This fragmentation led to the creation of a large variety of purely local art styles. Although the majority of the Ibo make their living by agriculture, very many of them are travelling traders and craftsmen, often moving in distant and alien ethnic milieu. Ibo art owes many of its features to these wide-ranging contacts.

Among the large repertory of Ibo styles and subjects, a few demand to be mentioned as outstanding and representative. In figure carving there are the painted ancestor figures, sometimes more than life-sized, from the area around the city of Onitsha. With some reservations their style may be called realistic, but whereas the general African tendency is to enlarge the head in relation to the body, the opposite trend prevails here. The heads are usually comparatively small, sometimes perched on a column-shaped neck, and the legs are somewhat longer than normal. These figures, which were probably the objects of a public village cult, appeared in large numbers in western collections only after the disastrous Nigerian civil war of the late 1960s. Worth attention is their exact reproduction of the traditional Ibo *itchi* scarification in the form of dense oblique grooves on the forehead. This is the same scarification that we saw in the rare bronze heads (fig. 7) from the 5th century, excavated in Igbo-Ukwu.

The *itchi* scarification marks are also often reproduced in the famous masks of the *mmwo* secret society (fig. 26) from the same area. These masks have elongated white (and very occasionally black) faces with fine features and represent the spirits of dead young women. This is why their helmet-shaped tops are carved in the form of rich coiffures with ornamental combs stuck in, sometimes even decorated with a figure on top. The performers wearing these masks dance in close-fitting woven costumes with small breasts attached to them. Besides these girls' masks, the *mmwo* society uses masks of an altogether different type which display stylistic affinities with Ibibio masks. These are male face masks with horns sticking upward in an exponential curve. According to William Fagg, this curve is a frequent symbol of strength, growth and fertility in African art.

An analogous case of two entirely different styles within a single ethnic group of the Ibo may be found in the north-eastern part of the Ibo territory, among the sub-tribe of the Afikpo. On the one hand they have masks called *mba*, allegedly named after the sort of wood they are carved from. This type is a convex face mask, the outline of which forms a re-

142 Pipe bowl in the form of a human head surmounted by a three-faced half-figure. Bamum, Cameroon. Brass cast by the lost-wax method. **Height 28.7 cm.** Náprstek Museum, Prague.

gular narrow oval. The stylized white face, representing a young girl, has the almond-shaped eyes cut through it and a narrow sharp nose. The drawing of the arched eyebrows and the scarification marks of the cheeks and temples are black, as is the rounded smooth top of the mask, representing the hair. The mask is surmounted by a standing or seated human figure, or sometimes only by a blade-shaped object carved geometrically, as in some masks of the western Sudan. These masks appear in identical pairs in celebrations of the annual agricultural cycle; the dancers wearing them imitate girls' movements.

By contrast, the Afikpo have also created a mask representing one of the highest points of abstraction ever achieved by African art. This mask is rounded, convex and relatively small, so that it does not even cover the whole face of the person it is attached to. Upwards from its forehead grows a seemingly stuck-in

blade, curved backwards and reminiscent of a rhino's horn, but flattened at the sides. This horn in fact represents the knife used in harvesting the yam bulbs. There are two horizontal slots in the middle of the mask. Along the vertical axis of the mask, under the blade, are three or four cylindrical protrusions, interpreted as teeth by the Ibo but more probably resulting from a stylization of the nose, mouth and chin. These masks, called *maji*, are used in the boys' initiation ceremonies and the festival of the yam harvest. Similarly conceived masks, obviously abstractions of animal heads — perhaps antelope — are to be found among the north-western Ibo in the area around the city of Nsukka. In the vicinity of the city of Abakaliki, north-east of the territory of the Afikpo, there are very remarkable elephant masks called *ogbodo enyi* (fig. 27), treated in an obviously cubistic way; their style is so different from all their neighbours' artifacts that their origin was for a long time sought far from here, in the north-eastern part of Nigeria.

Among the best Ibo works of art are the ritual carvings called *ikenga*, which serve the cult of the right hand of their owner, that is, the head of the household. The carving is a human torso, or sometimes a complete figure, out of which two carved horns symbolizing strength usually stick out upwards. Of equivalent symbolic significance are various attributes, especially weapons, which the figures sometimes hold in their hands. This carving is in fact a personal altar on which offerings are placed and which is begged for spiritual support and vital force during crises; it is made when a new household is set up, and destroyed after the death of its head. The cult of the right hand and altars for practising it are also known among other tribes of the Lower Niger region. They may be found, for example, among the Bini, where altars of this cult, called *ikebogo*, take the form of low cylindrical objects with the whole surface decorated with figure carving in low relief. From the rounded upper surface, an eccentrically placed apex juts out.

In this brief, simplified survey of the art of south-eastern Nigeria, we have been able to mention only the main stylistic trends, the

131

are therefore not surprised to find, among the Igala and Idoma, settled on the southern bank of the Benue River, similarities not only with the art of the northern Ibo who are their immediate neighbours, but also with the art of the southern Ibo, the Ibibio and the tribes inhabiting the Upper Cross River area.

This process of permeation is constantly intensifying. The last strong impetus was the civil war in Nigeria, when the art of entire regions was devastated. Many masks and figures were burned, stolen or, in the later stages of the war, sold to travelling traders by people who would not otherwise have been able to survive. After peace had returned to the area, such people started to replace the lost ritual objects in the traditional style by new ones. But while making new carvings, the artists frequently copy alien models (the choice being often a matter of fashion), work with bright imported pigments, make new sets of masks in eclectic style, and so on.

Until the 1960s, our knowledge of the art of south-eastern Nigeria was very fragmentary. It was more or less confined to the art of the coast of the Niger Delta, the Kalabar Coast and the Upper Cross River area, and dated from before the First World War, when two exceptional colonial administrators were active here, the German Mansfeld and the Briton, P. A. Talbot, both men who were deeply interested in understanding the life and culture of the local people. It is said that our deeper knowledge of the art of this area was brought about by the civil war, because of which a mass of artifacts came on to the international art market and into museums and private collections. In recent years that knowledge has been enriched by a number of detailed studies based on field research, notably by G. J. Jones (1984), K. Nicklin and H. M. Cole (1982), and J. S. Boston (1977).

THE BENUE RIVER BASIN

The third area of the East Guinea art province is the Benue River basin. Until recently, almost no art works were known from this area, apart from a few dozen objects brought from there by Leo Frobenius early in the present

144 Face mask with a movable lower jaw. Ibibio, Nigeria. Black-grey stained wood and raffia fibres. **Height 35.5 cm.** Linden-Museum, Stuttgart.

main centres, and a few types of masks and figures. Obviously a very long time ago, in the pre-colonial period, a tremendous inter-penetration of styles took place here, operating even over very great distances. For example, in the earlier art of the Cross River Basin tribes, apparently so pure in its isolation, the scarification in fact derives from the Tiv milieu to the north; according to Nicklin, the local carvers copied it from the bodies of Tiv slaves. The pacification of south-eastern Nigeria in the colonial period, and the modern way of life in general, made a far freer movement of people and ideas possible. We

143 Face mask. Bamum, Cameroon. Light-brown heavy wood with grey-black stained surface and functional patina. Hair and beard formed by wads made of cord with intertwined human hair. **Height 41 cm.** Náprstek Museum, Prague.

145 Helmet mask. Bekom or Babanki, Cameroon. Heavy pale wood with brown-stained surface. Deep incisions are left in the natural colour of the wood. **Height 38.5 cm.**
Náprstek Museum, Prague.

146   Buffalo mask. Bamileke (?), Cameroon. Light-brown wood with surface stained brown. Deep incisions filled up with white clay. This mask is worn horizontally on the top of head. **Height 43.5 cm.**
Náprstek Museum, Prague.

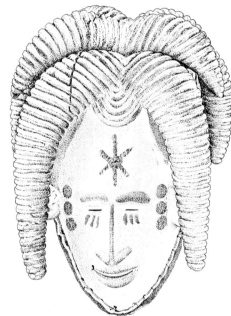

Fig. 26 Mask of a girl spirit of the *mmwo* society.
Ibo, Nigeria.
Height 33 cm.
Metropolitan Museum of Art, New York.

century, and a handful of others in the historic British collections. Some of the tribes in the Benue River basin appeared on the art map of Africa only after the Second World War, and a number of them only a few years ago. Nevertheless it was in the very heart of this area that the ancient Nok culture was discovered. However, the art of the present-day inhabitants is definitely not a continuation of Nok art, whose affinities were rather with the court art of the old Yoruba kingdoms and Benin.

The southern bank of the Lower Benue River constitutes a transitional area, in which influences from the south-east are felt. For example, the repertory of the Igala, who dwell at the Niger-Benue confluence, includes altars of the hand cult called *okega*, which are variants of the *ikenga* altars of their southern neighbours, the northern Ibo. This influence has been felt even more strongly by the Idoma, the eastern neighbours of the Igala. Some of their masks closely resemble the masks from Ikot Ekpene; and the dance headpieces in the form of a number of human heads are reminiscent of Ibibio carvings from the Cross River estuary and the Umuahia region in composition, style of carving and use of colour. At the same time, the art of the western Sudan

has clearly made an impact here. Whereas the animal masks of the Igala look like very simplified and geometrized versions of the Senufo *kpeliugo* masks, their doors carved in relief might easily be attributed to the borderland between Mali and the Ivory Coast, because of a similarity in style and a number of almost identical animal motifs.

In spite of these analogues and echoes, both of these tribes have created a number of original types of masks, figures and other carvings that are independent in style and very impressive as art. Among the Igala there are, for example, the *amdo* masks with a geometrically segmented hair area surmounted by a small low headpiece, and with arched eye-

135

147 Cylindrical stool. Bamileke (?), Cameroon. Pale wood with surface stained brown.
The openwork outer side of the cylinder is composed of animal heads, perhaps those of jackals.
The stool was part of the furnishings of a palace.
Height 39.5 cm, diameter 33 cm.
Náprstek Museum, Prague.

148 Stool. Duala, Cameroon. Pale wood with no surface treatment. **Height 28 cm, length 44 cm.** Náprstek Museum, Prague.

brows in relief and oblique marks of scarification in the face. There are also figures intended to safeguard the family which are small but give an impression of monumentality; their concave faces, also seen in some masks, are unambiguously independent works of this area. Similarly original phenomena, found among the Idoma, are ritual dishes, the lids of which are decorated with a small human head, a hornbill's head on a high neck, or entirely abstract dance headpieces in tower-like forms. The main carving centre of this tribe is the city of Otobi.

Further along the same bank of the Benue we reach the territory of the Tiv, whose art has received very little attention. Only a few wooden figures have so far appeared in the scholarly publications. Most of these are of women, and are widely different in size (48-120 cm), style and hair-styling. Their only common traits appear to be a rounded head, a vertical scarification lump in the middle of the forehead, and (only in the female figures) scarification in the form of a couple of concentric circles around the navel. Some of them exhibit stylistic features typical of the figure carving of other tribes in this area, such as a column-shaped neck which continues as a sharp ridge into the body. The arms loosely

hanging down stick out very little, the hands being placed on the hips. Female figures are said by Frank Willett to be set up in front of the house of a man's senior wife as a magical means of protecting the earth. The stylistic diversity of Tiv carving may have resulted from the fact that the Tiv, like the Lobi in Burkina Faso, have no professional carvers.

The eastern neighbour of the Tiv is the rather small tribe of the Jukun, the only one of this area (apart from the Igala) to have created a state of the sacred kingship type, with its capital at Wukari. The king, elected for a maximum period of seven years, was strangled when this period had elapsed, or even earlier if his physical powers seemed to be declining or if harvests were poor. In certain circumstances his face had to be veiled. It may have been this prescription which inspired the iconography of Jukun masks of the *aku-onu* type (fig. 28), known from the Frobenius collection (they are called *aku-maga* by C. K. Meeck, 1931). In surveys of African art these masks are repeatedly referred to as examples of abstract art. But if we look at them from the side which is not usually photographed, instead of abstraction we shall see a schematic negative of a human face with a long cone-shaped nose, which might

137

be better described as a beak, with an attached stylized leaf, corresponding both in outline and size to the face of the mask which it covers. It may not be mere chance that the name of this mask includes *aku*, which in the Jukun laguage means 'the king'. The *aku-onu* mask was taken over by the Goemai, the northern neighbours of the Jukun, who call this type *mongop*. The evidently erroneous interpretation of these masks has probably resulted from the fact that they are worn horizontally on the top of the head, the face covered by the leaf being turned upwards. However, many face masks are worn in this way in West Africa. (The term 'face mask' is used here in the iconographic sense, not as a description of function.) If our interpretation is correct, this is an exceptional, isolated case of a vegetal motif in traditional African sculpture.

During the past twenty years, certain wooden human figures assigned to the Jukun have become known; they are about 70 cm high and supposedly represent ancestors (plate 156). Among their characteristic traits are a high cone-shaped head-dress and a face around a vertical axis like a part of the lateral area of a cone, on which only the nose and the mouth are marked in very low relief. The small rounded eyes are prominent, however. The strong column-shaped neck emerges from a trunk with a horizontal shoulder-line, as on some Tiv figures. The trunk proper is formed by a slender cylinder. The outer sides of the arms, standing apart from the body, have preserved the smooth and unbroken round surface of the log from which the figures was carved. The arms and trunk give the effect of being interlocked cylinders. The legs are relatively short and straight, but apparently broken up by diagonal incisions into geometric form — pyramids and prisms — to create a cubistic impression.

These stylistic principles are characteristic of the art of the Benue River basin. Combined with various other stylistic elements, they may be found in the carving of various local tribes; for example, the columnar neck emerging from horizontal shoulders is also seen in the figures of the Wurkun and Mambila, and the 'cubist' legs in those of the Mon-

tol, Mumuye and Mambila. The double-cylinder arrangement of the trunk and arms appears in several hundred Mumuye figures (fig. 29), which were acquired for European and American collections as late as the 1960s. A comparison of Jukun and Mumuye figures reveals another common trait in the flap-like formations on the sides of the head, under which, in Mumuye figures, the small face is almost lost. According to a monograph by Philip Fry, these flaps represent the stylized traditional hairstyle of the Mumuye. These common traits raise the question — which can hardly be answered at present — as to whether they derive from the former dependence of the Benue basin tribes upon the Kororofa empire of the Jukun. Matters are complicated by doubts about the correctness of attributing these figures to the Jukun, since none of the known Jukun figures is completely documented.

The immediate eastern neighbours of the Jukun are the Chamba, renowned for two genres of carving in different styles. The first are buffalo masks connected with the worship of bush spirits. The second are human figures carved in pairs connected by a base. There are sometimes only half-figures seated on a wide prism, out of which a single pair of legs extends downwards. These rare carvings either serve the cult of ancestors, or represent one of the numerous variants of the West African cult of twins. The latter interpretation seems more probable, since some of these pairs are of the same sex. The small spherical heads of these figures have a hairstyle in the form of a high, narrow ridge running from front to back, similar to examples found in some Tiv figures. The most significant stylistic features are the arms, somewhat bent at the elbows, carved in low relief on the trunk and hanging loosely down so that together they form a lozenge design, or else standing slightly apart from the body in the same position. The breasts of the female figures appear as inverted V-shapes inside the upper half of this lozenge.

The Mumuye are the next tribe we meet as we travel east along the southern bank of the Benue River. We have already dealt with the stylistic aspects of these figures, which ob-

138

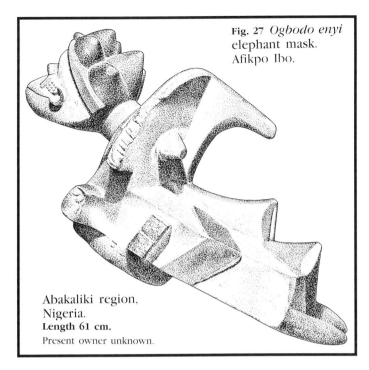

Fig. 27 *Ogbodo enyi* elephant mask. Afikpo Ibo.

Abakaliki region, Nigeria. **Length 61 cm.** Present owner unknown.

149 Zoomorphic food box with a flat lid. Bamileke (?), Cameroon. White-yellow light wood with surface stained brown. Deep incisions left in the natural colour of wood. The box probably formed part of the luxurious furnishings of a palace; it represents a stylized panther, a symbol of the ruler's authority. **Length 70 cm, height 35 cm.** Náprstek Museum, Prague.

viously served a number of purposes. They were used to cure diseases and bring rain, and were at least partly connected with the cult of ancestors. The rainmaker who looked after them and presented them with offerings always placed them beside the ancestral skulls for some time.

The Mambila live south of the territory of the Chamba and Mumuye, near the Cameroon border. They are well known for their human, animal and bird figures, which are unique in Africa. Some of these are made from small pieces of wood pith, pinned together into a flat surface from which the contours of a figure are carved, the front being schematically rendered in low relief. However, by far the most outstanding Mambila works are pieces carved in wood, especially helmet-shaped painted animal masks, so highly stylized that it is difficult to identify the creature they represent. Their distinctive stylistic features are most obvious in the masks with horns, representing a buffalo or an antelope (fig. 30). The horizontal orientation of these masks is broken by a number of vertical surfaces (the

139

150, 151 Spoon with a figure handle. Fang, Gabon. Light brown wood, eyes made of glass beads, ornaments of brass wire. The handle is a miniature replica of the well-known type of *bieri* reliquary figure.
Height of the spoon 13.5 cm, height of the figure 7.3 cm.
Náprstek Museum, Prague.

front side of the open mouth, the sides of the ears, the two disc-shaped planes behind the mouth). A similar stylization of the eyes may be seen also in human figures made by this tribe and representing ancestors. In the rare helmet-shaped human masks, the face is usually stylized into a concave, heart-shaped object, as is also done by the Kaka, who are the southern neighbours of the Mambila.

We shall meet this practice several more times in Central Africa, and it also appears here and there in West Africa. According to Douglas Fraser this is an ancient Bantu way of stylizing the human face, current throughout West Africa before the Bantu tribes migrated from this area into Central and South Africa. The fact that this mode of stylization is found among the tribes settled on the northern bank of the Benue is accounted for by the re-migration of some Bantu tribes from Central Africa to this particular region.

North of the Benue River, African art tradi-tions are preserved by minor 'pagan' tribes — that is tribes that are pagan from the point of view of the Muslims, who failed to subdue and convert them because of the difficult, hilly terrain. For the same reason their art is comparatively little known, such knowledge as we have being patchy and fragmentary, so that the attribution of many carvings to individual tribes is only provisional. Whether adequate research can be carried out before the area is plundered for its art, remains open to question. Here as elsewhere, the necessity for protecting traditional art is proclaimed by everybody, but little is done to counteract the rapacity of the world art market.

If we now move in the opposite direction, from east to west along the northern bank of the Benue River, the first tribe we encounter from whom a few wooden figures are known are the Wurkun (plate 139). This is one of the tribes that only appeared on the art map of Africa in the 1970s. The figures assigned to

140

152 Spoon. Fang, Gabon. Pale wood with glossy patinated surface. The handle imitates the shape of the hilt of a European dagger or a Fang knife. **Height 15.2 cm.** Náprstek Museum, Prague.

153 Head with stylized face in the shape of a concave heart. Fang, Gabon. The characteristic hairstyle is divided into three tresses falling to the nape of the neck. A harp decoration. **Height 53 cm.** Náprstek Museum, Prague.

the Wurkun, supposedly representing ancestors, are typical pole sculptures. The arms, which are the most distinctive stylistic elements, are treated in a similar way to those of the Chamba double-figures. Also present are features known from the art of other tribes in this area, such as the comb-shaped hair ornament and the same treatment of eyes as in figures mentioned as assigned to the Jukun. Unique in style is the male head from the former Tara collection, published by Gillon. It might, in fact, be typical of Wurkun art, but our lack of documentation and comparative material makes it impossible to reach any conclusion. The Wurkun are also the makers of yoke masks, erroneously assigned to the Waja group.

In discussing Jukun masks, mention has already been made of the Goemai, who live to the west of the Wurkun. Besides masks of Jukun type, collected and described *in situ* by Roy Sieber, this tribe became famous as a result of the terracotta figures made by the woman potter Azume, who died around 1950.

Among the Montol, north of the Goemai, a few human figures (*komtin*) are known, mostly collected by Roy Sieber in the 1950s; they were used for healing or divination, some of them also supposedly representing ancestors. It is unclear whether their stylistic variety resulted from the various purposes for which they were used. They seem to be works of self-taught artists, and their attraction lies

154 Torso of a *bwete* female figure. Mitsogho, Gabon. Light wood, surface painted red with a vegetable pigment, hair stained black; a line made with white clay divides the forehead and the hair. The head was separated from the trunk and attached again by means of wire (?) clamps. The trunk probably served as a reliquary or as a container for magical substances. The figure was originally holding something, most likely a vessel fixed to the hands by means of pegs, the holes for which can be seen. The legs were broken off and are lost; they were obviously bent in a squatting position, like those of some Fang *bieri* figures. The *bwete* figures served the same purpose, guarding the relics of revered ancestors. This piece from the collection of the writer Karel Čapek was bought in Paris towards the end of the 1920s.
Height 37.5 cm.
Private collection, Prague.

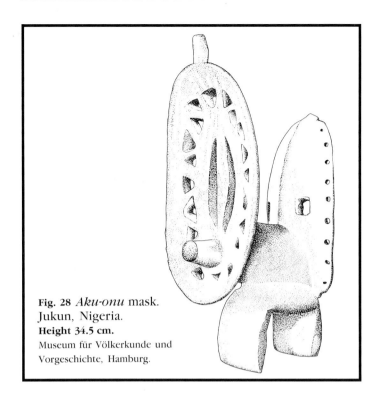

Fig. 28 *Aku-onu* mask.
Jukun, Nigeria.
Height 34.5 cm.
Museum für Völkerkunde und
Vorgeschichte, Hamburg.

in or the individual talents displayed rather than a traditional style, although stylistic features characteristic of this whole area can be discerned in them. Some carvers have succeeded in endowing their works with an extraordinary inner tension by curving the figure or by vigorous treatment of the upper part of its body.

West of the Montol live the Kantana, often incorrectly called the Mama; they are renowned for highly stylized buffalo masks (fig. 31) which are used in the *mangam* cult dances. The local carvers are said to supply them also to the neighbouring tribes. These masks take the form of a low wooden helmet worn on the top of the dancer's head. It is surmounted by large, horizontally protruding, flattened horns forming an almost closed, oval wreath on one side; on the other it ends with a short and, in relation to the horns, very small, stylized mouth. The symbolic significance and spiritual force of this mask are undoubtedly carried by the curve of horns, which is why carvers were able to minimize the size of the animal's actual head.

The area around the city of Jos, where the Nok culture was first discovered, is occupied by the Ham, who are also known as the Jaba.

The *gbene* human figures, very variable in size, are assigned to this tribe; their depressed dish-shaped bellies are used for ritual palm-wine drinking. The style of these figures — their hair, their angular shoulders, the way the neck is connected to the trunk — conforms to the general principles of this style area. These figures are in fact believed to be made by carvers of the neighbouring tribe of the Koro, who supplied the Ham with them. Inter-ethnic relations of this kind are known not only from other places in Africa, but also, for instance, in India. The truth of this theory seems to be proved by the entirely different abstract style in which the dance head-dresses of the Ham are made (plate 161). They are flat and two-dimensional, their stylization sometimes going so far that the original anthropomorphizing intention has become unrecognizable. For decoration, quantities of tiny red seeds of the Sudanese abrus are used, fixed in a layer of wax. This decorative technique is popular among many tribes in the Benue River basin, especially for masks; but it may be also found, to a lesser extent, in the western Sudan.

Four remarkable female figures made in the 19th century are generally assigned to the small tribe of the Afo, who live in the region between the city of Nasarawa and the Benue. However, only one of the figures is sufficiently well documented for us to be certain that it originated in the territory of this tribe; the rest were found in other places, one as far away as the Jukun capital of Wukari. The explanation may be sought in the fact that Afo carvers also worked for neighbouring tribes, and especially for the Jukun, whose power once extended far to the west. These stylistically identical figures were probably made in a single workshop, perhaps even by the hand of a single carver. They are worth mentioning because they are among the finest works of traditional African carving. Best known is the seated figure of a mother nursing her child, about 50 cm in height, in the Horniman Museum in London. This is a frequent subject in the north-eastern part of Yorubaland; and an association with Yoruba carvings is also suggested by the scarification of the face in the form of parallel broken lines, the oblique

position of the bulging eyes (the outer corners being lower than the inner), and the large coniform breasts. Nevertheless the style of these figures is characterized by a number of significant independent traits. There are large pouches under the eyes; the small slot-like mouth protrudes, while the small chin recedes; and the heavy breasts, covered with parallel incisions of scarification marks, jut out downwards and sideways. In the wedge-shaped gap left between the breasts, a bone-like protrusion appears; it probably represents an enlarged, protruding version of the navel, which is frequently seen in African figures.

However, the maternal figures assigned to the Afo that do not come from the same workshop, achieve nothing like the artistic conviction of the four classic examples. Whereas the female figures are akin to the art of southwestern Nigeria, the dance masks of the Afo unambiguously fit into the framework of the north-western area. These are slightly reminiscent of the Bambara antelope dance headdress *chi-wara*. They consist of small wooden helmets with a high openwork ridge composed of a number of curved horns, the points of which are surmounted by the figure of a chameleon. Like the dance head-dress of the Ham, this kind of helmet is richly decorated with glued red abrus seeds.

In our tour through the style area of the Benue River basin, we have now reached our point of departure, the Niger-Benue confluence. Immediately to the north of it live the small tribes of Basa-Nge and Basa Komo, of whom only single, though interesting, examples of figures and masks are known. On the right bank of the Niger, near the confluence, live the Igbira, whose masks, so far not documented in any systematic way, display a

155 Face mask. Mitsogho or Bavuvi, Gabon. Pale wood with traces of paint. The shape of the eyes probably imitates that of cowries, which were used by some tribes in this area. **Height 33.5 cm.**
Náprstek Museum, Prague.

156 Standing male figure. Jukun, Nigeria. Wood, eyes made of nail-heads. **Height 62 cm.**
Néprajzi Múzeum, Budapest.

145

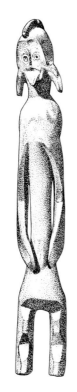

Fig. 29 Standing
female figure.
Mumuye, Nigeria.
Height 34.5 cm.
Dallas Museum of Fine Arts.

Fig. 30 Animal mask. Mambila, Cameroon. **Height 44.5 cm.**
Metropolitan Museum of Art, New York.

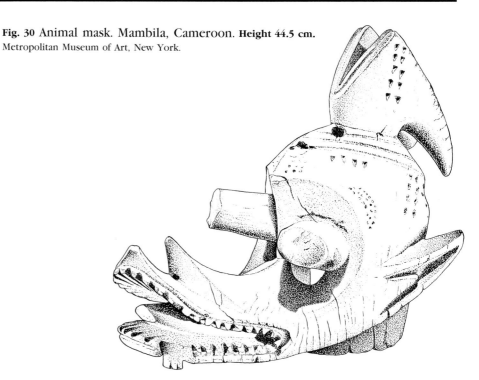

mixture of various neighbouring styles and iconographic loans.

Our survey of this area can be concluded with the masks of the isolated tribe of the Nupe, settled on the northern bank of the Niger-Benue confluence. These are convex and egg-shaped face masks with an almost unbroken facial surface in which rounded eyeholes are dominant. The tops of these masks carry slender hair ornaments of various shapes, which are the distinguishing attribute of the individual figures during dance performances. Leo Frobenius collected about seven of these masks in the town of Mokwa in 1911. Except for a single example in the British Museum (fig. 32), they are now all in German museums. Because of the enforced conversion of this tribe to Islam in 1830, these masks were believed for half a century to be the last remnants of Nupe art. But in the 1960s another set, still in use, was discovered in the town of Mokwa. Their function, however, has changed. They were once requisites of tribal ritual, but have now declined into objects used for general entertainment, even during Muslim festivals. These masks are the only relics of traditional carving in the Islamized territory of northern Nigeria.

THE CAMEROON GRASSLANDS

The final area of this art province lies in Cameroon, between the frontier of Nigeria and the Sanaga River. The art centre here is the Cameroon Grasslands, undulating grassy uplands, more than 1000 metres high, from which rise wooded mountains. This region is inhabited by tribes of varied ethnic origins who arrived there from the north-east only in the 17th—18th centuries impelled by population movements originating in the Lake Chad area. The main political institution was sacred kingship of the type with which we are already familiar from West Africa. However, large centralized states with autocratic monarchs did not develop; instead there were almost twenty small states whose armies were often no larger than a palace guard. These were in effect village-based kingdoms and chiefdoms with a very small hinterland. The power of the rulers was limited by the existence of a number of secret societies whose function was mainly concerned with religious ritual. Since the colonial period, this has been their exclusive function, left to them in order to preserve the tribes' cultural continuity and identity. Although many features of their social organization

157 Face mask.
Ashira-Bapunu,
Gabon.
Light-coloured
wood with glossy
patinated surface,
stained black. A
black variant of the
'white-faced' Gabon
masks. The cult
significance of
these black masks is
not known.
Height 21 cm.
Náprstek Museum,
Prague.

158 Face mask.
Ashira-Bapunu, Gabon.
Pale wood, painted.
These 'white-faced'
masks represent the
spirits of dead girls.
Height 27 cm.
Náprstek Museum, Prague.

148

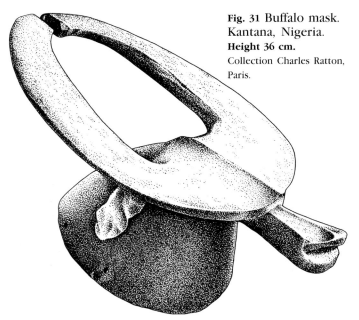

Fig. 31 Buffalo mask. Kantana, Nigeria. **Height 36 cm.** Collection Charles Ratton, Paris.

159 Face mask. Bavuvi, Gabon. Pale wood, painted. Whereas the mask of the same type in plate 155 displays an affinity with the figure and relief carving of the neighbouring Mitsogho, this one unquestionably bears the stamp of the Bavuvi style: the double line of the eyebrows, less arched than in Mitsogho carving; small eyes set close together in the centre of the mask; and the pyramidal nose. **Height 30 cm.** Private collection, Prague.

also bronze casting, pottery and the decoration of wood-carvings and ritual or prestigious objects with glass beads were employed in the service of the ruler and the court dignitaries, the cult of the ruler's ancestors, and the secret societies linked with the power élite. The artifacts constitute the output of professional craftsmen working to order, or bringing their works to the rulers as gifts to be repaid with presents.

Determining the origin of works from the Cameroon Grasslands is often difficult or downright impossible. Complicating factors include the frequent exchange of gifts between the rulers of the individual mini-states, the practice of inviting renowned carvers to alien courts far from their home territories, and the fact that some carvers had to work for alien rulers as slaves. All of this resulted in the development of an art style which is to a large extent uniform and unique. Given the prevailing political fragmentation, it is not even always possible to distinguish between ethnic groups and political units that may turn out to be quite small. This is why, for the practical purpose of classifying works of art, the populace is usually divided into three large ethnic groups, each of which includes a number of tribes or small kingdoms. The art of all of these three groups shares many common traits, but less diffused, distinctive features do exist.

resemble those of the Yoruba states of western Nigeria, no religious or political ties of the Yoruba type have been created here, and there are no acknowledged centres of religious authority comparable with Ife or Old Oyo. Nevertheless, cultural and commercial links between the Grasslands tribes are so strong that, in spite of their varied ethnic origins they have developed a more or less uniform and independent culture which is characteristic only of this relatively small area.

As might be expected in such conditions, the art of the Grasslands is a genuine court art. Not only carving in wood and ivory, but

The south-western area of the Grasslands is inhabited by the Bamileke group. The most outstanding art is produced by the Bangwa, already mentioned in connection with the art of the Upper Cross River region. The figure sculpture of the Bangwa is characterized by an extraordinary dynamism. Movement is often expressed by a disturbance of the otherwise normal symmetry — a slight turning of the trunk, an inclination of the head, or straddling of the legs.

The north and the east are inhabited by the Tikan group. Most renowned of the group in respect of carving are the Bekom, whose finest works are symbolic thrones of the ruling king and queen of the Kom kingdom. The backs of the thrones are formed by rigid life-sized standing portrait figures of the king and his senior wife. Four such thrones, collected by German colonial soldiers in the palace of the Kom *fon* in 1904, are among the most valuable relics of African culture (plate 170). All of them were originally in the Berlin Museum für Völkerkunde; now two are still there, one is in the Museum für Völkerkunde in Frankfurt, and the fourth is in a private collection in the United States. But undoubtedly the best known is a fifth throne, less outstanding as a work of art, which was stolen from the royal palace in obscure circumstances towards the end of the 1960s, appearing suddenly in the collection of a private American gallery in 1973. After prolonged diplomatic and legal arguments reported by the press all over the world, the throne was returned to its place of origin.

The third group is represented by the art of the Bamum, a tribe and kingdom situated in

160 Standing male figure. Ashira-Banupu, Gabon. Pale wood, painted; loin-cloth woven from fine raffia fibres. The head is a miniature replica of a 'white-faced' mask; the precise carving of the details contrasts with the schematic treatment of the trunk and limbs, notably the legs rising directly from the base without feet. The neck is disproportionately broad, too. A possible explanation is that the figure was originally meant to guard a bundle with magical ingredients, out of which only its head protruded. **Height 47 cm.** Náprstek Museum, Prague.

161 Dance head-dress. Ham, Nigeria. Painted wood, basketwork helmet-shaped cap covered with abrus seeds. **Height 60.4 cm.** Koninklijk Museum voor Midden-Afrika, Tervuren.

Fig. 32 Face mask.
Nupe, Nigeria.
Height 65.5 cm.
British Museum, London.

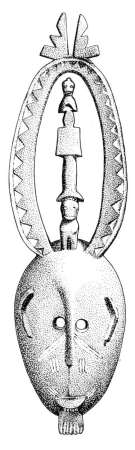

162 Figure of a kneeling woman (?). Ashira-Bapunu, Gabon. Brown wood with a glossy patinated surface, a fragment of a mirror glued to the chest. Although the head of the figure exhibits all the stylistic characteristics of Ashira-Bapunu carving, this is obviously a mirror fetish, evidently taken over from the Lower Congo region, where such fetishes were widely used. **Height 12.2 cm.**
Náprstek Museum, Prague.

the centre of the Cameroon Grasslands. This kingdom, with its capital at Fumban, is undoubtedly the best known of the Grasslands states. Historical events are responsible for this. King Njoya of Bamum was an exceptional personality who was forced to face more than one difficult problem that could only be solved by unenviable compromises. First he had to resist the pressure of the Muslims from the north. But German colonialism was far more difficult to cope with. Njoya realized that he was helpless against the German army, and submitted to the invader; his conciliatory policy even led him on occasion to parade in German military uniform. As a result, in 1902 he was recognized as the Sultan of the entire Grasslands by the German emperor. After the First World War this part of Cameroon became a French mandate. The French preference for direct rule over their colonies led them to regard Njoya an obstacle to the colonial administration, and in 1930 he was deported from the Grasslands to the city of Yaunde, in the southern part of the country, where he died in exile three years afterwards.

While buying time with his policy of collaboration, Njoya made substantial contributions to Cameroon culture. He supported the traditional arts and the development of education, even founding a small museum in Fumban. Perhaps his most remarkable initiative was the devising of a local alphabet, independent of both the Roman and Arabic forms. Njoya gained a permanent place in the history of African art by a present he gave to the German emperor: a large throne decorated with sculptures and coloured glass beads. This throne, still one of the prime exhibits of the Museum für Völkerkunde in Berlin, is a variant of the thrones used by Cameroon monarchs on ceremonial occasions. Njoya's support for traditional culture also indirectly brought new life to other political and cultural centres in the Grasslands.

163 *Mbulu-ngulu* reliquary figure. Bakota-Mindasa, Gabon. Brown wood, with brass sheets on the front; the back emphatically patinated. Figures of this kind were placed in a basket containing the bones of ancestors. **Height 59 cm.**
Náprstek Museum, Prague.

In the entire area, carving was extensively used in the decoration of palace architecture. The palaces are ostentatious versions of the local type of wooden house, with a square ground plan and a high pyramidal roof (originally covered with straw, now usually with corrugated iron). The supporting wooden columns and the door frames of the palaces are covered with figure carving in high relief. Its subjects are totemic animals or animals symbolizing the ruler's power; war-like subjects, such as figures of warriors or a ruler with a war trophy, usually the de-capitated head of a conquered enemy; and execution scenes, designed to deter those who might be inclined to trespass against traditional law. Some subjects, such as figures of women giving birth, symbolize fertility. Perhaps even more varied is the carvers' treat-ment of palace furnishings, including the thrones already mentioned. Also of great im-portance were stools, which served as sym-bols of royal authority. One such stool is rounded, having been carved from a stout log. Its seat is supported by human or animal cary-atids, especially popular being the figure of a panther, one of the symbols of royal power. In other examples the stool takes the form of a hollow cylinder, the area around the sides being carved into several rows of human fig-ures, intertwining bodies of snakes, totemic animals or their heads (plate 147), human heads, or simple diagonals that in fact represent rows of stylized spiders. The spider was used in Cameroon for a special kind of divination, and was originally also a royal symbol. Large oblong beds and rounded tables were similar-ly treated, and other luxury equipment in-cluded carved dishes on figure caryatids, and vessels in the form of stylized animals for serv-ing and preserving food (plate 149); dishes held

164 *Bwiiti* reliquary figure. Mahongwe, Gabon. Wood, brass sheet and wire. These figures, serving the same purpose as the Bakota *mbulu-ngulu*, used to be erroneously attri-buted to the Ossyeba. **Height 62.5 cm.** Náprstek Museum, Prague.

165 Figure of a standing woman. Bwaka (Ngbaka), Zaire. Light-brown heavy wood with surface, stained black. This rare figure from northern Zaire shows in a pure form a feat-ure characteristic of a larger area — the face stylized into a concave heart-shape. **Height 54.5 cm.** Náprstek Museum, Prague.

167 Anthropomorphic water jug. Mangbetu, Zaire. Terracotta, grey-white surface. The traditional deformation of the skull, achieved by binding the heads of small children of this tribe, was utilized by the maker of this jug for the oblique spout. **Height 28.5 cm.** Náprstek Museum, Prague.

166 Box whose lid is decorated with a human head. Mangbetu, Zaire. Box made of strips of bark sewn together; head and base made of light wood. Head glossy and stained brown on the surface, base stained black. These boxes are said to have been used for keeping wild-bees' honey, but the state of preservation of those in collections suggests that they were put to a wide variety of uses. **Height 50 cm, the head 18.5 cm.** Náprstek Museum, Prague.

by seated human figures were intended to carry offerings to the spirits.

There are also the wooden figures exhibited on festive occasions under an overhanging roof outside the outer palace wall. These comprise a sort of gallery of portraits of the ruler's ancestors and predecessors, symbolizing the continuity of the state. In the Bamileke group, favourite subjects are figures of the parents of twins with their children and nursing mothers, because they symbolize fertility and prosperity. Figures of pregnant women are believed to have magical properties that make childbirth easy.

The iconographic repertory of the dance masks used by secret societes is unusually rich. The most frequently encountered are the masks representing a human head (plates 143, 145). They usually have no eyeholes and, by comparison with other African masks, are heavy. This is because they are not worn in front of the face but in a slanting position above the forehead or on the top of the head, so that the dancer can see through his masking costume or the raffia fibres tied to the edge of the mask. It is in these human masks that the wide variations in stylization, characteristic of Grasslands art, are perhaps most obvious. The rare wooden elephant masks show a high degree of stylization, whereas the commonly found buffalo masks are often very realistic.

The wooden sculpture of the Cameroon Grasslands has nothing of the precise detailing, perfect finish and intentional prettiness seen, for example, in the carving of the Baule in the Ivory Coast. Grasslands art is explicitly masculine in character, a trait noticeable not only in the heaviness of all the sculptures including the masks, but also in the brutally impressive forms and the technique of carving. On the surface, the strokes of the wide adze are left without any modification, in a manner reminiscent of the visibly energetic strokes of a wide brush in a modern painting. The effectiveness of the sculptures, especially the masks, is often enhanced by the sharp contrast between the smoothness of the blackened surface and the wide and deep grooves of outlines and incised decorative pattern, which are either filled up with a white clay pigment (plate 146) or are left to shine with the natural bright colour of the wood. These modes of treatment occur in both masks and palace furnishings. Court art here has not yet had time to become a matter of rococo trifles.

Cameroon bronze casting probably originated among the northern group of the Bamileke, but it flourished most in the Bamum group. The best-known objects are pipe-bowls in the form of human heads, often very large indeed (plate 142). These pipes are part of the royal insignia, with a ritual function. In their wooden figure portraits, the rulers of the Grasslands states are often shown pipe in hand, because smoking a pipe is considered to be one of the magic means of securing the fertility of fields. Decorative handles of ceremonial fans and even large dance masks are

also cast in bronze. Most of these artifacts originated in the city of Fumban, being marked by a characteristic Bamum style, recognizable by the large, wide-open eyes and seemingly inflated cheeks. In the 1920s the French colonial administration concentrated the bronze-casters in a single street in Fumban, and many subsequent products of the traditional type in fact represented secularized souvenirs made for the tourist trade.

The dignitaries' pipes were originally made of terracotta. They are similar in type to the bronze pipes, but the subjects are more varied. The bowl is often carved in the form of a seated figure, which sometimes wears a ceremonial mask on its head (plates 140, 141). Towards the end of thee last century, the Bali were famous for the manufacture of these clay pipes, supplying not only other tribes but also the developing tourist market. Large clay pipes are made also in Bamum.

We have already mentioned the thrones on to which glass beads are sewn. This technique was also applied on various smaller royal insignia, and especially to cover the bottle-shaped calabashes used as vessels for storing palm-wine in palaces.

Whereas the art of the Grasslands is in a sense a continuation of that of the Upper Cross River, the coastal belt of tropical forest, about 150 km wide, is closely linked with the art of the Niger Delta. This belt is inhabited by a number of tribes whose traditional art has now probably disappeared altogether. Study of it is therefore confined to museum collections, especially German ones, and many important works are doubtless irretrievably lost. The only reasonably full information we possess concerns the art of the Bafo and Bakundu. Some of the carvings of these tribes, for example their dance headpieces, reveal an undeniable influence from the southern Ibibio. The face masks of the Bafo (fig. 33) are reminiscent in their outlines of a drop turned by 180°; they have spherical eyes set in rounded depressions, as in some Grasslands masks, where this element of stylization is to be found in much enlarged form, in accordance with the robust character of the local carving tradition. A closer parallel is

157

probably to be found in the stylization of the eye area of some masks of water spirits made by the Kalabar tribes. Typical of the Bafo and Bakundu are small human figures standing with legs and arms bent and the hands joined under the chin. They have no parallels in the northern part of the continent, belonging rather with the art of Equatorial Africa. They are said to have been used at the taking of ceremonial oaths.

Finally there is the art of the Duala, who live around the mouth of the Sanaga River. Their masks, in the form of stylized and rather flattened buffalo heads, served the *ekongolo* secret society. The rich colours, done with imported paints, break up the surface of these masks into large geometric areas. They are a variant of the buffalo masks of the Cameroon Grasslands and probably the southernmost example of this major subject of western Sudanese art. By contrast, unique in Africa are the prow ornaments carved almost in filigree and used on festive occasions by Duala merchants and fishermen to adorn their large boats. These rare and complicated carvings belong to a now distant past. Their brilliant colours were also done with imported paints, and here too the technique is the non-African one of assembling the work from several independently carved parts, as in some already mentioned carvings from the Kalabar Coast. It is probably impossible to determine whether the Duala carvers took over this technique from there, or whether they copied it from the work of European ships' carpenters.

The third genre of Duala carving consists of stools (plate 148), the basic form of which was probably copied from the Akan type of dignitaries' stools, spread along a large part of the Guinea coastal belt. The seat takes the form of a wide strip that curves upwards at each end. The support does not consist of a caryatid or three-dimensional ornament, but of a sort of box with openwork walls decorated with figures and patterns. The openwork is supplemented with carving in low relief.

168 Standing male figure. Mangbetu, Zaire. Pale, heavy wood. Hair, feet and end of penis stained black-brown. As in this piece, the free-standing human figures of the Mangbetu are often paedomorphic. **Height 27.5 cm.** Náprstek Museum, Prague.

EQUATORIAL AFRICA

The fourth and last large province of traditional African art includes the territory of Cameroon south of the Sanaga River, Equatorial Guinea, Gabon, Congo, Zaire, and the northern part of Angola. It also extends into the margins of territories belonging to some other states. A large part of this province is covered with tropical rain forest, which in the east gradually changes into a park savannah, with forests alternating with moist savannahs. All of this vast area is traversed by a large number of rivers. The basins of some of these provided natural migration routes, along which moved Bantu tribes and, in the northern half of the province, central Sudanese tribes. The fertile soil along the water courses made agriculture possible, and there was also abundant game and fish; whereas the watersheds were often covered with impenetrable forests. For this reason, the geographical variety of the landscape exerted a stronger influence on the development of traditional art than it did elsewhere. The larger river basins represent vast style areas within which a common basic culture gave rise to innumerable local styles and sub-styles. These evolved along the tributaries of large rivers, sometimes taking different forms on each bank of the same water course, as well as in its lower and upper part.

The western coast of this art province was known to Europeans as early as 1482, when the Portuguese landed at the mouth of the Congo River. According to their testimony a developed art of carving already existed here, but there are no surviving works of art such as we possess from Ife and Benin. The moist tropical climate did not allow the preservation of wood — the fundamental medium of African artists — over a period of centuries, and the use of other materials was minimal or non-existent. Moreover, the interior of this part of Africa stayed closed to the outer world until the second half of the 19th century. The tropical forest was an impenetrable obstacle even to Muslim-Arab conquerors on horseback, so we have no written accounts

159

169 Free-standing female figure. Azande, Republic of Sudan. Pale wood with surface stained brown. This figure and two others were collected by a Czech professional hunter and safari guide, Richard Štorch, between 1909 and 1914.
Height 32.6 cm.
Náprstek Museum, Prague.

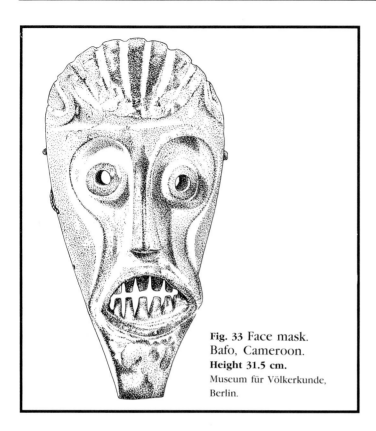

Fig. 33 Face mask. Bafo, Cameroon. **Height 31.5 cm.** Museum für Völkerkunde, Berlin.

of the area by learned Arab geographers of the kind to be found concerning the western Sudan. Some idea of the ancient art of this part of Africa can be formed only from the stone tomb figures (*ntadi*) from the Lower Congo region, and rare small figure carvings in ivory which originated in the same area. But it is difficult to ascertain their age, since sculptures made of the same materials and in the same style continued to be manufactured almost up to 1900. A few exceptions, datable to the time of their collection, enable us to state that the style of the Lower Congo region did not change considerably between the 16th and 19th centuries.

The artistic history of Equatorial Africa is also obscured by other historical circum-

170 Symbolic throne: standing female figure with a stick and a stool. Bekom, Cameroon. Wood, the face of the figure covered with copper sheeting. One of four similar figures collected in 1904, two male and two female. They represent the ancestors of the ruling *fon* of the Bekom, probably forming pairs. Judging from its identical stool base supported by buffalo heads, the figure made a pair with the male figure now in the Museum für Völkerkunde, Frankfurt-am-Main. The stool was probably not meant for sitting, offerings such as calabashes with palm wine being placed on it. **Height 185 cm.** Museum für Völkerkunde, Berlin.

161

171 Figures of a standing man and woman. Azande, Republic of Sudan. Pale wood stained brown. This couple, made by a single carver, is the most beautiful example of the tribal style in which arms and shoulders are treated as a horseshoe and the legs are stylized in cubistic fashion. These figures probably served the cult purposes of the *mani* secret society. **Heights 34.5 cm and 35 cm.** Náprstek Museum, Prague.

stances. In West Africa Europeans confined themselves for a couple of centuries to conducting their trade from fortified coastal stations, operating through local rulers who were enriched thereby; the bronze alloy imported by the Europeans as a medium of payment even provided an incentive for great progress in the artistic use of this metal. A different situation prevailed in Equatorial Africa. When the Portuguese arrived, they found relatively developed states in the Lower Congo region (especially the Loango empire in the coastal part of the present-day People's Republic of Congo, and the Congo empire, situated to the south of the mouth of the River Congo), exerting a political as well as a cultural influence far inland. The ruler (*manikongo*) of this empire accepted baptism in 1491 and entered into diplomatic relations with the Portuguese court. For more than two centuries after this, the Lower Congo region was exposed to the influence of Christian missionaries, who suppressed ancestor worship and belief in the supernatural power of fetishes. Wood-carvings were heaped up and burned as works of the devil, and a messianic fanaticism devastated anything that had been spared by the tropical climate.

In 1717 the Portuguese were expelled from the Congo area and the old beliefs were revived. Local art also flourished again; but we shall never know to what extent it was related to the earlier, vanished traditions, rather than Christian iconography and European models. Moreover a new disaster for traditional art arrived with 19th century colonialism. The French and — even more emphatically — the Belgian colonial administrations followed a policy of direct rule; that is, they did not exercise control via traditional African institutions, but suppressed them. Christian missionary activity and the destruction of cult objects furthered these objectives. The almost complete disappearance of traditional art was also brought about by the demand for 'primitive' and 'Negro' art, which arose in Europe (and especially France) in connection with artistic modernism in the early 1900s. 'Idols' and fetishes thus became a welcome source of additional income to the clerks and officials of the French and Belgian administra-

tions in Central African colonies. This is why, right up to the present, only fragmentary remains and isolated enclaves in inaccessible places are left of the entire equatorial province of traditional African art. Even these are quickly exhausted as transport improves, collectors become ever more demanding, and the African economy and African society undergo modernization. Knowledge of the art of Equatorial Africa is therefore dependent on the study of European and American collections and archive material to a far greater extent than in the case of West African art.

THE OGOWE RIVER BASIN

The first large style area of this equatorial province is the Ogowe River basin in Gabon. This area also includes Equatorial Guinea and southern Cameroon, extending into Congo in the east and south. The inhabitants are composed of two groups, the Bantu tribes which have come to this area from the south and the Sudanese tribes called by the common name of the Beti or Pangwe. The Beti penetrated into this region over a period of three hundred years from central Sudan, along the Ivindo River, which is a north-eastern tributary of the Ogowe River. During their progress they assimilated the older Bantu settlers, or drove them either southwards or westwards. This migration stopped only around 1870, when the Beti reached the coast. The styles of these Sudanese tribes are usually referred to under the collective ethnic denomination of the Fang, although this is in fact the name of only one tribe belonging to the group.

In spite of this ethnic dualism, and a range of styles including both highly abstract and notably realistic tendencies, the art of this area is characterized by an unusual uniformity in terms of basic types. One, serving the ancestor cult, is the reliquary figure (fig. 3); this is attached to the boxes containing the bones of the founder of the family and village, the mother of many children, and other noteworthy individuals. This practice has no analogue in other parts of Africa, although it is almost universal here. A second basic type consists of white-faced masks representing

163

172 Spoon. Balega (Warega), Zaire. Ivory with the reddish brown patina, which such spoons acquire from red palm-oil. **Length 17.8 cm.** Náprstek Museum, Prague.

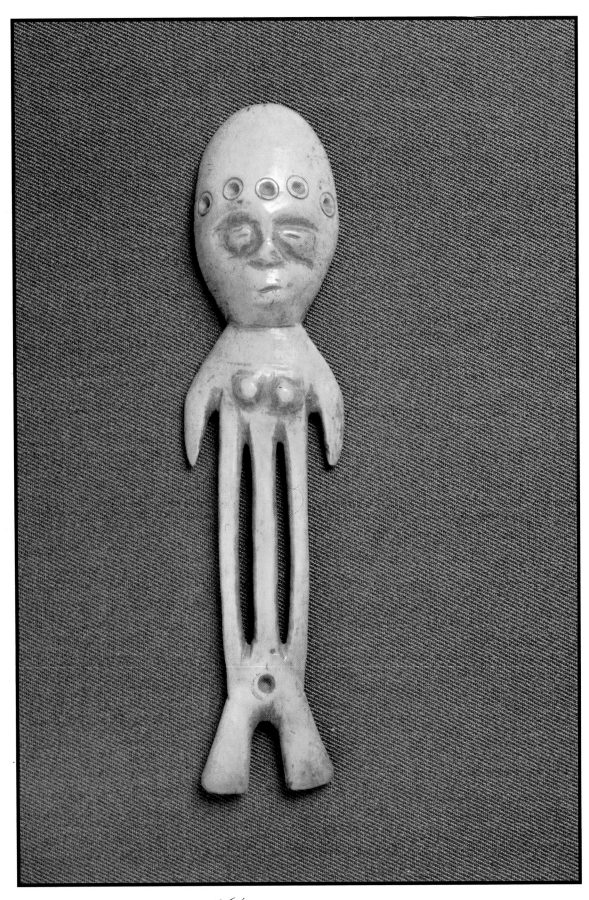

the spirits of dead girls. A performance with a white-faced mask gives these spirits an active role in the life of the community, thus placating them. This type is concentrated in the southern half of the area. However, a considerable uniformity also appears in the choice of another, though less frequent and less conspicuous technique which is to be seen in the insignia of various chiefs; this is the decoration of harps with a little human head.

In the northern part of the area, the dominant ethnic factor is the Beti. From a stylistic point of view they can be divided into three groups: northern (the Bane, Bulu and Jaunde in southern Cameroon), central (the Ntumu and Mwai in Gabon and Equatorial Guinea), and southern (the Fang in Gabon). The outstanding subjects of all these tribes are human heads and entire figures, attached to the lids of cylindrical reliquaries made of bark for preserving the bones of ancestors. These reliquaries are called *bieri*, but the name is also often used to describe the reliquary figures. Independent heads attached to the centre of the reliquary's lid are believed to be an earlier phenomenon, since they are mostly female heads with an older type of hairstyle.

The *bieri* figures, both male and female, are rightly considered to represent one of the apogees of traditional African art. They are rounded, about 45—70 cm in height, with supple musculature, long trunks, elbows bent at right angles, the male figures usually holding in front of them an antelope's horn representing a magic box. The short legs are bent at the knees as though the figures were seated, because they were attached to the edge of the reliquary lid in a sitting position by means of a projection under the figure's back. The *bieri* figures are strictly symmetrical, with well-balanced proportions and a perfect finish attained by rubbing in palm-oil mixed with powdered charcoal or a certain kind of powdered

173 Drum with a caryatid in the form of a woman holding a bottle. Bakongo, Zaire. Soft pale wood with glossy surface patinated brown. The realistic style of the Lower Congo region is characterized by the inlaying of the eyes with ceramic shreds, and the indication of the collar-bones, a rare feature in African sculpture. **Height 94 cm.**
Náprstek Museum, Prague.

174 Handle of a ritual rattle.
Basundi, Lower Congo region, Zaire.
Brown wood with surface stained grey-brown and patinated.
Rattling fruits were tied to the bar under the figures.
The rattle is used at the initiation dance
af the Bakkimba sect.
Height 46.7 cm, figures 20 cm.
Náprstek Museum, Prague.

wood. Among the tribes of southern Cameroon, the important parts of these figures are further decorated with sheathing made from brass. In some cases this decoration enhances the artistic effects of the work, but it can also seem quite unsuitable; this depends on the extent to which the maker was able to harmonize these different materials into an organic whole.

The *bieri* figures of southern Cameroon display some cubistic tendencies. These are apparent in the transformation of the rounded parts of the body into faceted segments, and in the geometric stylization of the mouth into tetragonal forms. Such tendencies appear to have derived from the influence of certain small local tribes, such as the Ngumba and the Yabassi, in whose rare and very little known sculpture these tendencies are dominant.

The *bieri* reliquaries were deposited in a special shrine in a corner of the chief's house, where they were regularly presented with offerings. Both women and uninitiated youths were forbidden to look at them. Originally they probably represented ancestors, functioning as a refuge for their souls. Gradually their protective function prevailed, and their task became that of guarding the contents of reliquaries and protecting the community against hostile magic. The reliquary figures of all the other tribes in this area probably had similar functions.

The art of the Beti also includes a number of types of mostly white masks with two or more faces. These are found as both face and helmet masks. Most outstanding as works of art are the elongated white masks called *ngel*, the abstract features of which are reduced to a long vertical line of the nose and, growing out of its base, two large arches of eyebrows that reach the edges of the mask. The eyes are small horizontal slots and the mouth is a horizontal oblong. These masks, very effective in their simplicity, serve the *ngi* secret society. Their purpose is to discover and punish sorcerers and law-breakers.

Although much attention has been paid to Beti art, some fundamental questions remain unanswered. These tribes are said not to have known the art of carving in their original homes, which they left in relatively recent

175 Fetish figure. Bakongo, Zaire. Brown wood with glossy patina, eyes inlaid with small fragments of glass. The top of the head is completed with modelled magic materials, into which a strip of ivory and the tip of an antelope horn are inserted. Further magical ingredients are put into the rounded glazed box in the chest.
Height 22.7 cm.
Náprstek Museum, Prague.

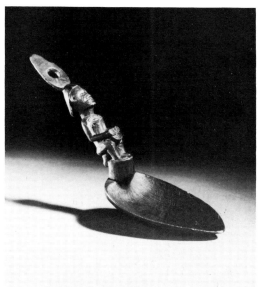

times; yet it would be surprising if they had been able to create such fine works, in mature styles, so quickly and in a new and hostile environment. Their art would be an admirable achievement even if they had taken over ready-made styles and subjects from the earlier inhabitants. It is also hard to believe that the carvers of this tribe were amateurs, working without formal training or a craft tradition to direct their energies.

The reliquary figures of the tribes in eastern Gabon are unique creations. The most famous are the highly abstract works of the Bakota-Mindasa from the Upper Ogowe region (plate 163). The fundamental and commonest type is a two-dimensional figure, reduced to a mere head surmounted by a crescent which may represent either stylized hair or a stylized head-dress. The face is usually slightly concave, figures with a convex face occurring more rarely. The entire front of the head is covered with brass sheathing. The head is placed on a narrow neck joined to a lozenge-shaped frame which was set into a basket containing ancestor's remains. These figures, known as *mbulu-ngulu*, were among the first works of African art to fascinate and inspire European artists at the beginning of the 20th century. A rare variant, with two faces turned in opposite directions, is called *mbulu-viti*. One of the faces, the female one, is usually concave, the other, male one is convex. The *mbulu-ngulu* figures appear in

176 Spoon with a figure handle in the form of a man with a pipe. **Length 22 cm.** Náprstek Museum, Prague.

177 Spoon with a figure handle in the form of a drummer. **Length 15.2 cm.** Náprstek Museum, Prague.

178 Spoon with a figure handle in the form of a standing woman. **Length 13.7 cm.** Náprstek Museum, Prague.

Bakongo, People's Republic of Congo; according to the original labels of the spoons in plates 177 nad 178, which still survive, they were collected in the Niari River basin. Hard dark-brown wood with patinated surface. The bowls of the spoons are set at an angle of about 60° to the handles. Their shape was probably influenced by European models. Some spoons of this type may also come from southern Gabon.

numerous stylistic variants among different Bakota tribes and obviously also in localities not defined in a more exact way. The most abstract reliquary figures of all, called *bwiiti* (plate 164), originated among the Mahongwe living east of the Middle Ivindo River region. Formerly they were erroneously ascribed to the Ossyeba.

Bakota masks are very rare. They are characterized by the absence of a lower jaw, the lower edge following the line of the mouth. The top of the mask is surmounted by two high ridges in the form of two vertical planes intersecting at right angles. The doubled arches of the eyebrows, connected to the top of the nose and reaching all the way to the edges of the mask, stand out high in the white face. These masks represent evil spirits who must be placated by sacrifices and prayers.

The culture of reliquary figures extends into the territory of the Bakota's neighbours, the Ambete in the Congo. However, there the ancestors' bones are deposited directly in the hollow trunks of the figures themselves, each of which has a lid on its back. These rare figures are about 70 cm in height and are covered with white pigment. They have column-shaped necks and trunks, arms with elbows bent at right angles forming a relief on the trunk, and shoulders showing a tendency towards a cubistic treatment. The head is widest at the level of the mouth, tapering upwards; the top is decorated with a ridge running from back to front. The face is almost flat, a full half of it being occupied by the very slightly raised forehead. The eyebrows are represented by a single arch occupying the entire width of the face, the eyes being formed by inset cowrie shells or carved in relief.

Figure reliquaries of this type may have been inspired by fetish figures from the Lower Congo region, into the hollow trunks of which various magic substances are put.

The Mitsogho live in the hardly accessible hilly interior of Gabon, west of the Bakota territory, between the Upper Offoue and Upper Ngounie Rivers. Their reliquary figures, called *bwete* (plate 154), are somewhat reminiscent of the *bieri* figures of the northern Gabon Fang. They are all half-figures, rounded in

179 Group of a drummer with six listeners (five men in European dress and an African woman). Bakongo, Zaire. Soft painted wood. The figures are nailed to a circular base cut from a board. Some male figures probably represent Asians, since the group represents a cosmopolitan party in a coastal town at the turn of the century. The long drum hollowed from an entire tree trunk is a characteristic musical instrument of the Lower Congo region. An early souvenir carving in traditional style. **Height 26 cm, diameter of the base 34 cm.** Náprstek Museum, Prague.

outline, with round inset eyes made from various materials, the eyebrows consisting of two high arches meeting over the nose (a feature frequently found in the carvings of this area). The facial expression of the *bwete* figures resembles the look of a wondering child. The surfaces of the figures are painted with a red vegetable pigment. Only a few reached European collections before the Second World War, the example illustrated here being one of them. Moreover, this is probably the only known figure of this type which was originally complete. Its legs have unfortunately disappeared, but they were probably bent in a sitting position like *bete* figures, since the *bwete* and *bete* were used in the same way.

It was only after the Second World War that the carvings of the Mitsogho in French collections, until then unknown, were published. These formed a part of the decoration of cult houses, such as doors and supporting columns carved in low relief. The main decorative element is a stylized human face, closely resembling the masks from the area of the white-faced masks of southern Gabon, mentioned at the beginning of this chapter.

The white-faced masks representing the spirits of dead girls (plate 158) were among the most ardently sought-after objects in the pioneering days of African art collecting. They are still much admired, but their exorbitant prices make them much harder to acquire. A few of these masks are enlivened by a slight asymmetry, creating the impression that they are idealized portraits of real people. Most, however, are strictly symmetrical, with black hair divided into three sections, the middle one being the largest. The areas of scarification are square-shaped on the forehead and lozenge-shaped on the tem-

180   Figure of a moustached European in ceremonial uniform. Bakongo, Zaire. Pale wood, painted. Judging by a similar piece published by F. M. Olbrechts in 1959, this figure represents the Belgian King Albert. In the colonial period, European rulers were a frequent subject of local artists. Sometimes — as here — the figures were souvenirs; in other cases they were incorporated into the local cultural stock. Especially frequent are figures representing Queen Victoria; among others represented is the German Kaiser, Wilhelm II. In some, an intention to caricature is apparent. **Height 81 cm.** Náprstek Museum, Prague.

ples; they are painted with red pigment and divided into small cicatrices by crossing incisions. The lips of these masks are sometimes also reddened. Masks with a more complicated scarification, forming long lines (for example horizontally across the face and over the nose), are rarer. Owing to their fine carving, combination of colours, and expressive faces, these masks were compared with the Japanese masks used in *No* plays, although the idea that these Japanese masks might have been a source of the Gabon masks is now rightly considered absurd. These masks also exist — although there are only a few — in black versions (plate 157), the iconographic significance and ritual use of which are completely unknown. William Fagg suggested that these were not a separate type of object, but ordinary white-faced masks which had been kept under hut roofs and blackened by smoke from the fireplace. This hypothesis is obviously wrong, however, because there is no trace of any previous whitening and the black surfaces are smooth and polished, indicating that the masks had been blackened intentionally.

For decades the white masks were assigned to the M'pongwe inhabiting the Lower Ogowe River region; but this turned out to be wrong. Europeans did buy them from this tribe, which lived in an area accessible to foreigners; but the masks had originated deeper in the interior. French authors usually ascribe them to the Balumba from the southernmost part of Gabon, on the basis of a few examples from documented collections. But white masks identical in both style and function, were also used by other tribes in southern Gabon such as the Mashango, Ashira, Bapunu, Banzabi, Balali and even Bakota. This is why British scholars give these

181 Souvenir carving on a hippopotamus tusk. Bakongo, People's Republic of Congo, Loango Coast. Souvenir carvings like this were made at a relatively early period in this part of Africa. They consist of elephant and hippopotamus tusks decorated with reliefs of walking Africans, at least partly clad in European dress, and scenes of everyday African life, going round the tusk in a rising spiral. Although they were made in quantities, there were no standardized series: every piece is an original with its own naïve charm. **Length 33.8 cm.** Náprstek Museum, Prague.

171

masks the names of two of the above tribes, calling them Ashira-Bapunu, a practice that will be followed here. In these tribes, white-faced masks are connected with the *makui* secret society; the dancers who wear them sometimes perform on stilts.

The same tribes made rare and probably exclusively female figures without a base. They stand on bent legs, their arms hanging loosely at their sides, with bottle-shaped gourds held in their hands. Their faces are stylized in the same way as the white-faced masks, but the carving is executed with even more finesse. The carvers have taken great care over not only the head but the entire figure, and in particular the exact reproduction of complicated scarification marks on the body. This phenomenon is also seen in the figures made by various Zaire tribes. To my knowledge, no information is available concerning the function of these figures. Those whose bodies are obviously more schematic and less elaborate (plate 160) probably served a purpose similar to that of reliquary figures, guarding bundles containing magic substances from which only the head and torso of the figure protruded.

The afore-mentioned white masks of the Mitsogho are different in style from those of the Ashira-Bapunu group. They are more stylized, representing a kind of rusticized form of the latter. This rusticizing process has taken place even more consistently in the masks of the Bavuvi, who are the Mitsogho's neighbours (plates 155, 159). These masks, general knowledge of which dates only from the last few decades, are almost flat and oval. The eyebrows consist of two large connected arches, while the nose is a small triangle and the strikingly small almond-shaped eyes are placed closely together in the middle of the face.

Now let us return once more to the north of Gabon. In some of the Fang white-faced masks and *bieri* figures from that region, a very significant and obviously ancient element of stylization appears, namely the heart-shaped, slightly concave face (plates 150, 151). We have already met this kind of stylization in south-eastern Nigeria, drawing attention to Douglas Fraser's hypothesis that this might be the orig-

182 Fetish figure of a man carrying a stick and a gun. Babembe, People's Republic of Congo. Pale wood with glossy surface stained dark brown. Thin brass wire bound around the neck. **Height 14.5 cm.**
Náprstek Museum, Prague.

inal style of the central Sudan, carried by the Bantu tribes in their migration to Equatorial Africa some two thousand years ago. This kind of stylization of the face is also to be found in the tribal art of other continents, and cannot therefore be attributed with certainty to a single centre; but its frequent occurrence in the long belt stretching from northern Gabon eastwards, across the Congo to the northern and eastern parts of Zaire, is striking indeed. The last-mentioned is the second large style area of this art province, and will now be considered.

183 Object of uncertain purpose. Babembe, People's Republic of Congo. Pale wood; both the tops of the figures' heads and the dancers in low relief on both sides of the 'box' have been blackened, perhaps by burning. The two figures on the sides have anal orifices burned deep so that a magical paste can be inserted in them. The same purpose was probably served by the double row of holes in the bodies of these figures. This object was most likely a gong used during magical ceremonies. The pointed chins indicate that the figures are male, although their gender is not marked in any way. **Length 28 cm, height 14.5 cm.**
Náprstek Museum, Prague.

NORTHERN AND EASTERN ZAIRE

The Bakwele are settled immediately to the east of the Fang, in the territory of the Congo. Among this tribe, the carving style featuring heart-shaped, concave faces has developed to an extraordinary level. The carvings of the Bakwele are at first sight different from those of other tribes working in this style. Bakwele masks are characterized by oblong bulging

184 *Butti* fetish figure. Bateke-Sise, People's Republic of Congo. Sexless figure with male hairstyle; a box with magical substances in the chest. Pale wood with a thick layer of dark ritual patina; necklace of brass rings. **Height 36.7 cm.** Náprstek Museum, Prague.

185 *Butti* fetish figure. Bateke-Fumu, People's Republic of Congo, or Zaire. Pale wood with thick, dark ritual patina. The leather cover of the trunk contains magic ingredients. **Height 44 cm.** Náprstek Museum, Prague.

eyes with slit-like eyeholes, usually diagonally placed. The eyes are sometimes repeated one or more times in a single mask, or in the chief's insignia, as a symbolic element. Bakwele masks (fig. 34) represent both human faces and stylized heads of animals such as antelopes and gorillas. The masks with human faces in fact represent elephants. All the known masks in this style were formerly said to belong to two collections (one from the early 20th century and the other from 1930) and have been found in a single locality. But newly collected examples seem to have been added during recent decades. Some masks were used in dance performances, whereas others were made only to decorate the walls of cult houses. Helmet masks with other kinds of faces, similar to those of the Fang, also originated among the Bakwele after the Second World War.

The tribe of the Bwaka (or Ngbaka) is scattered throughout the area between the large bend of the Congo and its huge tributary, the Ubangi River. The style of their initiation masks, ancestor figures and heads adorning harps, is heterogeneous. It oscillates between almost rudimentary forms, and works in a mature style, for instance the extraordinarily fine female figure illustrated here (plate 165). It is among these high-quality carvings that we again meet the heart-shaped concave face. In some masks and figures, the tribe's traditional scarification — a row of stone-shaped cicatrices — is represented by a vertical line of wedge-shaped incisions running down the middle of the forehead.

186 *Kebe-kebe* dance requisites in the form of human heads. Kuyu, People's Republic of Congo. The two pieces were purchased in Africa by the same collector in 1910. A piece with black and white triangles on the neck was published for the first time by C. Kjersmeier in his classic book, *Centres de style*.
Heights 50.3 and 50.5 cm.
Náprstek Museum, Prague.

187 Figure of the primordial mother of the tribe, used at the initiation ritual. Kuyu, People's Republic of Congo. Pale wood, painted.
Height 80.5 cm.
Náprstek Museum, Prague.

176

The Mangbetu, extremely prolific carvers, live further east, in the area south of the Upper Uele River region. Besides less numerous and stylistically rather varied figures of both sexes (plate 168), the art of this tribe consists of a number of functional objects decorated with human heads. They are necks of harps of the current Central African type, knife-handles, and especially cylindrical boxes, used to preserve wild bees' honey and probably for other purposes too (fig. 166). Many of these carvings maintain the style with a concave heart-shaped face, and eyes in the form of coffee-beans. But the dominant feature in the form of the Mangbetu is the replication of an artificial deformation of the skull, achieved by the use of tight wrappings round a baby's head. In carvings of women this artifical deformation is optically enhanced by a wreath-shaped coiffure on the top of the head. Convex rather than concave faces, seen in some heads and figures, probably represent a retreat from the older style, influenced by this very deformation; that is, the heads represent an effort to cope realistically with the actual physiognomy of the tribe's members. The backward elongation of the skull, along with the marked ethnically characteristic prognathism, strikingly emphasize the convexity of the face.

The Azande live to the north of the Uele River, their territories also extending into the Central African Republic and the Bahr-el-Ghazal province of the Sudan. They have taken over some carvings made by the Mangbetu in their own style; and, moreover, either the Azande themselves evolved a special local style, or the carvers of the Mangbetu devised a sub-style for export to the Azande in which a certain number of wood-carvings are made; most of them originate at Yambio in the Sudan. This city is also the place of origin of an extraordinarily beautiful pair of human figures in the Náprstek Museum in Prague (plate 171).

188 Free-standing figure of a woman with a child. Bambala, Zaire. Pale wood with surface stained brown. A mother with a child is the commonest subject of this tribe's art. The protruberant lower half of the face is characteristic of the traditional style of the Bambala. **Height 40.5 cm.**
Náprstek Museum, Prague.

189 Figure of a standing woman. Bayaka, Zaire. Hard brown wood with glossy patinated surface. The exceptional height of the figure probably indicates that it represents a clan or village ancestor. The Bayaka style is characterized by an egg-shaped head, protruding ears, 'spectacles' around the eyes, and the concave profile of the slightly upturned nose.
Height 53 cm. Náprstek Museum, Prague.

Characteristic features of this style are the horseshoe-shaped arms and shoulders, and the cubistic treatment of the lower torso and legs. However, even in these figures, the archetypal heart-shaped concave face appears, albeit not very strictly defined. In the past these figures may have served the cult purposes of the *mani* secret society; but this cannot be proved, and it has been surmised that they have always been made for the tourist trade. This is possible, since the area where they probably originated, Bahr-al-Ghazal, became a staging-point for European safaris in the late 19th century. On the other hand, there is no known case of a mature style in the best traditions of African art developing without a more profound inner motivation; so the theory is unlikely to be correct. Moreover, the number of visitors around 1900 was scarcely large enough for the carvers to have acquired such skills by working for this market alone.

The vast tropical forest inside the large Congo Bend has made continuous settlement impossible, and that is why we cannot follow the spread of the heart-shaped-face style in an unbroken line. It appears isolated among the Bambole from the large Bantu group of the Mongo, dwelling above the confluence of the Lomami and Lualaba Rivers. (The latter is the name of the Congo River in its upper reaches.) This mode of stylization appears in a pure form in the figures of hanged men in the *lilwa* secret society, discussed already in another context (fig. 35).

The last large domain of this super-tribal style is among the Balega (Warega), east of the Lualaba. Instead of a central political authority, they have the *bwame* initiation society, which is not secret since its membership comprises all adults including women. The *bwame* society is divided into eight initiation grades, five for men and three for women. Practically all carvings in ivory and wood serve the purposes of this society. Both figures and masks (fig. 36) are insignia of the individual initiation grades. Spoons called *kalu* (plate 172), carved of ivory in the form of highly stylized human heads, are said by Cornet to have been used by the members of the highest grade of the *bwame* society for the ritual consumption of pangolins.

190 Slit drum. Bayaka or Bankanu, Zaire. Pale wood stained brown. The right side of the drum has been damaged by insects. There are five rings of brass wire and a loop made of raffia cord on the neck. The human-headed handle exhibits traits characteristic of the Bayaka style, but the convex ridge of the nose suggests a possible origin among the Bakongo tribe of the Bankanu, who have taken over the Bayaka style. **Height 44 cm, head 19 cm.** Náprstek Museum, Prague.

THE LOWER CONGO REGION

The next independent style area is the Lower Congo region, comprising the coastal territory of the Congo, the Cabinda enclave, the Lower Congo River basin roughly as far as Kinshasa (the capital of Zaire), and northern Angola. This area is inhabited by a number of tribes. The Bavili live on the Congo coast, the Bawoyo in Cabinda, the Basundi in the Mayombe district, north of the city of Boma, and the Basolongo in northern Angola. Many other minor tribes are settled on the eastern border of this area.

For practical reasons the style of the whole region is called Bakongo, which in fact denotes a linguistic rather than an ethnic unit, the Bakongo being the people who speak the common Kikongo language. The name of an individual tribe tends to be used only where some localized genre is involved. For instance, the Bawoyo in Cabinda are renowned for their carved wooden lids of pots and food bowls (plate 199), which are therefore usually given the tribe's name, although stylistically the name Bakongo would be perfectly appropriate. These lids are decorated with a carving in high relief on the upper side; it represents various symbols, animals or scenes of everyday life, usually involving husband and wife (for example a man sitting at the bed of his sick spouse). A woman is given these lids — either new ones or family heirlooms — as a part of her dowry. All the carvings have a symbolic meaning, expressed in a rebus-like form but comprehensible to every member of the community. As with the gold weights of the Akan tribes, this meaning is based on a well-known proverb. When serving the husband a meal, the wife selects a lid to cover the food, choosing one through which she can voice an idea, opinion or comment without uttering a single word. Bawoyo men eat apart, and this is the only way in which a woman can interfere in their discussion. Although these lids are somewhat anecdotal in character, this does not detract from their artistic originality and masterly execution; and as a harmless channel for ventilating family grievances, they are quite remarkable.

Also confined to a single tribe are the cere-

191 Comb with a handle in the form of a human head. Bayaka, Zaire. Brown wood. **Height 15.1 cm.** Náprstek Museum, Prague.

192 Initiation mask. Bayaka, Zaire. Basketwork covered with cloth. The face, a painted horned animal head, is carved from pale wood. A figure of a naked woman made of stuffed cloth is attached to the top of the mask; the head, arms, legs and sexual organs are carved in wood. Human hair is glued to the head and belly of the figure. **Height 56 cm.** Náprstek Museum, Prague.

monial masks of the Bavili, characterized by a half-opened mouth with a small tongue carved in low relief on the lower lip. These masks, now practically impossible to find outside the older museum collections, are usually called *Joango*, after the name of the coast where Europeans acquired them. Another local speciality is the ritual rattle used by the Bakhimba sect of the Basundi at initiation ceremonies (plate 174); the upper part of the wooden handle is decorated with figures of twins standing back to back. But like the commemorative ancestor figures of the same

tribe, formerly placed under special shelters on the ancestors' graves, these rattles are simply called by the geographical name of Mayombe. From the same area come the well-known wooden gunpowder flasks with hinged lids, which are unique in Africa.

180

193 Initiation mask. Bayaka, Zaire. Basketwork and raffia. Instead of the face, a seated male figure with a bottle is attached to the mask, perhaps representing a European. The figure is undoubtedly intended as a caricature to amuse the spectators. Collected in the 1920s. **Height of the figure 28 cm.** Náprstek Museum, Prague.

Let us now return to the general characteristics of the Bakongo style. This may be termed realistic or naturalistic. It shows a predilection for full, rounded forms, but without any exaggerations or deformations such as characterize, for example, the naturalism of the Cameroon Grasslands. With the exception of a few objects whose function determines their size (for example the caryatids of drums or some fetishes), the figures are rather small and certainly do not produce an impression of monumentality. There is a wide variety of precise miniature carvings in wood as well as in ivory, including spoons with figure handles (plates 176, 177, 178), figure carvings on staffs and sceptres, and carved handles of ceremonial fans and fly-whisks; all of these point to a long tradition of court art,

produced in the service of the tribal aristocracy. The figure carvings do not usually display the rigidity and strict symmetry that is the case elsewhere in Africa. Although it can hardly be proved, this may have resulted from a centuries-long contact with Europeans. However, it is also to be seen in the *ntadi* stone figures from the area around Matadi on the Zaire-Angola border, and these figures may date from before the arrival of the Portuguese.

Common subjects of Bakongo wood-carving are seated cross-legged figures representing members of the tribal aristocracy. Some are asymmetrical, often showing the figure, chin in hand, with the elbow resting on the knee, or dangling a leg from the base to the ground. The closed eyelids emphasize their pensive mien. From the point of view of iconography, they are an exact analogue of the *ntadi* stone figures, also sharing their function. But this type of Bakongo figure was probably made during the lifetime of its subject, serving as a symbolic substitute for his authority during his absence, and becoming an ancestor figure only after his death. The seated figures of a woman with a child at her breast probably represent the mothers of the tribe's great men. They have been interpreted as influenced by Christian art, but this seems unlikely in view of the fact that the subject is an all-African one that occurred among many tribes deep in the interior, where Christianity was demonstrably never heard of till the 20th century. In this case the source of inspiration was rather the fertility cult and an effort to ensure welfare by magic means.

The Lower Congo region is one of the classic areas of fetishism. One of its specialities is the *konde* nail fetish, which is either a human figure (male, or without sexual characteristics) up to a metre high, or an animal, most frequently a standing or sitting dog. The human figure often has its right arm raised in an aggressive gesture; the hand probably originally held a spear or knife. Both the trunks and limbs of these fetishes sometimes bristle with embedded nails, knife blades, or pieces of iron. We have already encountered embedded nails in some West African masks, where they

194 *Mbuya* initiation mask. Bapende, Zaire. Pale wood, painted, and raffia. This mask with a tongue-shaped elongated chin represents the chief, one of about twenty characters of farcical plays performed at the end of an initiation at the 'Bush school'.
Height 43 cm.
Private collection, Prague.

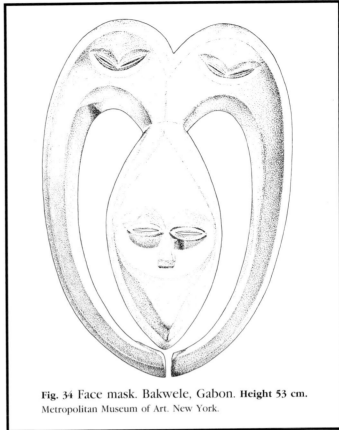

Fig. 34 Face mask. Bakwele, Gabon. **Height 53 cm.**
Metropolitan Museum of Art. New York.

195 *Hemba* initiation mask. Basuku, Zaire. Pale wood, painted, and raffia. **Height 37 cm.** Náprstek Museum, Prague.

are imbued with magic properties; and here too there is a belief in the supernatural power of iron. The second type consists of the mirror fetishes (plate 175).These are small human figures with a hollow in the front of the trunk which is a box for various magic ingredients. The hollow is usually capped with a glued piece of glass or mirror. The magic power of fetish figures of this type is further enhanced by applying layers of a paste made of magic ingredients to the head as well the trunk; or by tying some objects which are believed to be endowed with supernatural power to the fetish, such as snail shells; by attaching bird feathers to its head; and so on. Hybrid fetishes, combining the magic principles of both types, are also frequently seen.

Even these two types of fetish figures have been suspected of displaying European influences, a possibility which cannot, of course, be excluded. A superstitious belief in

the magic properties of iron was widespread in medieval Europe, and survives to this day in certain customs. And the mirror fetishes might have been inspired by the glazed boxes containing the relics of Christian saints. But if the local mirror fetishes owe anything to European inspiration, it is probably only the glazing, since the placing of magical substances in tetragonal boxes forming a part of a figure is known in distant parts of Africa (for example the Cross River region) and in many other parts of the world, such as southern India and Sumatra. Such a box may even be found in the stone figures of the Mexican Olmecs, made long before the arrival of Europeans in America. This practice is obviously connected with the universal belief that the soul resides in the heart or chest, so that if a fetish is to be activated, the magic ingredients must be put into this part of the body.

On the northern border of this area, two styles intersect. Here we find typical mirror fetishes as well as other figure genres characteristic of the Lower Congo region, but with

196 Free-standing figures of a man and a woman. Bapende, Zaire. Pale wood, painted. Although these figures were probably made by the same carver, it is unlikely that they were intended as a pair, since the artist did not give the same attention to the details of each body.
Height 54.5 cm.
Náprstek Museum, Prague.

197 Detail of plate 196.

faces carved in the style of the white-faced masks from southern Gabon (plate 162). Northeast of Brazzaville, the capital of the Congo, the Babembe live in the Sibiti district of the Upper Niari region. They are renowned for their fetish figures which, with rare exceptions, are miniatures, belonging to the style of the Lower Congo region in their naïve realism and in their use of various materials, mostly bones, for the figures' eyes. Nevertheless they also have stylistic peculiarities of their own, for example oval beards on the male figures, and high trunks on which the tribal scarification marks are reproduced in detail. This is a practice current among many tribes of the equatorial province, but not when applied to fetish figures. Another anomaly is that Babembe fetishes are activated by the insertion of the magic paste into their anal orifices. These figures usually hold in their hands various objects such as sticks, guns, knives and vessels, probably connected with their protective function. This is because they are made for the protection of children (plates 182, 183).

Just north of Brazzaville live the Bateke, who are also known for fetish figures intended to protect children until adolescence. The fetishes are made on the birth of the child and, besides other things, a part of the placenta is placed in the box in the chest of the figure. The Bateke figures are either male or sexless, on average about 30 cm in height; but miniatures around 10 cm high are common, and rarer figures exist reaching about 50 cm in height. The head is usually adorned with a coiffure with a high ridge, sometimes reminiscent of a sort of helmet. The male figures have

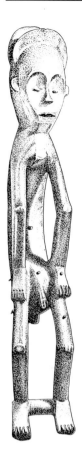

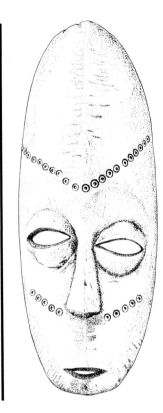

198 Free-standing male figure. Bapende, Zaire. Pale wood, painted. The figure was probably made in the same workshop as the pair in plate 196. All three figures were in Prague collections before the Second World War. **Height 58.7 cm.**
Náprstek Museum, Prague.

Fig. 36 Mask of the *bwame* society. Ivory.
Balega, Zaire.
Height 21.5 cm.
Metropolitan Museum of Art, New York.

Fig. 35 Figure of a hanged man, used by the *lilwa* secret society. Bambole, Zaire. **Height 92 cm.** Koninklijk Museum voor Midden-Afrika, Tervuren.

trapezium-shaped beards. The tribal scarification marks of the eastern Bateke are reproduced on the faces of some fetishes in the form of dense oblique parallel incisions. (When carried out in reality, this scarification is produced by scoring the skin with iron combs.) The figures' legs are bent at the knees, and the elbows are bent at right angles, forming a low relief on the trunk. However, they are mostly hidden, along with the entire trunk, under a crust of clay and powdered bark. The fetish, finished and activated in this way, is called *butti*; a figure with a hole in its chest, without any magic ingredients, bears the name *tege*. There are two principal tribal sub-styles. The main distinguishing mark is an oval framing of the face, typical of the carving of the Bateke-Sise sub-tribe (plate 184) dwelling in the north-western part of the tribal territory; in the figures of the Bateke-Fumu sub-tribe, settled close to Brazzaville, this framing is missing (plate 185). The heads of the fetishes of the Bateke-Sise, with their more rounded forms, have affinities with the style of the Lower Congo region.

186

199 Wooden lid. Bawoyo, Cabinda. Relief of a woman being embraced and swallowed by a python. **Diameter 24 cm.** Museu de Etnologia do Ultramar, Lisbon.

The painted *kidumu* masks from the westernmost part of the tribal territory, near the frontier of Gabon, are in no way related to the other ethnic styles. They are flat and disc-shaped. Their plasticity is exhausted by a slight raising of the upper part, which stands out above the lower part by about a centimeter. The small peg-like nose appears to hang from the centre of this 'step' across the middle of the mask. In other respects this mask is a graphic work rather than a three-dimensional one. All the lines are incised and the areas between them are painted in various colours. Apart from the large white ovals of the eyes, and the small circular mouth, the whole mask is covered with geometrized sym-

bols. A frequently occurring symbol is a stylized lizard in the centre of the forehead. These masks have been known only for the last three decades.

The Kuyu live on the river of the same name around and to the north of Fort Rousset, in the Congo. At least some of their carvings, which possibly have a longer history than the *kidumu* masks, approach the realistic feeling of the Lower Congo region style. They exclusively serve the ritual purposes of the serpent cult of a male secret society. The best-known items here are club-shaped objects used in the dance, called *kebe-kebe* (plate 186). The thick end of the club is carved in the form of a human head which is set on a columnar neck; the thin end represents a handle, by means of which the dancer clad in a long robe holds the *kebe-kebe* over his head. It re-

187

presents the great serpent Ebongo, whose protection is begged for in the dance, and the primordial parents of the tribe, the first mother Ebotita and the first father Joku. This primordial pair are also featured in rare column-shaped figures with the arms hanging down close to the trunk, obviously in order to give the strongest possible impression of a snake's body (plate 187). Apart from some very rare realistic heads and figures with heads, the plasticity of these carvings is confined to the horizontal eyes in low relief, the small nose, and the mouth with a visible row of upper teeth. More attention is paid to the variously shaped hair-style with holes drilled for the strings that

200 Ornament made of glass beads on the *mboom* mask in plate 201.

201 *Mboom* helmet mask. Bakuba, Zaire; carver Sefryano. Acquired in 1950. Pale wood with surface stained black, copper sheeting, raffia mat, glass beads, white animal hair, fur tongue with elephant hair tied into its edges.
Height 30 cm, width 27 cm. Náprstek Museum, Prague.

represent braids of hair and are whirled around the head during the dance. This hair has only seldom been preserved in the *kebe-kebe*. Both the masks and the figures are painted, and various geometric shapes appear in them that probably represent a stylization of the original, and perhaps forgotten, tribal scarification. The latter is documented in a

188

189

few surviving old figures. The dominant colour is ochre. The only known helmet mask carved in this style is in the Museum für Völkerkunde in Frankfurt-am-Main. It is not known whether this is the unique survivor of an older genre or an exceptional attempt at innovation.

The *kebe-kebe* dating from various periods of the 20th century bear witness to a general decadence. Compared with earlier examples, those from 1930s grew in size and lost much of their formal rigour, while the colouring was intensified. Then, after the Second World War, they were miniaturized, declining to the level of airport art. From the 1960s some miniaturized examples are known in which the great Ebongo appears in the guise of a naïve portrait of President de Gaulle.

The traditional art of the Lower Congo region was one of the first in Africa to respond to European demand, a tendency that began towards the end of the 19th century. On the coast, painted figures from contemporary life as well as entire groups began to be made from light woods (plates 179, 180). In the stylization of the face, and in the proportions, they have preserved the traditional style. The eyes are often inlaid with bone or ceramic shards; they look as though they are fixed on something outside time and space, as in the old woodcarvings from this area. But their subjects are new. They were made to remind visitors from overseas of their romantic experience of an exotic milieu in which they were able to see themselves as representing a higher level of civilization. Therefore these figures feature subjects such as an African servant taking his master's dog for a walk and black bearers with a European lounging in a palanquin. Black men are almost always shown clad in dark European suits, but the women are depicted à l'Africaine, that is, topless. African ivory carvers also oriented themselves towards new customers. For this purpose a new genre was created — elephant tusks and hippopotamus teeth carved in relief (plate 181) as a rising spiral of small marching figures and everyday scenes, the protagonists of which were again men who had borrowed foreign fashions (including top hats) and excitingly half-naked African women.

203 Pipe. Bakuba, Zaire. Wood, brass wire and bone. Bowl and stem decorated with a current Bakuba geometric ornament; the end of the stem under the bowl carved into a human hand gripping the bowl. An antelope mask is carved in relief on the inner side of the curve of the stem. **Length 50.5 cm.**
Náprstek Museum, Prague.

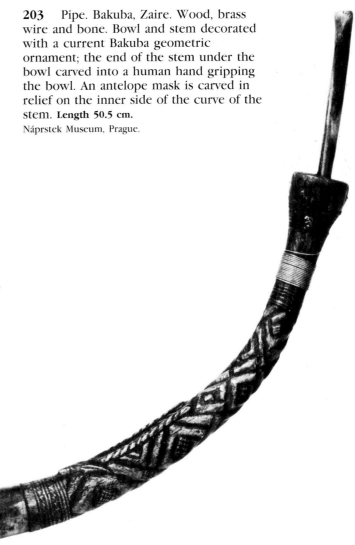

202 *Mwaash a mbooy* helmet mask. Bakuba, Zaire. Basketwork covered with raffia cloth; a mosaic of lozenge-shaped pieces of fur sewn together on the flat face. Ears, nose and mouth carved in wood. Decorated with cowries and glass beads. The projection on the top of the head represents an elephant trunk with small tusks. **Height 46 cm.**
Náprstek Museum, Prague.

191

SOUTHERN ZAIRE

Another large style area of Equatorial Africa is southern Zaire, in the vast basin of the Kasai River, a tributary of the Congo. The basins of the rivers emptying themselves into the Kasai

204 Palm-wine cup standing on human legs. Bakuba, Zaire. Brown dark-stained wood with slightly glossy patina. The fine relief carving imitates a thinly woven mat.
Height 21 cm, diameter 10 cm.
Náprstek Museum, Prague.

divide this area not only geographically but also culturally. Although the western and northern borderlands of this area receive some influences from the old centres of power and culture on the banks of the Lower Congo, the tribes settled along these rivers have created a number of characteristic styles of their own, which may be divided into a small number of distinctly different groups.

The first group is composed of the tribal styles of the Kwango and Kwilu administrative provinces. The boundaries of this area are the southern tributaries of the Kasai, the Kwango River in the west and the Luangue in the east. The most prolific carvers are undoubtedly the Bayaka, the westernmost of these tribes, dwelling in the Middle and Upper Kwango regions. Centuries long contacts with the Bakongo tribes of the Lower Congo region led not only to hostilities — the Bayaka conquering San Salvador, the capital of the Christianized Congo empire, in 1568 — but also to the operation of mutual cultural influences. Whereas the eastern Bakongo tribe of the Bankanu has taken over the Bayaka art style, among the Bayaka we find fetish figures in a purely local style, the chest being hollowed for putting in a quadrangular box for magic substances. Boxes of this kind seem to have been taken over from the Lower Congo region.

The most distinctive stylistic features of Bayaka wood-carving are the treatment of the nose with its upward curving tip which in extreme cases even turns right back like the trunk of a trumpeting elephant, and the Bayaka 'spectacles', an oval frame around the upper half of the face. The origins and significance of these stylistic features are not known.

Small figure sculptures of both sexes are made as fetishes with special protective functions; some magic material is often attached. Large figures, such as the example reproduced here (plate 189), are very rare, and nothing is known of their meaning. We can only surmise that they represent ancestors. Among magical items, the most remarkable in terms of carving are cylindrical slit drums, used by a sorcerer to call together the villagers for a performance (plate 190). The handles of the drum

205 Human-headed cup for ritual palm-wine drinking. Bakuba, Zaire. Brown wood stained black. A number of features are characteristic of the Bakuba style: the shaved hairline above the forehead, the bow-shaped markings on the nostrils, and the bridge connecting the upper lip with the nose. **Height 18.7 cm.**
Náprstek Museum, Prague.

cers are arranged in pairs with identical masks, performing dances to amuse the watching villagers. These are painted helmet masks, with a projection below the chin by which the dancer holds the mask in position. The carved face is attached to a basketwork skeleton capped with vividly coloured raffia fibre. The top of the mask consists of a bizarre hairstyle conveying the wearer's social position within the initiation system. A figure of a comic or even satiric nature is sometimes tied in front of the face. These figures are usually stuffed mannequins made of raffia fibre, only the heads and hands being carved in wood. Whereas the faces of the masks are subject only to slight changes, the figures on the masks are modified in order to surprise and amuse the spectators (plate 192). The face is sometimes entirely missing on the basketwork helmet, being replaced by a comic figure (plate 193). Long raffia fringes are tied to the edge of the mask.

The masks called *kakunga* are very rare. Unlike those of the initiation masks, their faces are enlarged many times, their characteristic feature being large and seemingly inflated cheeks. The *kakunga* masks are credited with extraordinary magic powers, and are kept therefore in a special hut outside the village. They are used for curing illnesses or controlling the weather, being worn in the initiation camp on the day when circumcisions are performed. According to evidence recorded by Himmelheber, the Bayaka have taken over these masks from their western neighbours, the Bankanu of the Bakongo tribal complex, although similar masks from the Lower Congo region are not known. However, this does not exclude the possibility of the *kakunga* masks having originated in that area, since the Bayaka art tradition was created so long ago that the Bayaka themselves have forgotten its origins and significance.

Although relatively little known, perhaps the most remarkable Bayaka carving is the decoration of the circumcision huts, which can also be found among the Bankanu. The decoration consists of painted panels with a figure decoration in high relief. Its mostly sexual themes are expressed either in naturalistic hyperbole or symbolically.

are carved in the form of small human heads in typical Bayaka style. Among everyday objects, the Bayaka have perhaps treated artistically only combs ornamented with a human head (plate 191) and headrests supported by caryatids in the form of standing animal figures or humans holding the headrests aloft.

The best-known Bayaka works are initiation masks. After attending the bush school, the initiated boys (*tudansi*) return to the village in a triumphal procession. The best dan-

The Basuku, who dwell on the Inzia River, are the eastern neighbours and near relatives of the Bayaka, and have created a style very similar to theirs. Their painted helmet masks (*hemba*) are carved entirely in wood in the form of a human head surmounted by an animal or bird figure (plate 195). A dense, short raffia collar is tied to the mask. All Basuku figures, whether sexually defined or not, probably represent fetishes. Their striking stylistic trait is high-raised shoulders, between which the head is sunk.

To the north of the Bayaka, in the area between the Kwango and the Inzia Rivers, dwell the Bambala, who are renowned for their realistic figures of a standing or sitting mother with a child at her side (plate 188) or at her breast, as well as other figures including drummers. They are notable for their inner tension and dynamism. The hairstyle consists of a ridge on the top of the head running from front to back; the forehead bulges outwards and the small, half-opened mouth is thrust forward. In its realism, asymmetry and to some extent its subject matter, this art has affinities with that of the Lower Congo region. Many figures of a woman with a child are said to represent the founder of the tribe.

Worthy of special notice is the little-known art of the Bahuana (also Bahuangana) settled north-east of the Bambala around the Inzia-Kwilu confluence. Their fetish figures are

206 Box for the preparation of a *tukula*, cosmetic red paste made from powdered wood. Bakuba, Zaire. Brown wood with emphatically patinated surface. The bottom is inset and glued with resin; three duiker horns (believed to possess magic properties) are carved in relief on the lid. A hole in the lid allows a string to pass through; the box was hung by it on the wall of the hut. **Length 23 cm, height 4.5 cm.**
Náprstek Museum, Prague.

sometimes difficult to distinguish from the fetish figures of the Basuku, although their other figures are carved in an obviously autochthonous tribal style. The main characteristic of the latter is the hairstyle divided into three front-to-back ridges and falling far down the back in a long tress; the arms are bent at the elbows and the hands support the chin. Among the masks ascribed to this tribe, the most remarkable is a unique wooden helmet mask with a pair of flat horns, to be seen in the Staatliches Museum für Völkerkunde in Dresden; it was acquired by Leo Frobenius in 1905. But best known are small, flat bone

207 Toy doll in the form of a stylized human head. Bakuba, Zaire. Brown unstained wood. Carved on the top is a traditional flat Bakuba head covering, its borders sewn with cowries. The line separating the forehead from the hair is sometimes considered to be a characteristic Bakuba stylistic feature, but is in fact an accurate rendition of the traditional way of shaving the upper forehead. This toy, collected in 1949, is almost identical with a piece acquired by Torday early in the present century; Torday's doll is now in the British Museum. **Height 21 cm.**
Náprstek Museum, Prague.

194

195

pendants in the form of kneeling figures, the heads of which take up more than a half of the overall height. Their faces are strikingly reminiscent of the style of the Bambala figures. Nothing is known of their function (or of that of any other Bahuana carvings). They may have served as initiation badges, like the miniature ivory replicas of the masks made by the Bapende, higher up the Kwilu River.

The Bapende are the last large tribe renowned for its carving in this group. In terms of style they are usually divided into the western and the eastern Bapende. The western Bapende live on the Kwilu River and the eastern Bapende on the Kasai, the dividing line being the Luangue River. The western Bapende are especially known for their initiation masks. These are used in various farce-like plays performed when the initiation at the bush school is over. In spite of their seemingly secular function, these plays symbolize the ritual rebirth of the previously uninitiated child as an adult member of the tribe. These masks (*mbuya*) represent about twenty main characters including chiefs, culture heroes and village dignitaries. Their wooden faces are more or less identical, except for the chief's masks, the chin of which is lengthened into a tongue. This lengthening may originally have represented the beard (plate 194). It is covered with geometric carving consisting of small black and white triangles. The individual figures are mainly differentiated by the hair, which is made of raffia cloth embroidered with blackened raffia fibres.

The style of both the masks and the figures of the Bapende is heterogeneous. The forehead is emphatically bulged; the eyebrows are connected above the nose and open out in a wide wedge; the cast-down upper eyelids convey the impression of a pensive or sleeping face; and the ridge of the small nose is slightly concave. The cheek-bones are strikingly emphasized. The lips of the small closed mouth stand out from the face in relief. The basic colour of both the masks and the figures is ochre-brown or brown-red, supplemented on the masks with white clay.

The figure sculpture of the western Bapende (plate 196) is less well-known and far rarer. These figures represent both ancestors

208 Standing figure of indeterminate sex. Bena Lulua (?), Zaire. Brown dark-stained wood. Although the body and limbs of this undocumented figure are highly stylized in an unusual fashion, it can be provisionally attributed to the Bena Lulua because of the eyes, inset in concave ovals, and the lavish, highly schematized scarification of the face and neck. The original Czech collector acquired this figure in the 1920s from a missionary living in Metadi. **Height 20 cm.** Náprstek Museum, Prague.

209 Comb. Bena Lulua, Zaire. Pale wood with slightly glossy patina. A human half-figure is carved in relief on the handle. Although the miniature size restricted the carver's stylistic repertory, the coffee-bean-shaped eyes and the characteristic arms with elbows bent at right angles indicate a Bena Lulua origin. **Height 13.7 cm.**
Náprstek Museum, Prague.

and fetishes. The figures of a woman, with a child at her side and holding an axe in her right hand as an insignium of the chief's authority, are famous. These figures were placed on the roof ridge of the chief's house. Other small figures form the heads of chiefs' staffs and the caryatids of important people's seats, while entire groups decorate the backs and ties of armchairs of the European Renaissance type, which the Bapende have taken over

from the southern Bachokwe along with their decorative style. Heads in the style of *mbuya*-masks may also be seen on objects such as hunters' signalling whistles and the helves of chiefs' axes.

The most outstanding artistic product of the eastern Bapende is the mask called *gi-phogo*. This is a wooden helmet mask used by the chief for shamanistic healing practices. Western Bapende influence can be discerned in it (bulging forehead, small, slightly concave nose, painting technique), as can the influence of Bachokwe models (shape of the eyes, the horizontal collar under the chin) and that of eastern neighbours belonging to the large tribal complex of the Bakuba (shaved line of the hair above the forehead). The other masks of the eastern Bapende, both human and animal, are rather flat and are sometimes stylized into a concave heart-shape like that of carving in northern and eastern Zaire. Some masks are rounded and slightly convex. The eyes are either tube-shaped or take the form of horizontal slits. The painting of all of these mask types is identical to that of the other Bapende carvings.

The second style group in southern Zaire is unusually homogeneous. It is concentrated in the area above the confluence of the Kasai River with its right tributary, the Sankuru. The main representatives of this group are the Bushongo, who have gathered about ten neighbouring tribes under their cultural — and partly also political — leadership. Their common art style is usually called by the ethnic name Bakuba, which is a Baluba denomination of the Bushongo. Stylistic differences between the products of the individual tribes are, with a few exceptions, hardly noticeable; therefore exact tribal attribution is seldom possible, and is based on some tribes' specialization in certain genres, rather than on stylistic peculiarities.

Geographically the Bushongo occupy a central position in this area. To the west of them, on the opposite bank of the Kasai, is the large tribe of the Bashilele. They have preserved their political independence, but in respect of style they belong to the Bakuba complex. South of them, between the Luangue

210 Face mask. Basalampasu, Zaire. Pale wood, the face covered with oblong strips of copper sheeting, the hair consisting of seventeen balls woven from brown-stained pliable grasses. A raffia cord with a single woven ball hangs from the chin.
Height 31 cm.
Náprstek Museum, Prague.

and Kasai Rivers, dwell the Bawongo, who are similarly independent but artistically subordinate to the Bushongo. North of the Bashilele live the small but artistically prolific tribe of the Bashobwa, and close to them another minor tribe, the Bakele. The eastern neighbours of the Bushongo are the Babinji, who are different in language, and the southern neighbours are the Bakete. It is these tribes, including other groups who may or may not properly be regarded as separate tribes, which constitute the Bakuba stylistic complex.

To these must be added the Ndengese to the north of the Bushongo, between the Bankuru and Lukenie Rivers, and the Bena Biombo, dwelling between the Kasai and Lulua Rivers. These tribes exhibit a strong Bakuba influence, but one that is modified by the presence of non-Bakuba subjects and certain stylistic peculiarities.

The Bushongo have created a state of the sacred kingship type, headed by a king (*nyimi*) who resides with his court in the city of Mushenge. As in Benin, oral tradition has preserved a history of the tribe in the form of a king-list going back 1500 years. According to tradition, the aristocracy is supposed to have come from the north (that is, the Nile Valley) at some time in the first millennium AD. But a number of Bushongo cultural objects, especially works of art, show the influence of western cultural models, which must have been encountered among the kingdoms of the Lower Congo region.

Tradition names the *nyimi* Shamba Balongongo (fig. 43), who ruled the Bushongo at the beginning of the 17th century, as the tribe's great cultural hero. He is said to have made a kind of study trip to the Lower Congo region and brought the art of weaving raffia cloth from there. The renowned Bakuba velvets, still manufactured by the tribes belonging to this style complex, are (like the countless Bakuba wood-carvings) decorated with geometric patterns strikingly similar to those of some old fabrics that have survived from the Lower Congo region, and also to the scarification designs to be seen on old Bakongo figures. Shamba Balongongo is also said to have introduced conventionalized portraits

of the ruling kings, as described in the chapter on the history of African art. It is certainly no coincidence that these portrait figures show the ruler seated cross-legged in exactly the same manner as the old *ntadi* stone figures, as well as the wooden figures from the Congo kingdom. The style of these portrait figures is also closely related to the realistic style of the Lower Congo region. Other cultural innovations are ascribed to Shamba's wife Kashashi. Shamba Balongongo must have been an exceptional man, but there is little doubt that tradition has simplified the past by crediting him with the achievements of other rulers as well as his own.

Apart from the royal portraits, there is almost no figure sculpture in the proper sense of the term among the Bakuba tribes. Nor do we find ancestor figures or fetishes. But there is an immensely rich decorative art whose character reveals its undoubted court origin. It was created for the court aristocracy, but in the 19th century it was already found among all the tribes of the Bakuba complex. Utilitarian objects, beautifully shaped and decorated with ornamental reliefs, have become the property of the common people, and despite the existence of the royal statues there is no gulf between the court and 'folk' (that is, tribal) styles of the kind that existed in Benin.

The common stylistic denominator of all of these objects is the geometric ornament covering their surfaces in countless variations. This was probably derived from various types of basketwork, some patterns being perhaps a legacy of the ancient Mediterranean, brought by the ruling aristocracy from their original home many centuries ago. The Bakuba carvers know how to incorporate into their geometric designs even such alien elements as stylized antelope heads, the favourite motif of the 'knot of wisdom', spread also among the West African Asante, and the motif of an oblong, probably derived from Muslim leather talismans (Himmelheber). Among objects decorated in this way are oblong razor boxes reminiscent of the wooden pen-cases that European children used to have; numerous wooden boxes for the preparation of the cosmetic paste called *tukula*, made from the powdered red wood of the pterocarpus tree and palm oil (plate 206); the bowls and stems of large pipes (plate 203); ladles with wide handles, ceremonial drums, and even such profane objects as enema funnels. The greatest variations in form occur in the boxes for the preparation of *tukula*; some of them are polygonal, while others take the form of a hut, the roof of which forms the box's lid; and so on. The boxes are most often crescent-shaped.

The Bakuba carvers produced a class of objects unique in traditional African art — human-headed and -bodied (cephalomorphic and anthropomorphic) cups for ritual palm-wine drinking (plates 204, 205). Their prototype is also to be sought in the ancient cultures of the Mediterranean. Rare two-faced cups are said to have been used at weddings. A speciality of the Bashilele and Bashobwa are cups, or rather mugs, with a handle in the form of a figure, reminiscent of European beer mugs. The handle sometimes takes the form of a human hand, a motif also found in the form of handles on the sides of ceremonial drums, or in the centre of the lid of a razor box. Objects on which the hand motif appeared were the property of the members of an aristocratic military society, the *yolo*; a condition of membership was to have acquired the left hand of an enemy.

Some authors rightly compare the great range of Bakuba artifacts with that of the Baule tribes of the Ivory Coast. Both of these ethnic groups produced disfunctional replicas of aesthetically appealing utilitarian objects, thus indulging in a form of 'art for art's sake'. Among the tribes of the Bakuba complex, such objects are not carvings but models, made with the red *tukula* powder mixed with some jointing substance, which were then dried above a fire. These *bongotol* were distributed among those present at a funeral as mementoes of the dead person. Another speciality of the Bakuba style complex is an instrument of divination and detection (*itombwa*); this is a small, stylized figure of an animal, most often a crocodile, the sides of which are decorated with the usual geometric ornament. A wooden peg was swiftly rubbed to and fro on its straight, smooth back; the point at which it stuck was taken to single out a sought-after culprit, or to indicate the

211 Fetish figure, sexless. Basongye, Zaire. Pale wood with no surface treatment and no patina; eyes made of inset cowries, strips of copper wire and five cone-headed copper nails on the figure's head. It was collected before the fetish had been activated by the placing of a magic ingredient (usually an antelope horn) into the hollow on the top of the head. The mouth, shaped rather like a horizontal figure eight, is characteristic of the tribe's style. Skirt made of raffia cloth.
Height 23 cm.
Náprstek Museum, Prague.

200

212 Dance (?) shield. Basongye, Zaire. Yellow-white light wood with the front stained brown. The fragility of the wood indicates that the shield was not used in battle, but at a *kifwebe* (or *kalebue*) dance, because a miniature of the mask worn at these dances appears in the centre of the shield. The masks were worn at initiations and on other occasions. No precise information exists concerning the purpose of these shields. **Height 74 cm, width 34.5 cm.** Náprstek Museum, Prague.

answer to one of a series of questions asked in quick succession.

The three most current types of Bakuba mask are connected with the mythological origins of the ruling caste. The *mwaash a mbooy* mask represents a king, the primeval ancestor of the Bushongo, named Woot, who married his sister Shene Malula (plate 202); the mask representing her is called *ngady a mwaash*. The king's mask is constructed from rods covered with raffia-work and richly decorated with sewn-on cowrie shells and coloured glass beads to form a typical Bakuba decorative pattern. The flat face is covered with leopard skin, onto which cowries and a wooden nose and mouth are sewn; wooden ears are attached to the sides of the mask. The high curving superstructure obviously represents an elephant trunk, as is proved by the presence of two miniature tusks sometimes sewn on to the base of the trunk.

This *mwaash a mbooy* mask is associated with a large wooden helmet mask called *mboom* (plate 201); it has a flat top and a large bulbous forehead which, like the mouth, is covered with a sheet of copper. The metal sheathing of the mask is supplemented with glass bead decoration. A long fur tongue is attached under the chin. Some scholars suppose that the large forehead and wide nose represent the physiognomy of the original Pygmy inhabitants of the area.

Whereas the iconography of these two types of mask is very conservative, the third, *ngady a mwaash* type shows considerable variation in both the carving of facial details and the use of colour. This variability, and the frequency with which the mask type occurs among tribes of the Bakuba style complex, has led some writers to speculate that it was taken over from them by the Bushongo. These masks, like the royal portrait figures, reproduce the traditional Bakuba shaving of the hair above the forehead into a straight line ending in sharp wedges on both sides. The eyes are mostly conical, enclosed in the rings

of small holes through which the wearer can see. This type of eye probably imitates the eye of a chameleon. The nose has nostrils cut away into a flaring bow; a small bridge links the nose partition to the mouth. These masks too are decorated with glass beads. They are used at funerals and initiation ceremonies, functioning as guardians of the initiation camps. The painted decoration often takes the form of small, alternating black and white triangles.

The repertory of Bakuba masks was originally larger, as demonstrated, for example, by a rare basketwork figure mask covered with coloured raffia cloth (Hamburgisches Museum für Völkerkunde und Vorgeschichte). This represents a half-figure of a mother holding a child in her arms. It is a helmet mask with eyeholes in the belly of the figure. Practically nothing is known about its purpose.

The Ndengese owe much to the Bakuba in terms of style, but apply it to independent genres of their own. They are renowned for commemorative figures of chiefs, about 50 to 150 cm high. These figures are in fact legless torsos ending just under the sexual organs in a rounded base. They were placed on the graves of chiefs and in the houses of elders (fig. 38). The trunk is disproportionately elongated, cylindrical and covered with traditional scarification marks, among which the motif of raised discs is most common. Carvings also typical of this tribe are large forked tools whose purpose is unknown (plate 216). Their figure handles are analogues, reduced in size, of the commemorative figures. Each figure handle has two holes in front — on the chest and under the middle spike — for tying with raffia string. The spikes of these forks are usually ground down, leaving only stumps considered to represent the legs and sexual organ (Delange). A beautiful example, admitting of no other interpretation, can be seen in the collection of the Rautenstrauch-Joest Museum in Cologne.

The southern tribe of the Bena Biombo, whose style derives from the Bakuba, carve helmet masks that are of the Bakuba type but much larger. Characteristic is the black-red-white colour scheme with rows of black and white triangles. Through the mediation of

213 *Kifwebe* face mask. Basongye, Zaire. Hard light-brown wood stained dark-brown; white clay pigment in the parallel grooves, a red paint on the raised parts. **Height 47 cm.** Náprstek Museum, Prague.

this tribe some Bakuba stylistic features reached the eastern Bapende settled on the opposite western bank of the Kasai River. The eyes of some of these masks, which are used at the circumcision ceremony, imitate those made by the Bachokwe in southern Zaire and northern Angola. Ancestor figures placed in front of their huts are a speciality of the Bena Biombo. These are tree trunks with the upper and lower parts untreated, the middle being turned into a monumental human face carved in the Bakuba style.

To the south of the tribes of the Bakuba complex live a few minor tribes who have created very original styles in spite of being surrounded on three sides by politically and artistically powerful neighbours. (Apart from the Bakuba, there are the Baluba in the east and the Balunda-Bachokwe complex in the south and south-west.) Stylistic and other influences do appear from time to time, but most of the local carvings bear witness to the existence of a longstanding independent art tradition.

The most important of these tribes, the Bena Lulua (literally 'People from Lulua'), have created one of the most beautiful of African art styles. Their slender male and female figures are carved precisely and with a great feeling for detail, manifested by the scarification marks that often cover the whole figure but are densest on the forehead and cheeks (fig. 37). The erect postures create a haughty, aristocratic impression, modified by a certain lyricism. In spite of their stylization, they convey a great sense of life. The hair often tapers off to a point. The head is slightly inclined, as if in pensive mood, and the upper lids of the eyes are heavy and drooping in harmony. The neck is high and slender, mostly covered with scarification marks. In many figures, the protruding navel is emphasized. The arms, with elbows bent at right angles, are carved in relief on small figures but stand apart in the larger ones. The hands are placed on the

214 Chief's staff with a head in the form of a man carrying a woman on his shoulders; a chief's insignium. Baluba-Hemba, Zaire. Brown wood with brown-black patina. The woman's hair is decorated with iron points. The staff is provided with an iron tip, and strengthened with brass wire and a strip of copper sheet in the middle. Baluba art, in its day one of the most prolific of African arts, to a large extent served and glorified the chiefs and tribal dignitaries. The figures decorating the chief's staff represent a young woman whose initiation is over, carried on the shoulders of her suitor. **Height 134 cm, figures 25 cm.**
Náprstek Museum, Prague.

204

abdomen or hold an object, usually a bowl. The figures stand directly on the ground without a base. A frequent subject is a mother with a child on her arm. These figures are said to have been carried by women to protect their children, including those yet unborn. Male figures with long pointed beards and holding chiefs' insignia, especially weapons, were placed in front of a chief's house during his absence. Their purpose was both to guard the house and to protect the chief on his journey. As among the Bachokwe, a favourite subject is a squatting human figure resting its elbows on its knees and supporting its chin with its hands. This appears as a small caryatid on miniature tobacco mortars, or in the figure bowls of pipes. Free-standing versions of these figures were probably used by sorcerers.

The masks of the Bena Lulua, representing the spirits of the dead, have knitted covers for the neck tied to their edges. They are rather distinctive in style — oval, painted in several colours with a distinctly concave eye area on the face; the scarification marks, which are carved in relief on figures, are painted on the masks.

South of the Bena Lulua, near the Zaire-Angola frontier, dwells the small tribe of the Balwalwa, known for their remarkable wooden face masks. The outline is roughly lozenge-shaped and the profile of the face concave. The chin tapers off to a point. The narrow nose rises high into the forehead, especially in the male masks (fig. 39), reinforcing the aggressive impression made by the mask's bow-shaped profile. The eye slots and the lips are horizontal, and there are cylindrical projections of scarification marks on the temples, where the mask is widest. These masks were used for propitiating the victims of head-hunting, performances involving their use being connected with a ritual transition into a higher grade of initiation.

The southern and south-eastern neighbours of the Balwalwa are the warlike Basalampasu, who have remained politically and artistically independent of the powerful neighbouring Bachokwe. Their best known works are wooden or finely woven masks executed in the same style; the huge numbers that have appeared in Europe during recent decades demonstrate the long reach of modern communications. The masks have a strikingly bulbous forehead, a small nose in the form of a short cylinder or cone, cut through lengthwise, and eyes hidden under

215 Profile view of the chief's staff in plate 214.

205

the forehead; they are oblong, like the mouth, which is provided with saw-like teeth. The hair consists of tied-on balls, made of pliable split grasses, which are roughly the size of a table-tennis ball. In many masks an identical ball hangs on a raffia strip under the chin. The face is black or white, but its entire surface is sometimes covered with sheets of copper (plate 210). The masks are used at the initiation circumcision ceremony as well as in encounters with evil spirits. Rare standing human figures, in a style identical to that of the masks, have their surfaces painted red.

The last important tribe of this stylistically independent group is the Bena Kanioka, dwelling to the east of the Basalampasu. In style and subjects the figure carving of this tribe is influenced by Baluba art. Their extremely rare masks are known through the Hamburg Museum examples (fig. 40), acquired by Leo Frobenius at the beginning of the century and published several times. These are wooden face masks in black, white and red, round in outlines, with a large crosswise bow-shaped ridge. They have a large bulging forehead, horizontal eye-slits, a small nose, and a large open mouth in the shape of a horizontal lozenge with two rows of long teeth. On the temples, at the level of the eyes, there are small triangular projections, probably vestiges of scarification marks corresponding to the cylindrical projections on the Balwalwa and some Basalampasu masks. The huge, almost spherical forehead, which often appears in this whole area and which we have already met in the *mboom* masks of the Bakuba milieu, seems to be a kind of stylistic archetype of south-eastern Zaire.

The southernmost large style group is formed by a tribal complex called Balunda-Bachokwe. This denomination is incorrect in principle, since it is based on historical and political criteria, rather than artistic affinities. The Balunda, at one time, created a powerful empire in south-eastern Angola and southern Zaire, maintaining close contact with the Congo kingdom in the west and the Baluba empire in the east. The Bachokwe, a tribe of hunters and warriors dwelling in Angola, were vassals of the Baluba but eventually destroyed the Baluba empire and founded a state

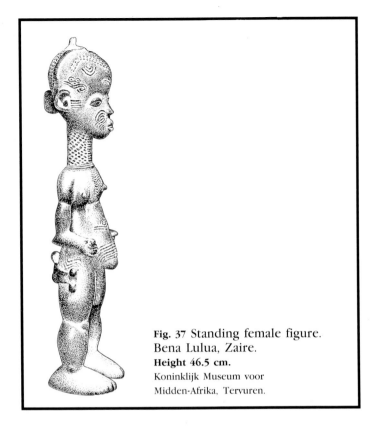

Fig. 37 Standing female figure. Bena Lulua, Zaire. **Height 46.5 cm.** Koninklijk Museum voor Midden-Afrika, Tervuren.

of their own in the 1880s. However, the contribution of the Baluba to the local art style was negligible; since all the outstanding carvers were probably Bachokwe in origin. The territory of the tribe is situated mainly in Angola, extending into the border areas of Zaire. The Bachokwe style was adopted by many tribes in Angola, even reaching those of western Zaire. There are almost no stylistic differences between the productions of the individual tribes; a precise attribution is sometimes possible only from the evidence of the figure's hairstyle and scarification, where this follows the fashion of a particular tribe. Somewhat more obvious deviations can be distinguished in the work of tribes dwelling on the periphery of the Bachokwe's sometime sphere of influence, for example among the Ovimbundu in the mountainous area of Benguela in West Angola (plates 225, 226) and among the Baholo in the Upper Kwango region. Some traits, especially the way in which the eyes are stylized, spread far beyond the original sphere of influence and may be identified in such diverse carving styles as those of the

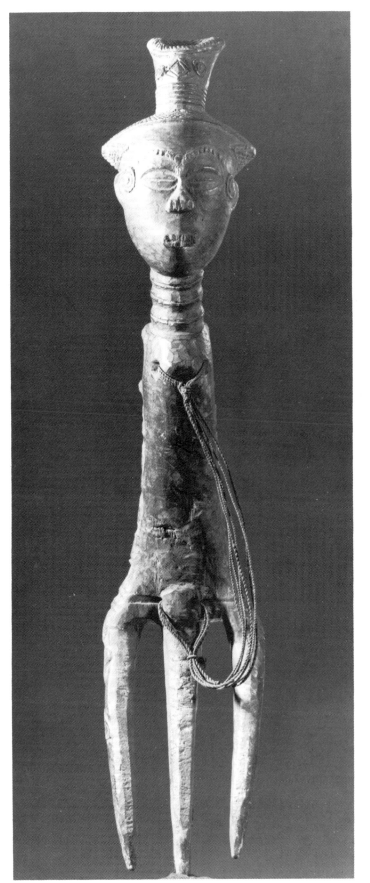

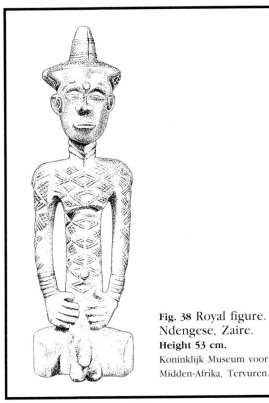

Fig. 38 Royal figure. Ndengese, Zaire. **Height 53 cm.** Koninklijk Museum voor Midden-Afrika, Tervuren.

Bena Lulua, the eastern Bapende and the Baluba.

The outstanding figure works of the Bachokwe are inspired by the traditions of the tribal aristocracy. These are male figures representing great chiefs of remote antiquity, and especially the legendary hero, great hunter and founder of the dynasty, Tchibinda Ilunga. The bodies of these figures are rounded and muscular, standing on legs very bent at the knees, as if the figure was about to pounce upon an adversary. The hands and feet are disproportionately large, with exaggerated joints and nails. The surface is perfectly smooth and polished. This very realistic appearance is sometimes enhanced by genuine human hair. But the majority of figures wear on their heads the characteristic chief's hat (*chihongo*), reminiscent of a large bonnet whose edges and ends form curves boldly encircling the head.

A number of other carvings are also connected with chiefs and village notables. These

216 Trident fork with anthropomorphic handle. Ndengese, Zaire. Wood and twisted string. **Height c. 50 cm.** Rautenstrauch Joest-Museum, Cologne.

are insignia such as staffs with a figure at the top (plate 220), axes with figures carved on the hafts, spear helves also decorated with human figures, and fly-whisk handles. Worthy of special attention are the chiefs' armchairs, copying European Renaissance models. Rows of figures and scenes of everyday life are carved

on their ties and back-bars. Frequent subjects are figures wearing typical initiation masks, copulating couples, palanquin bearers, and sick-bed attendants. Other dignitaries and village elders made use of low rounded stools with caryatids in the form of standing or squatting human figures with their elbows

217 Headrest with a caryatid in the form of a kneeling woman. Baluba-Hemba, Zaire. Pale wood with polished patinated surface. Chain made of brass wire round the neck. Collected around 1900.
Height 17 cm, width 13.9 cm.
Náprstek Museum, Prague.

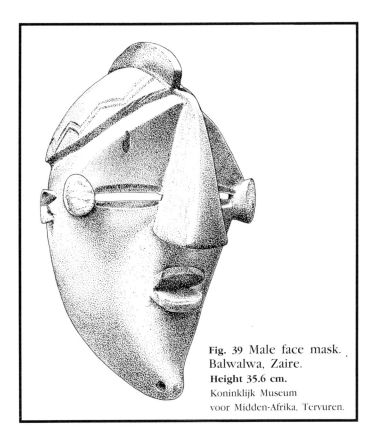

Fig. 39 Male face mask.
Balwalwa, Zaire.
Height 35.6 cm.
Koninklijk Museum
voor Midden-Afrika, Tervuren.

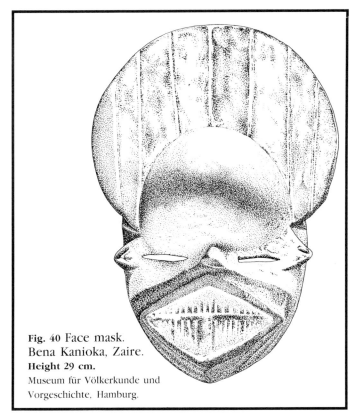

Fig. 40 Face mask.
Bena Kanioka, Zaire.
Height 29 cm.
Museum für Völkerkunde und
Vorgeschichte, Hamburg.

resting on their knees and their hands either supporting their chins or placed on the temples (plate 221). A bird caryatid often appears in carved headrests, which are decorated with brass hobnails.

Miniature human heads decorate a number of other objects such as hunting signal whistles (plate 223), combs (plate 224), musical instruments and pipes. Miniature tobacco mortars rest on the heads of human and animal caryatids. The Bachokwe carvers used every possible opportunity to display their virtuosity. If an object could not be given an anthropomorphic form, they covered its surface with geometric decoration consisting of oblong segments filled with parallel grooves and tiny lozenges.

This tribe's repertory of ceremonial masks is rich and varied. There are several types made with basketwork frames, originally covered with bark cloth (*tapa*), nowadays with sackcloth or even paper. Their high 'coiffures' are coloured, the faces being very simply modelled in a black resinous stuff and covered with glued-on white and red fabric cuttings. The outstanding type of these masks is called *chikunza*; it represents a protective spirit and supposedly induces fertility. The top of this mask is lengthened into a high cone. No less important is the type called *chikungu*, which takes the form of a chief's hat. These masks with slit-eyes and a strikingly wide mouth appear in various functions in the initiation camps. The wooden masks which once served some ritual purpose have declined into mere objects of entertainment. They are used in the *makishi* dances (which take place after the end of the initiation) and on other important occasions. Among these masks, of most importance is the type called *mwana pwo*, representing a beautiful young girl (plate 222). The dancer wearing this mask is dressed in a close-fitting knitted costume with wooden breasts attached to the chest. In some tribes of this style complex, he performs an acrobatic dance on poles from two to ten metres high. The male counterpart of this mask has a beard rather reminiscent of a flat horizontal collar under the chin. As with the stylization of the eyes, this element has extended beyond the style boundaries, appearing among the eastern Bapende and sometimes

218 Free-standing female figure. Bachokwe, Zaire. Hard brown wood with red-brown stained patinated surface. Notice a very distinctive feature of the tribe's style: the eyes in the form of coffee-beans set in sharply defined lentil-shaped holes. **Height 40.5 cm.** Náprstek Museum, Prague.

also in the masks of the Bakuba complex. In the wooden *makishi* dance masks, the stylization of the eyes is particularly emphatic. These take the form of coffee-beans, sometimes elongated, in other cases 'split' lengthwise, and are placed in the centre of concave ovals, in extreme cases jutting out in relief from the face. In the *makishi* masks, the special tribal scarification appears in the form of a Maltese cross placed in the centre of the forehead and sometimes also on the cheeks. It probably represents a memory of a Christian model, since the Bachokwe were in contact with Europeans for centuries, supplying the slave market.

The art of the Bachokwe and the tribes influenced by their culture is the most intensely studied in Africa, thanks in particular to the work of the Belgian scholar Marie-Louise Bastin.

THE LUALABA BASIN

The last large style area of this African art province is in south-eastern Zaire, in the basins of the Upper Lualaba (Congo) and its tributary the Lomami, extending along the western coast of lake Tanganyika. Although this was one of the areas richest in art, it is now amongst the most devastated. This is partly the doing of the Africans themselves, since an iconoclastic, hemp-smoking cult spread among the Baluba in the late 19th century, leading them to destroy objects connected with ancestor cults. Apart from tourist souvenirs and fakes, no new works of significance are likely to be discovered in this area. In style it is not so uniform as the Bakuba complex region or other areas stylistically dominated by a single tribe. There are two main factors here, represented by the art of the Baluba tribal confederacy in the south and of the Basongye in the north. Stylistically, they are directly antithetical. Although both the

219 Free-standing male figure. Baluba, Zaire. Light-brown wood with glossy patina. The rudimentary trunk and limbs suggest that this is a fetish figure, the body of which was intended to be kept concealed in a bundle containing magic ingredients. **Height 18.2 cm.**
Náprstek Museum, Prague.

Baluba and the Basongye created states of the sacred kingship type in the past, Baluba art conforms to the tendency of the other state-forming African tribes in its realism and socially representative motifs, whereas Basongye art serves the tribal secret societies, supplies the demand for fetishes, and may be described as cubistic in style. These two fundamental tendencies intersect in the areas of contact and have many local and ethnic variants.

Surface decoration, so significant in the style areas of the Bakuba and Bachokwe, plays a secondary role in Baluba art. The central subject of the complex of the Balubized tribes (at one time politically dominated by the Baluba) is the human figure; in the overwhelming majority of cases these represent important ancestors, especially female ones. The ancestor cult is served not only by free-standing figures, but also by caryatids supporting chiefs' stools and headrests, and by figural motifs in the chief's insignia. In accordance with the polyethnic composition of the former Baluba empire, Baluba art comprises many local styles as well as a number of identifiable, though anonymous, workshops, 'schools' and carvers, including the famous Master (or Masters) of Buli (fig. 1) and the Master of the Cascade Coiffures (fig. 2), both of whom have been mentioned in an earlier context.

220 Staff surmounted by a figure. Bachokwe, Zaire or Angola. Brown wood with patinated surface. A variation on the favourite subject of a seated figure supporting its head with its hands. This subject also appears among the Bena Lulua and, obviously, as a result of Bachokwe influence in Baluba art. **Height 78.3 cm, figure 9.8 cm.** Náprstek Museum, Prague.

In the central area of the Baluba-Hemba, the characteristic treatment of free-standing ancestor figures involved an idealization which enabled the carver to create a quite individualized human face with features ex-

221 Caryatid and base of a stool. Bachokwe, Zaire. The seat has broken off, and a retouch is visible on the top of the caryatid to conceal the break. A seated figure with elbows resting on its knees and supporting its head is a favourite subject of this tribal art. A coiled snake, two human figures lying facing each other, and an erotic couple are carved in relief on the base. Stools with human caryatids were reserved for important men among the tribes of southern Zaire. **Height 25.5 cm, diameter 29.5 cm.** Private collection, Prague.

pressing a particular mood. Among the tribes on the periphery of the Baluba complex, figures are more stylized and their facial expressions are stereotyped. Everywhere a predilection for rounded or even conical forms is apparent, especially (as we might expect) in the treatment of the head. This tendency is noticeable even in the realistic Baluba-Hemba style, although there it is modified by fluent transitions from one part of the body to another; the spherical belly is connected to the chest by a graceful curve, for example, so that the trunk thus becomes pear-shaped. The ancestor figures, up to a metre in height, are static and strictly symmetrical. In the female figures the hands are often placed on the breasts, or sometimes, as in their male counterparts, on the abdomen. The carvers have taken great care over the face and the complicated hairstyle, placed on the back of the spherical head. The anatomical structure of the trunk is also reproduced with remarkable fidelity, whereas the limbs are obviously stylized. The legs are disproportionately powerful in relation to the rest of the figure, whose weight they must support. The scarification marks, especially concentrated in the abdominal area, are reproduced in detail. These traits persist in the caryatids, including those supporting low headrests, in which the figure is very miniaturized.

Among the artistically executed objects of personal luxury there is a type of wooden food bowl held by two figures facing each other. Very frequently found is a seated or kneeling female figure holding a round vessel in her lap. These objects are given various names, depending on their functions — ritual or profane — in the different Baluba tribes.

The carved insignia of tribal dignitaries include axes whose hafts are decorated with human heads at the bottom end, and staffs with one or two figures on the top (plate 214). A speciality of the Baluba is the bow and arrow stand, which is stuck into the ground beside the chief on ceremonial occasions, or stands in front of his house as a symbol of his authority. Its lower end is shod with an iron point; the top is a female figure, out of whose head three spikes project to hold the weapons.

From an artistic point of view, the fetish figures are also worthy of attention (plate 219), especially the rubbing oracle (*katatora*). This is a small oblong frame with a human head carved on one of the shorter sides. The diviner and his client sat facing each other, with their forefingers in the frame, and rubbed the *katatora* up and down on a wooden base. When the oracle stuck fast on the base, the answer to the client's question became known. This is an analogue to the Bakuba rubbing oracle *itombwa*.

The Baluba masks are hemispherical, dark, and covered with white grooves in concentric circles. The highly stylized facial features stand out from the convex mask only in low relief, forming a graphic composition of white grooves. These masks are used at the funerals of chiefs and on various occasions connected with the chieftainship. The most frequently reproduced Baluba mask (Musée Royal de l'Afrique Centrale, Tervuren, Belgium), acquired towards the end of the 19th century, is among the most famous works of African art. But it is exceptional — a helmet mask in the form of a spherical male head with a trapezium-shaped beard and two winding horns, topped with a small bird figure. Nothing is known concerning its function.

A pronounced stylistic independence appears in the carving of the Balubized tribes dwelling beside Lake Tanganyika, although this independence diminishes the further south one looks. The northernmost outpost of Bakuba influence is represented by the commemorative figures of chiefs and notables of the Basikasingo, who live on the northwestern shore of Lake Tanganyika (fig. 41). Characteristically, the lower part of the face is elongated into an isosceles triangle. This, along with the large, high-placed eyes, gives the figure the appearance of a man wearing a

222 *Mwana pwo* face mask representing a beautiful woman. Bachokwe, Zaire or Angola. Pale wood, stained red-brown; turban-shaped hairstyle stained brown-black. The nape of the mask is knitted from a cord. The dancer wearing this mask performs in a close-fitting knitted costume to which wooden breasts are attached. **Height 25 cm.** Náprstek Museum, Prague.

214

223 Hunting whistle decorated with the head and torso of a human figure. Bachokwe, Zaire or Angola. Brown wood with remains of crusty patina. Collected before the First World War. **Height 15.8 cm.** Náprstek Museum, Prague.

224 Comb decorated with a human head. Bachokwe, Zaire. Hard red-brown wood with functional patina. **Height 15.8 cm.** Náprstek Museum, Prague.

gas-mask with the filter removed. The cheeks are edged with mouldings of saw-like projections representing the beard. The hands are placed on the chest. Some of the figures have been assigned to the Babembe, probably because examples were acquired from them. But these may well be works of the Basikasingo, commissioned by the Babembe. This view is strengthened by reference to the entirely different character of the highly stylized and almost oblong masks of the Babembe (*kalunga*), both helmet-shaped and flat. Their facial traits are reduced to the white ovals of the eye-sockets with small eyes inside them. The mouth is in the form of a small cylindrical projection.

The Babuye, settled further to the south-west, produce figures that are identical in function to those of the Basikasingo (fig. 42). However, their bodies are treated in a distinctly cubistic way, whereas their spherical heads and the stylization of the large bulging eyes point to a Baluba influence. The Baluba style is approached most nearly by the works of the Baholoholo and Batabwa on the south-western shores of Lake Tanganyika.

The territory of the Basongye is situated in the Lomami River basin, between the Baluba in the south and the Bakuba in the north-west. Their artistic style is the antithesis of the Baluba style, although some subjects are identical in both tribes; this is especially true of masks and chiefs' stools with caryatids. But in Basongye art, masks play a far more important role than they do among the Baluba. Whereas their highly stylized hemispherical masks are a somewhat alien element in the generally more realistic Baluba repertory, among the Basongye the style of these masks is almost omnipresent; for example, the human caryatids supporting the stools (mostly male, unlike Baluba caryatids) have faces carved in the style. Hence the probable correctness of the hypothesis that masks of this type (*kifwebe*; plate 213) are a Basongye contribution to the common inventory of subjects.

By comparison with Baluba masks, those of the Basongye are far more varied in form. The outlines are roughly keyhole-shaped. The more cubist examples have large goggling eyes, a pyramidal nose and a box-shaped mouth. The arched top of the head is sometimes divided by a long ridge running from back to front, down to the nose. The mask is convex from the horizontal axis of the eyes upwards, but concave down towards the chin. The whole surface of a *kifwebe* mask is covered with parallel grooves forming optically fascinating patterns. They are either left in the original bright colour of the wood or filled with a white clay pigment, in order to create a contrast with the stripes of the dark stained surface of the mask. Sometimes the mask is covered with coloured stripes along the lines of the grooves.

We lack information concerning the function of these masks, but they were obviously used at initiation ceremonies, and tribal sorcerers are said to have worn them when practising their art. The rare, oval wooden shields of the Basongye which carry a miniature *kifwebe* mask in the centre, carved in high relief, were certainly not intended for use in fighting, but were rather ritual objects, perhaps carried during dance performances (plate 212). Very rare are face masks without grooves, with the eyes made of inset cowrie shells and the mouth shaped like a horizontal eight.

The most famous African carvings in wood include the fetishes of the Basongye, some of which might be called assemblages, to use a modern art term (plate 211). These are sexless human figures, with the arms broken at right angles and pulled against the trunk. The eyes are made of inset cowries, or of small cones of rolled copper sheeting that give the fetishes an extraordinarily ferocious look. Magic ingredients are sometimes placed in hollows in both the trunk and the top of the head. An antelope horn often sticks out of the top; this is credited with tremendous magic power, which is further enhanced by strips of copper covering the face. The middle of the figure is girdled with snake skin with attached snail shells and other objects. Because of their dangerous magic power, these fetishes were kept outside the village.

As in many Zaire tribes, a ceremonial axe was used among the Basongye as a symbol of the chief's authority. In the other tribes the decoration of these axes was done by the carvers, but among the Basongye it had to be confined to the metal part and was the work of smiths. The blades of these axes are forged from iron rods, out of which miniature stylized human faces are also forged. More rarely found are axes with a compact copper blade, decorated with a miniature mask in relief.

The decoration of masks with parallel white grooves or painted strips has spread to the northern neighbours of the Basongye, the Batetela. But the masks of this tribe differ in form from the *kifwebe* masks. There are a small number of types, the product of different places and, perhaps, periods. These are helmet masks. Some of them are low with two faces turned in opposite directions, surmounted by horns or a miniature human head. In another type (fig. 43), the mask takes the form of a high cone with a schematically indicated face at the top and a wide ridge twined around it like a halo.

EAST AND SOUTH AFRICA

At the beginning of this book it was stated that East and South Africa are very poor in traditional sculpture; and in fact some parts of the eastern half of the continent have even been called lands without art. However, this is only a partial truth. Here we shall not argue about the existence of countless artifacts of traditional design made for everyday use, such as the products of basket-makers, smiths and jewellers, inlays, or objects sewn with glass beads, although in all of these the East and South Africans have displayed a highly developed sense of beauty of form and harmony of colour. Nor do we wish to argue about carved wooden objects made for practical purposes, such as headrests or stools. With a few exceptions, these are not decorated figuratively, although their abstract

217

ornamental treatment nevertheless reveals the existence of local traditions and an ability to blend functional with aesthetic considerations. Here we shall argue from figure sculpture. Ladislav Holý made the most recent attempt to sum up the known facts in the mid-1960s, concluding that there are very few tribes in this vast territory among whom no traces of sculpture could be found.

Unfortunately, in many cases they are nothing more than traces. These are often unique works, preserved in old museum collections and documented in a very unsatisfactory way. Even where reliable data exist concerning the purchase, there are sometimes justified doubts as to whether the object in question originated at the place where it was acquired.

However, Holý's work suggests some important conclusions. First, figure sculpture was not confined to a few small areas of East and South Africa, but was produced to a far greater extent than has generally been appreciated. Second, it was far from being just the offspring of major western centres such as south-eastern Zaire and northern Angola. And, finally, dozens of European museums possess examples of East and South African art hidden away in their collections and perhaps not identified so far; the study of these might broaden our notions about them as well as making them more precise.

If no great progress has been achieved in this field, that can be attributed to the fact that the traditional art of East and South Africa is a closed historical chapter, making collecting practically impossible — and collecting undoubtedly exerts a very positive influence on the study of art; students naturally tend to concentrate on the living art of West Africa since, among other things, they can hope to find the answers to questions which can never be supplied by collections of objects in extinct styles. Other reasons are the diffusion and consequent inaccessibility of collections, and the fact that any results laboriously achieved will be only provisional and uncertain.

In spite of these drawbacks, more information is available than can be included in a book of this size, and we shall have to confine our survey to the most important centres.

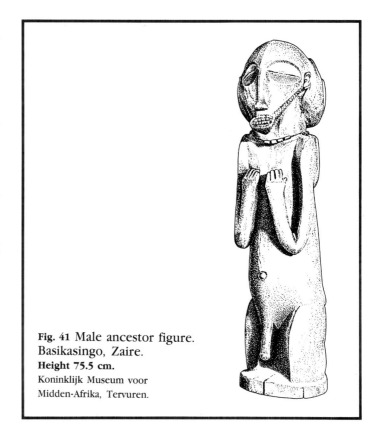

Fig. 41 Male ancestor figure. Basikasingo, Zaire. **Height 75.5 cm.** Koninklijk Museum voor Midden-Afrika, Tervuren.

Starting from the north, the first centre is the Upper Nile region of the southern Sudan. The best-known figure sculpture here is done by the Nilotic Bari tribe, who are credited with male and female figures that have not got beyond rudimentary representations (plate 227). These sculptures are relatively common and may be seen in at least ten European museums; most of them were acquired in the 19th century, some even before 1850. However, nothing is known about their origin, and our information concerning their function is not entirely clear. They were probably connected with ancestor worship and suspended in huts where offerings were made to them. The hypothesis of a possible connection with the Azande figures of north-eastern Zaire is not corroborated by any correspondence of form. In spite of the primitive schematic conception of these figures, at least two different styles can be distinguished; but we shall probably never known whether these have resulted from ethnic differences or only as a result of individual developments.

A stylistically isolated centre occurs in

Fig. 42 Standing male figure. Babuye, Zaire. **Height 99.5 cm.** Collection René van der Straete, Brussels.

225 Chief's staff surmounted by a human head, a chief's insignium. Ovimbundu, Angola. The carving style is related to that of the neighbouring Bachokwe, only the characteristic hairstyle being different. Collected before the First World War. **Length 52.6 cm.** Náprstek Museum, Prague.

south-western Ethiopia, among the Konso, Gato and Ometo. Commemorative figures of the dead, placed on their graves by the Gato (fig. 45), or at the entrance to the village by the Konso, are pole sculptures in the true sense of the term. The carving is done on the upper end of a pole lacking any indication of arms and legs, and consists only of a head wearing a helmet-shaped cap. Sometimes a phallic projection is placed above the forehead. The face is oval, in male figures adorned with an angular beard, and the prominent tube-shaped eyes are placed under the straight grooves representing eyebrow arches.

The first East African wooden masks on our north-south journey occur among the Was-siba (Haya) near Lake Victoria in south-western Tanzania. These are masks featuring a schematized human face with large rounded eyeholes and a large mouth into which human teeth are set. Some of these masks have a beard made of black monkey hair, the features of the face being outlined in white. Once more, the function of these masks is unclear. In the south-eastern part of the Lake Victoria

219

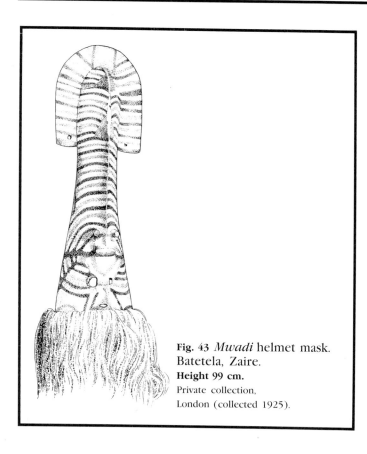

Fig. 43 *Mwadi* helmet mask. Batetela, Zaire. **Height 99 cm.** Private collection, London (collected 1925).

Fig. 44 Standing female figure. Wassukuma, Tanzania. **Height 50 cm.** Linden-Museum, Stuttgart.

226 Free-standing female figure. Ovimbundu, Angola. Brown wood with patinated surface, eyes made of glass beads, a row of brass hobnails above the forehead. Multiple strings of glass beads wound around the neck and waist; skirt made of blue cloth. The rounded little hollow on the chest was obviously made to hold some magic ingredients, as in the fetish figures from the Lower Congo region to the north, not far from the tribe's territory. **Height 38 cm.** Náprstek Museum, Prague.

region, commemorative figures of ancestors and tribal chiefs are known among the Wakerewe who live on Ukerewe Island and the adjacent mainland. Although different in style, these figures are identical, in a number of other respects, with those made by the Wassukuma, the southern neighbours of the Wakerewe (fig. 44). The figure sculpture of both of these tribes displays a predilection for long cylindrical trunks and proportionately long limbs, the heads being rather small and the sexual parts reduced to the minimum needed to differentiate between male and female. The hair is represented by vegetable fibres, sometimes with glass beads strung on them.

Among the tribes on the eastern shore of Lake Tanganyika, rare sculptures are known, distinctly influenced in style by the Baluba tribal complex from the opposite side of the lake in eastern Zaire. This is true, for example, of the sculptures of the Wajiji group belonging to the Abaha (Ha) tribe, especially the famous figure in the Berlin Museum für Völkerkunde, which was acquired among the Wabende; the pear-shaped trunk of this figure

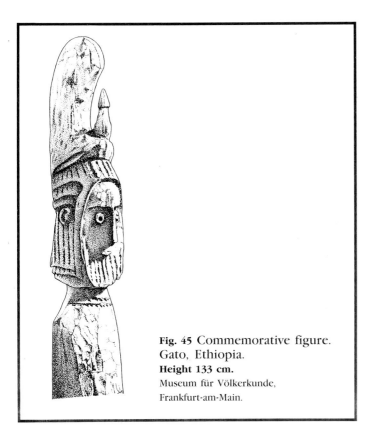

Fig. 45 Commemorative figure. Gato, Ethiopia.
Height 133 cm.
Museum für Völkerkunde, Frankfurt-am-Main.

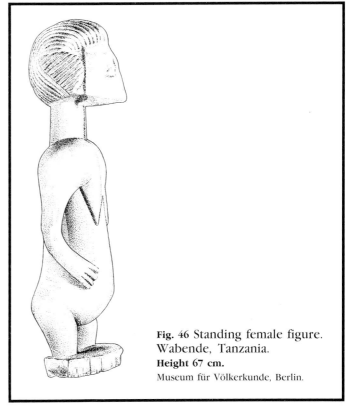

Fig. 46 Standing female figure. Wabende, Tanzania.
Height 67 cm.
Museum für Völkerkunde, Berlin.

is strikingly reminiscent of the similarly stylized bodies of Baluba-Hemba ancestors (fig. 46). A trunk conceived in an analogous way may be seen in the unique figure believed to have originated in central Tanzania among the Wahehe (Hamburg Museum), or in the figure of a kneeling woman, from the eastern shore of Lake Victoria, published from a private collection by Himmelheber. These three unique figures, in different mature styles yet connected by a common way of treating the trunk that is by no means current in Africa, are worth mentioning because they demonstrate how difficult it is to map the art of this part of the continent. Of course, the reliability of the data concerning their provenance remains questionable, but there seems little hope of future verification. Moreover, these are all female figures, so that the pear-shaped trunks may not be a result of stylistic affinity, but may simply be stylized representations of the body of a pregnant woman.

There was an interesting centre of court art in central Tanzania, among the Wanyamwezi and their eastern neighbours the Wagogo.

From the former comes the well-known armchair of the Sultana of Buruku, found in her palace in 1898 (fig. 48), and from the latter the similarly conceived armchair of a chief. They are in the Museum für Völkerkunde, Berlin, and the Museum für Völkerkunde, Vienna, respectively. Each of these chairs has a high full back, with a relief carving on the outer side of a human figure with long slender limbs embracing it. Probably of the same provenance are the horns, identical in style, published by Holý from a Belgian private collection. Their uniqueness, representational style and socially exclusive function make these objects reminiscent of the finest works of Abomey Fon court art. The objects appear to have been made in a single place, but we do not know which of the two tribes was responsible.

A mature sculptural tradition must once have existed along the shores of the Indian Ocean, as is demonstrated by a few uniquely preserved figures found among the Washambala in the Usambara Mountains in northeastern Tanzania. For example, one female

221

figure (fig. 49) bears comparison with the best works of West African art, and simply cannot be the work of some isolated individual.

Southward along the sea coast, the number of sculptural works increases, despite the fact that the region has been for centuries exposed to Arab-Islamic influences. The Wazaramo, dwelling north of the Rufiji River, have created figure sculptures in various styles. The *tambiko* staffs with carved figures at the top are for curing children; they may perhaps be considered a stylistic outpost of the rich art of the tribes settled between the ocean and Lake Malawi. But the small figures called *mwana kiti* (fig. 47) are certainly very original in style. Their schematic heads and limbless bodies comprise a premeditated design involving cones, cylinders, arches and segments of spheres. These are dolls, obviously endowed with sympathetic magic power, of a kind found in various styles in different parts of Africa. They were carried by unmarried girls and by wives until their first child was born. The Doe, settled further in the interior, have figures of the same type but the consistency of their geometric treatment is impaired by the concave faces with simply modelled details (in figures made by the Wazaramo, the faces are altogether absent). The Doe were probably also the makers of a unique but (alas) undocumented horn carved from an elephant tusk and kept in the collection of the Übersee-Museum in Bremen (plate 231). Its blow-hole is placed on the side, as is usual in all African horns, and the point of the tusk is carved into a typical *mwana-kiti* figure with a face. Nothing is known about the function of this instrument. Primitive human figures are made by the Wabondei, who are neighbours of the Washambala and Wazaramo dwelling further inland; these are remarkable for their concave heart-shaped faces, of the type known also from the western half of the continent. The same style prevails in the face masks of Mozambique tribes.

The area stretching from coastal southern Tanzania into the part of Mozambique between the Indian Ocean and Lake Malawi may be considered a single homogeneous style area. The keynote of the local style is set by the works of the Makonde (Wamakonde),

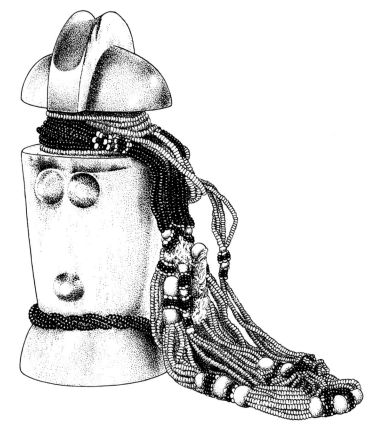

Fig. 47 Female *mwana-kiti* figure. Wazaramo, Tanzania.
Height 14 cm.
Museum für Völkerkunde, Berlin.

which are amply documented and represented in collections. Most of the Makonde inhabit the area south of the Ruvuma River, in Mozambique; a smaller section of the tribe, settled on the northern bank in Tanzania, was converted to Islam and therefore abandoned its traditional art at about the time of the First World War.

227 Free-standing figures of a human couple. Bari, Republic of Sudan. Wood with surface stained red-brown. Ten European museums hold about forty-five figures made by this tribe, all of which were collected during the 19th century and some even in its first half. In style they belong to at least four groups, which may reflect differences between individual carvers, different tribal origins, or different periods. Uncertainty surrounds the purpose of these figures. They either represented tribal ancestors, or served magical protective purposes. This undocumented pair, acquired a short time ago from a private collection in Prague, perhaps most closely resemble some figures in the Musée de l' Homme, Paris, collected in the first half of the 19th century.
Heights 32 and 34 cm.
Náprstek Museum, Prague.

228 Helmet mask. Makonde, Mozambique. Light yellow-white wood with ochre-stained patinated surface. Some human hair is set into the head. The *pelele* lip peg, a traditional ornament of the Makonde, is marked on the upper lip.
Height 26 cm.
Náprstek Museum, Prague.

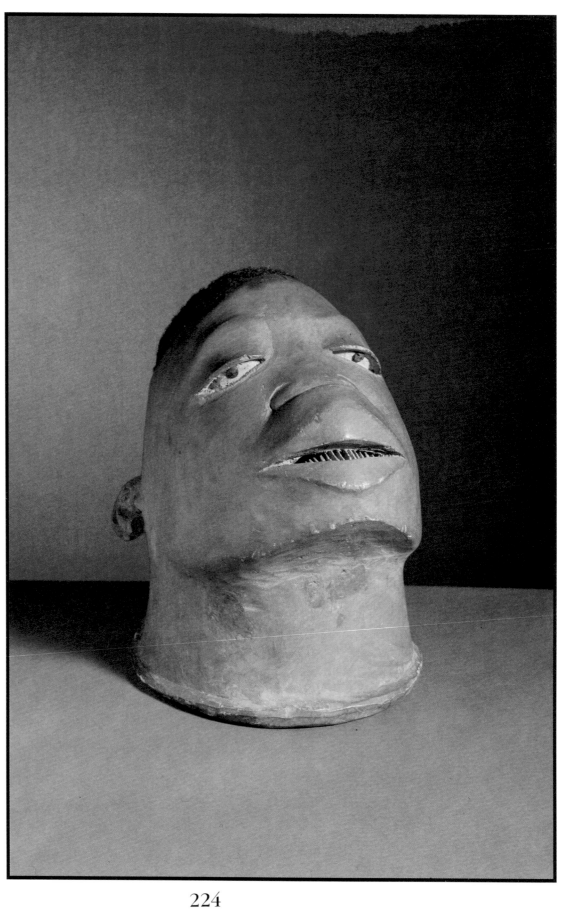

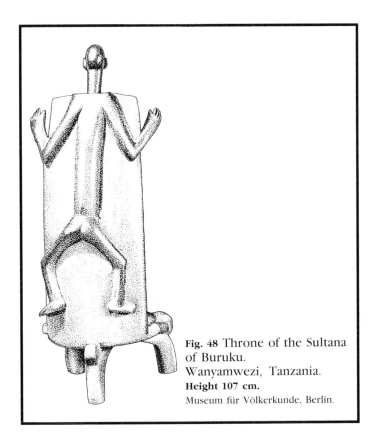

Fig. 48 Throne of the Sultana of Buruku. Wanyamwezi, Tanzania. **Height 107 cm.** Museum für Völkerkunde, Berlin.

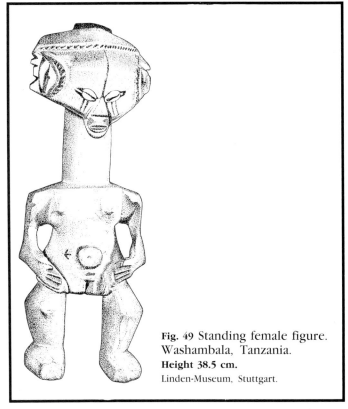

Fig. 49 Standing female figure. Washambala, Tanzania. **Height 38.5 cm.** Linden-Museum, Stuttgart.

Members of this tribe subsequently came from colonial Mozambique to work in what was then British Tanganyika, settling around Dar-es-Salaam. They created the art, so popular over the last few decades, consisting of fantastic figures and realistic column-shaped statues carved in ebony. However, this modern art has nothing to do with the traditional wood-carving of the Makonde, being motivated by the demands of the tourist trade. The best realistic works are based on modern styles, whereas the fantastic element probably derives in part from a folklore demonology, which found no expression in traditional sculpture.

The northern periphery of this style area is represented by the human and animal masks made by the coastal tribe of the Wamuera from southern Tanzania. The traditional sculpture of the Makonde, however, has developed many genres, to a degree comparable with the prolific artistry of some west African tribes. This sculpture includes face masks, masks in the form of human heads reminiscent of those of the Yoruba *gelede* secret society, figures, drums with human caryatids, staffs with figural heads, and pipes conceived in the form of figures.

In terms of quantity, masks dominate Makonde carving. The face masks have obviously originated in a large number of centres, since they exhibit a variety of distinctive traits. The outlines of these masks are round or oval, and the masks themselves are slightly convex and highly stylized, with the surface stained brown or brown-red. The lavish geometric tattooing of real Makonde faces is reproduced on the masks by markings made with black beeswax. The male masks are bearded; the female ones always have a disc-shaped peg (*pelele*) set in the upper lip. The female masks are supplemented with a wooden shield with breasts, which the dancer ties to his chest. Dancers wearing these masks performed in pairs, their dance consisting of a choreographed representation of copulation. At initiation ceremonies animal masks were also used, as well as diabolic masks with horns.

The helmet masks are more uniform in style, showing a strong tendency towards

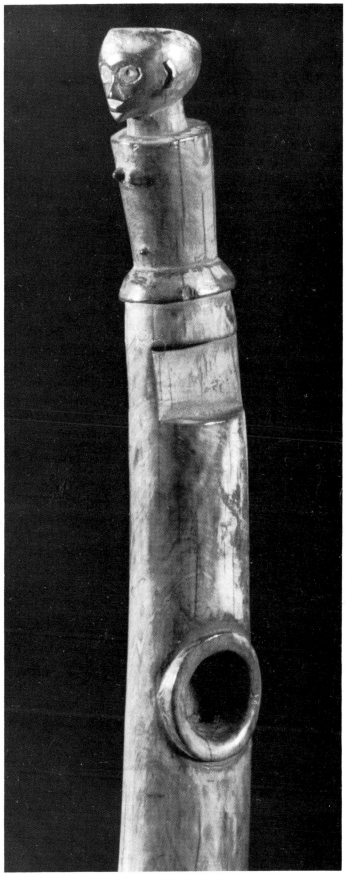

realism (plate 228). They represent fleshy human heads with wide, flat noses; the teeth are visible between the thick lips of a half-opened mouth. The female masks are again provided with the obligatory lip peg, while beards made of grass are attached to the male masks. An asymmetrical hairstyle is often represented by human hair pressed into incisions in the wood. The masks have the character of portraits, sometimes with an apparent intent to caricature; in some of them the racial

229 Figure of a kneeling woman. Makonde, Mozambique. Pale wood with no surface treatment and no patina, extensive tattoos indicated by burned lines. **Height 49 cm.** Náprstek Museum, Prague.

230 Detail of plate 229.

231 Horn made from an elephant tusk, ending with a stylized female figure. Doe, Tanzania. As the carved strip at the lower end of the tusk indicates, the mouthpiece of the horn was probably provided with a leather collar. **Height of the figure 8 cm.** Übersee Museum, Bremen.

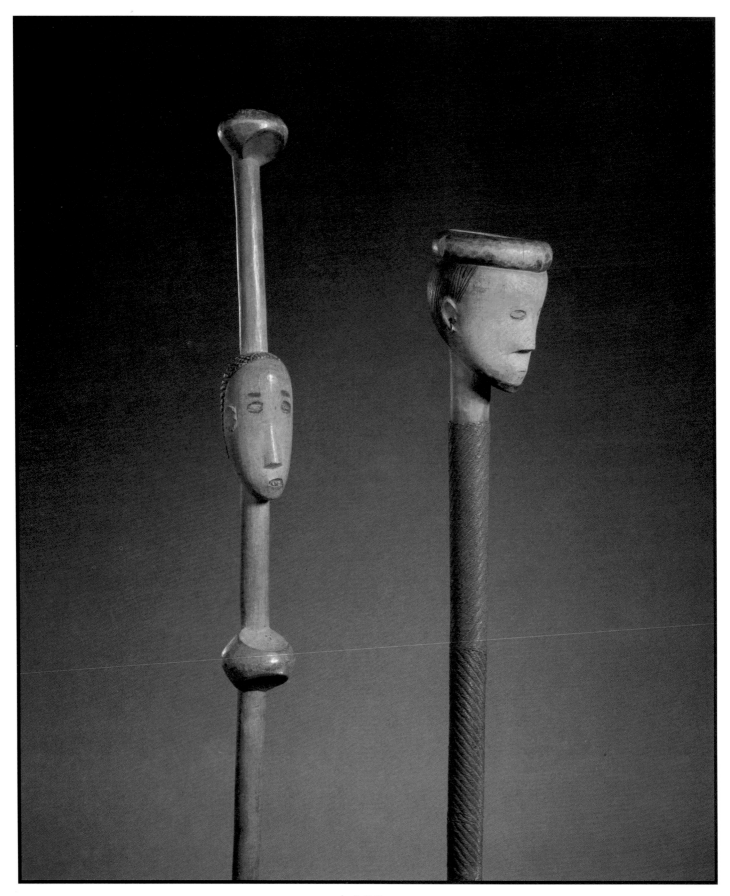

Fig. 50 Standing female figure.
Lomwe, Malawi.
Height 40.4 cm.
Museum für Völkerkunde, Berlin.

characteristics of foreigners — Europeans, Arabs, Chinese — are easily recognizable. The masks of the neighbouring Mawia are identical in style and indistinguishable from those of the Makonde. Masks with naturalistic lips which look as though they are extremely swollen are assigned to another neighbouring tribe, that of the Wayayo.

Makonde female figures, often made with a child on an arm or shoulder, probably represent the primordial mother of the tribe. Characteristic of them is a dance-like pose with legs straddled and the arms held away from the body. Male figures are much rarer. Like the masks the faces of the figures carry the tribal ornamentation, the tattoo again being reproduced with beeswax or burned lines (pyrography; plate 229).

Makonde art is often regarded as the easternmost extremity of Congo basin art — a kind of West African enclave in the artistic desert of East Africa. But we have seen that Makonde art is not such an isolated phenomenon as it is usually believed to be, and its style is altogether independent, even if we admit that in very general terms it displays some affinities with Baluba art.

Southern Malawi is where certain female figures, impossible to place more precisely, originated. They represent a 'rustic' form of Makonde art from the southern periphery of Makonde influence. The connecting link between them is the mother-and-child motif; in the southern Malawi figures the hair is replaced by fur, and widely straddled legs and bent arms that hang loosely, far from the body, give them a dynamic appearance. Similar female figures are made by the Lomwe in the Malawi-Mozambique borderland southeast of Lake Malawi. There are two unique examples of them, very different in style, in the Berlin Museum für Völkerkunde. In their stylistic maturity and unique character they are comparable to the wooden figures of the Washambala. Here, too, a long sculptural tradition must be postulated. This is particularly evident in a well-known figure with a concave face divided by the narrow, oblique eyes into sections; both the face and the body are covered with parallel geometric grooves representing tattooing (fig. 50).

232 Staff decorated with a human head. Zulu-Nguni, Republic of South Africa. Light-brown wood. Grooves of eyes and eyebrows additionally blackened by burning. The staff was probably made by the carver of the human couple in the Rijksmuseum voor Volkenkunde in Leiden.
Height 140.5 cm, head 7.9 cm. Náprstek Museum, Prague.

Staff surmounted by a human head Bathonga or Zulu, Republic of South Africa. Light-brown wood. Staff bound with copper wire. The little wreath around the head represents the traditional hairstyle of Bathonga men, but may also be found in the sculptures of other South African tribes.
Height 113 cm. Náprstek Museum, Prague.

A more important centre of traditional carving is situated in the Middle Zambezi River region. Its outstanding representatives are the Barotse (Lozi) who in the 17th century founded a state here on the ruins of the ancient Monomotapa empire. Their most original genre of carving consists of luxurious oval food bowls, the flat lids of which have handles in the form of bird, animal or human figures. These are essentially realistic, displaying excellent powers of observation. A frequent subject is birds floating on water, which are the most stylized of all Barotse figural subjects. This is probably why many writers believe that these figures continue the tradition of large bird figures made of steatite, which decorated the walls of stone buildings in the ancient city of Zimbabwe. In style and iconography, however, the Barotse figures do not correspond to these supposed models. Furthermore, the rare free-standing figure sculptures of this tribe have undeniable affinities with the style area of the Balunda-Bachokwe complex in the west. It was undoubtedly also from this complex that Barotse masks were adopted. They are made of bark cloth (tapa) stretched over a basketwork structure and painted in geometric patterns, and are worn during the *makishi* dances. The wooden masks of the Barotse are identical in style with those of their southern neighbours, the Masubia. Their most striking features are their bulbous foreheads (which are sometimes even hemispherical), their bulging cheeks, the opened mouths with two rows of sharply pointed teeth, and the few parallel wrinkles carefully carved on the foreheads. This type of mask is also found among some other tribes.

The last style centre in our survey is connected with a group of tribes given the common name of Bathonga. They live in the coastal areas of south-eastern Africa, in southern Mozambique and South Africa. In relatively recent times the works of these tribes have obviously inspired the development of carving among the Zulu (Amazulu) in South Africa. The Bathonga make male and female figures carved in pairs. These have slender cylindrical trunks and long limbs, especially the legs; the arms hang loosely along the body. The heads are rounded and relatively small, with round eyes. The male figures wear a hairstyle in the form of a small rounded wreath, and have a beard carved on the chin. The female figures have small breasts in the form of round caps. These figures do not serve any cult purposes. The surface is left the natural colour of the wood and only a few details, such as the male's hair and beard, are blackened by burning. Small human heads carved in this style adorn staffs which may have been symbols of social prestige (plate 232). Zulu carving is reminiscent of its Bathonga models, some male figures even having identically treated hairstyles; but they tend to display a greater freedom in applying and deviating from the canon of style. Most Zulu figure carvings have probably been made to be sold to foreigners.

230

LIST OF PLATES

231

a ceremonial shield. Private collection, Prague.

103 Akan gold weight in the form of a stool. Náprstek Museum, Prague.

104 Akan gold weight in the form of a basketwork ceremonial shield. Private collection, Prague.

105 Akan gold weight in the form of a 'knot of wisdom'. Náprstek Museum, Prague.

106 Akan gold weight in the form of a chief with a ceremonial sword and shield. Náprstek Museum, Prague.

107 Akan gold weight in the form of a dignitary on horseback and two drummers. Náprstek Museum, Prague.

108 Pipe bowl in the form of a quadruped devouring a fish. Gold Coast. Náprstek Museum, Prague.

109 Pipe bowl in the form of a chameleon. Náprstek Museum, Prague.

110 Pipe bowl with a standing male figure. Náprstek Museum, Prague.

111 Pipe bowl with a seated male figure. Náprstek Museum, Prague.

112 Figure of a standing woman. Ewe, Togo. Náprstek Museum, Prague.

113 Figure of a seated woman with two children. Yoruba, Nigeria. Náprstek Museum, Prague.

114 Sculpture of a hunter with a gun, taking aim at a lion. Fon, Republic of Benin. Náprstek Museum, Prague.

115 *Ere ibeji* figures of deceased twins. Yoruba, Nigeria. Private collection, Prague.

116 *Ere ibeji* figures of deceased twins. Yoruba, Nigeria. Náprstek Museum, Prague.

117 *Ere ibeji* female figure clad in a miniature version of the costume worn by a priest of the god Shango. Yoruba, Nigeria. Náprstek Museum, Prague.

118 *Ogo elegba* dance staff. Yoruba, Nigeria. Náprstek Museum, Prague.

119 *Ogo elegba* dance equipment. Yoruba, Nigeria. Náprstek Museum, Prague.

120 *Agere ifa* palm-nut bowl. Yoruba, Nigeria, or the Republic of Benin. Náprstek Museum, Prague.

121 *Opon ifa* tray. Yoruba, Nigeria. Náprstek Museum, Prague.

122 Hare mask of the *egungun* society. Yoruba, Nigeria. Náprstek Museum, Prague.

123 *Ikin ifa* miniature human head. Yoruba, Nigeria. Náprstek Museum, Prague.

124 Mask of the *gelede* society. Yoruba, Nigeria, or the Republic of Benin. Náprstek Museum, Prague.

125 *Ilari* dance head-dress of the *egungun* society. Yoruba, Nigeria. Náprstek Museum, Prague.

126 Mask of the *gelede* society. Yoruba, Republic of Benin. Náprstek Museum, Prague.

127 Box in the form of a duck. Yoruba, Nigeria. Náprstek Museum, Prague.

128 Mask of the *gelede* society. Yoruba, Republic of Benin. Náprstek Museum, Prague.

129 Door carved in low relief. Yoruba, Nigeria, Ilorin (?). Náprstek Museum, Prague.

130 Mirror case with a lid. Yoruba, Nigeria. Náprstek Museum, Prague.

131 *Opa osanyin* altar. Yoruba, Nigeria. Náprstek Museum, Prague.

132 Figure of a seated man. Yoruba, Nigeria. Opočno Castle, Czechoslovakia.

133 *Ogboni edan* pair of figures. Yoruba, Nigeria. Náprstek Museum, Prague.

134 Face mask. Bini, Nigeria. Náprstek Museum, Prague.

135 Face mask of the *ekpo* secret society. Ibibio, Nigeria. Náprstek Museum, Prague.

136 Head-dress of the *ekkpe* secret society. Ekoi (Ejagham), Nigeria, Cross River region. Náprstek Museum, Prague.

137 *Duen fobara* funeral panel. Kalabari Ijo, Nigeria. Museum of Mankind, London.

138 Tailor working at a Singer sewing machine. Ibibio, Nigeria, Ikot Ekpene. Náprstek Museum, Prague.

139 Free-standing female figure. Wurkun (?), Nigeria. Náprstek Museum, Prague.

140 Pipe bowl in the form of a seated man. Bali (?), Cameroon. Náprstek Museum, Prague.

141 Anthropomorphic pipe bowls. Bali (?), Cameroon. Náprstek Museum, Prague.

142 Pipe bowl in the form of a human head surmounted by a three-faced half-figure. Bamum, Cameroon. Náprstek Museum, Prague.

143 Face mask. Bamum, Cameroon. Náprstek Museum, Prague.

144 Face mask with a movable lower jaw. Ibibio, Nigeria. Linden-Museum, Stuttgart.

145 Helmet mask. Bekom or Babanki, Cameroon. Náprstek Museum, Prague.

146 Buffalo mask. Bamileke (?), Cameroon. Náprstek Museum, Prague.

147 Cylindrical stool. Bamileke (?), Cameroon. Náprstek Museum, Prague.

148 Stool. Duala, Cameroon. Náprstek Museum, Prague.

149 Zoomorphic food box with a flat lid. Bamileke (?), Cameroon. Náprstek Museum, Prague.

150 Spoon with a figure handle. Fang, Gabon. Náprstek Museum, Prague.

151 Detail of plate 150.

152 Spoon. Fang, Gabon. Náprstek Museum, Prague.

153 Head with stylized face in the shape of a concave heart. Fang, Gabon. Náprstek Museum, Prague.

154 Torso of a *bwete* female figure. Mitsogho, Gabon. Private collection, Prague.

155 Face mask. Mitsogho or Bavuvi, Gabon. Náprstek Museum, Prague.

156 Standing male figure. Jukun, Nigeria. Néprajzimúzeum, Budapest.

157 Face mask. Ashira-Bapunu, Gabon. Náprstek Museum, Prague.

158 Face mask. Ashira-Bapunu, Gabon. Náprstek Museum, Prague.

159 Face mask. Bavuvi, Gabon. Private collection, Prague.

160 Standing male figure. Ashira-Bapunu, Gabon. Náprstek Museum, Prague.

161 Dance head-dress. Ham, Nigeria. Koninklijk Museum voor Midden-Afrika, Tervuren.

162 Figure of a kneeling woman (?). Ashira-Bapunu, Gabon. Náprstek Museum, Prague.

163 *Mbulu-ngulu* reliquary figure. Bakota-Mindasa, Gabon. Náprstek Museum, Prague.

164 *Bwiiti* reliquary figure. Mahongwe, Gabon. Náprstek Museum, Prague.

165 Figure of a standing woman. Bwaka (Ngbaka), Zaire. Náprstek Museum, Prague.

166 Box whose lid is decorated with a human head. Mangbetu, Zaire. Náprstek Museum, Prague.

167 Anthropomorphic water jug. Mangbetu, Zaire. Náprstek Museum, Prague.

168 Standing male figure. Mangbetu, Zaire. Náprstek Museum, Prague.

169 Free-standing female figure. Azande, Republic of Sudan. Náprstek Museum, Prague.

170 Symbolic throne: standing female figure with a stick and a stool. Bekom, Cameroon. Museum für Völkerkunde, Berlin.

171 Figures of a standing man and woman. Azande, Republic of Sudan. Náprstek Museum, Prague.

172 Spoon. Balega (Warega), Zaire. Náprstek Museum, Prague.

173 Drum with a caryatid in the form of a woman holding a bottle. Bakongo, Zaire. Náprstek Museum, Prague.

174 Handle of a ritual rattle. Basundi, Lower Congo region. Zaire. Náprstek Museum, Prague.

175 Fetish figure. Bakongo, Zaire. Náprstek Museum, Prague.

176 Spoon with a figure handle in the form of a man with a pipe. Bakongo, People's Republic of Congo. Náprstek Museum, Prague.

177 Spoon with a figure handle in the form of a drummer. Bakongo, People's Republic of Congo. Náprstek Museum, Prague.

178 Spoon with a figure handle in the form of a standing woman. Bakongo, People's Republic of Congo. Náprstek Museum, Prague.

179 Group of a drummer with six listeners. Bakongo, Zaire. Náprstek Museum, Prague.

180 Figure of a moustached European in ceremonial uniform. Bakongo, Zaire. Náprstek Museum, Prague.

181 Souvenir carving on a hippopotamus tusk. Bakongo, Loango Coast, People's Republic of Congo. Náprstek Museum, Prague.

182 Fetish figure of a man. Babembe, People's Republic of Congo. Náprstek Museum, Prague.

183 Object of uncertain purpose. Babembe, People's Republic of Congo. Náprstek Museum, Prague.

184 *Butti* fetish figure. Bateke-Sise, People's Republic of Congo. Náprstek Museum, Prague.

185 *Butti* fetish figure. Bateke-Fumu, People's Republic of Congo, or Zaire. Náprstek Museum, Prague.

186 *Kebe-kebe* dance requisites in the form of human heads. Kuyu, People's Republic of Congo. Náprstek Museum, Prague.

187 Figure of the primordial mother of the tribe. Kuyu, People's Republic of Congo. Náprstek Museum, Prague.

188 Free-standing figure of a woman with a child. Bambala, Zaire. Náprstek Museum, Prague.

189 Figure of a standing woman. Bayaka, Zaire. Náprstek Museum, Prague.

190 Slit drum. Bayaka or Bankanu, Zaire. Náprstek Museum, Prague.

191 Comb with a handle in the form of a human head. Bayaka, Zaire. Náprstek Museum, Prague.

192 Initiation mask. Bayaka, Zaire. Náprstek Museum, Prague.

193 Initiation mask. Bayaka, Zaire. Náprstek Museum, Prague.

194 *Mbuya* initiation mask. Bapende, Zaire. Private collection. Prague.

195 *Hemba* initiation mask. Basuku, Zaire. Náprstek Museum, Prague.

196 Free-standing figures of a man and a woman. Bapende, Zaire. Náprstek Museum, Prague.

197 Detail of plate 196.

198 Free-standing male figure. Bapende, Zaire. Náprstek Museum, Prague.

199 Wooden lid. Bawoyo, Cabinda. Museu de Etnologia do Ultramar, Lisbon.

200 Ornament made of glass beads on the *mboom* mask in plate 201.

201 *Mboom* helmet mask. Bakuba, Zaire. Náprstek Museum, Prague.

202 *Mwaash a mbooy* helmet mask.

Bakuba, Zaire. Náprstek Museum, Prague.

203 Pipe. Bakuba, Zaire. Náprstek Museum, Prague.

204 Palm-wine cup standing on human legs. Bakuba, Zaire. Náprstek Museum, Prague.

205 Human-headed cup for ritual palm-wine drinking. Bakuba, Zaire. Náprstek Museum, Prague.

206 Box for the preparation of a *tukula*. Bakuba, Zaire. Náprstek Museum, Prague.

207 Toy doll in the form of a stylized human head. Bakuba, Zaire. Náprstek Museum, Prague.

208 Standing figure of indeterminate sex. Bena Lulua (?), Zaire. Náprstek Museum, Prague.

209 Comb. Bena Lulua, Zaire. Náprstek Museum, Prague.

210 Face mask. Basalampasu, Zaire. Náprstek Museum, Prague.

211 Fetish figure, sexless. Basongye, Zaire. Náprstek Museum, Prague.

212 Dance (?) shield. Basongye, Zaire. Náprstek Museum, Prague.

213 *Kifwebe* face mask. Basongye, Zaire. Náprstek Museum, Prague.

214 A chief's insignium. Baluba-Hemba, Zaire. Náprstek Museum, Prague.

215 Profile view of the chief's staff in plate 214.

216 Trident fork with anthropomorphic handle. Ndengese, Zaire. Rautenstrauch Joest-Museum, Cologne.

217 Headrest with a caryatid in the form of a kneeling woman. Baluba-Hemba, Zaire. Náprstek Museum, Prague.

218 Free-standing female figure. Bachokwe, Zaire. Náprstek Museum, Prague.

219 Free-standing male figure. Baluba, Zaire. Náprstek Museum, Prague.

220 Staff surmounted by a figure. Bachokwe, Zaire or Angola. Náprstek Museum, Prague.

221 Caryatid and base of a stool. Bachokwe, Zaire. Private collection, Prague.

222 *Mwana pwo* face mask. Bachokwe, Zaire or Angola. Náprstek Museum, Prague.

223 Hunting whistle. Bachokwe, Zaire or Angola. Náprstek Museum, Prague.

224 Comb decorated with a human head. Bachokwe, Zaire. Náprstek Museum, Prague.

225 A chief's insignium. Ovimbundu, Angola. Náprstek Museum, Prague.

226 Free-standing female figure. Ovimbundu, Angola. Náprstek Museum, Prague.

227 Free-standing figures of a human couple. Bari, Republic of Sudan. Náprstek Museum, Prague.

228 Helmet mask. Makonde, Mozambique. Náprstek Museum, Prague.

229 Figure of a kneeling woman. Makonde, Mozambique. Náprstek Museum, Prague.

230 Detail of plate 229.

231 Horn made of an elephant tusk. Doe, Tanzania. Übersee Museum, Bremen.

232 Staff decorated with a human head. Zulu-Nguni, Republic of South Africa. Náprstek Museum, Prague.

Staff surmounted by a human head. Bathonga or Zulu, Republic of South Africa. Náprstek Museum, Prague.

SOURCES FOR THE TEXT FIGURES

African Arts. Los Angeles: 6 (vol. XIV/2); 17 (vol. XII/2); 18 (vol. XIV/2); 29 (vol. XI/3)

Elisofon, Eliot, and Fagg, William. **The Sculpture of Africa**. London, 1958: 23

Eyo, Ekpo, and Willett, Frank. **Treasures of Ancient Nigeria**. London, 1982/3: 7-9, 12, 13, 15

Fagg, William. **African Sculpture**. Washington D. C., 1970: 10

Fagg, William. **Tribes and Forms in African Art**. New York, 1965: 5, 11, 16, 31, 33, 39-41, 48, 50

Galerie Wolfgang Ketterer, Munich (41 Auction, 1980): 22

Gillon, Werner. **Collecting African Art**. London, 1979: 43

Herold, Erich. **Zur Ikonographie der 'aku-onu' Masken (Jukun, Nigeria)**, in Abhandlungen und Berichte des Staatlichen Museums für Völkerkunde, Dresden, vol. XXIV. Berlin, 1975: 28

Holý, Ladislav. **Afrikanische Plastik**. Prague, 1967: 44-47, 49

Leiris, Michel, and Delange, Jacqueline. **Afrika: Die Kunst des schwarzen Erdteils**. Munich, 1968: 14, 21, 24, 32, 35

Leuzinger, Elsy. **Afrikanische Skulpturen**. Zurich, 1963: 2

Meauzé, Pierre. **African Art: Sculpture.** London, 1968: 37, 38, 42

Newton, Douglas. **The Nelson Rockefeller Collection: Masterpieces of Primitive Art**. New York, 1978: 25, 26, 30, 34

Trowell, Margaret, and Nevermann, Hans. **Afrika und Ozeanien**. Baden-Baden, 1967: 1, 4, 19, 20

Sotheby—Parke—Bernet, New York (May 26, 1978): 3, 27

View-cards published by the former Museum of Primitive Art, New York: 36

BIBLIOGRAPHY

Ninety years ago the first monograph on African art appeared — the now rare *Die Masken und Geheimbünde Afrikas* by Leo Frobenius. Since then the literature on the subject has swollen, and there are now thousands of books, articles and catalogues of some significance. In the early decades of study, sometimes only a single contribution was added in a year; but since the 1960s a veritable publication explosion has occurred in this field as in so many others. Until then it was not particularly difficult to keep up with the literature, whereas there are now hardly any libraries, including those of large universities, that can acquire everything of relevance that has been published. For at least the past twenty years the situation has been quite beyond the financial resources of an individual. All of this is due to an ever increasing interest in African art, the ever-growing number of exhibitions, the growth of independent museums specializing in this field, and the fact that at many universities African art has become a separate subject of study and research, involving many scholars and students. As in other subjects, no individual can master all the problems of African art, and specialization has become the order of the day.

For this reason the literature listed in the bibliography is confined to the most important items and to works mentioned in this book. The reader who wishes to dig still deeper is referred to L. J. P. Gaskin's *Bibliography of African Art* (1965), which records literature published down to the mid-1960s; many of the later works — although inevitably not all — are listed in the bibliographies in the tenth and fifteenth volumes of *African Arts*. This publication, produced since 1967 at the University of California in Los Angeles, is the most important specialist periodical, and an indispensable source for anybody who wants to follow the progress of the subject. Also very important is the French quarterly *Arts d'Afrique noire*, which has appeared since 1971 in Arnouville and concentrates on the traditional art of French Africa.

In all the books and magazines listed, the reader will find references to further literature, as well as the specialized bibliographies. In addition to catalogues of exhibitions, invaluable sources of knowledge about otherwise inaccessible materials in private collections are provided by the catalogues of large firms of auctioneers such as Sotheby's and Christie's in London, Sotheby-Parke-Bernet in New York, and Wolfgang Ketterer in Munich. Descriptions and commentaries in such catalogues are nowadays written by the foremost authorities on African art.

African Arts. Quarterly periodical from 1967. Los Angeles.

Allison, Philip. **African Stone Sculpture**. London, 1968.

Arts d'Afrique noire. Quarterly periodical from 1971. Arnouville.

Azevedo, Warren L. d' (ed.). **The Traditional Artist in African Society**. Bloomington, 1973.

Bascom, William. **Ifa Divination**. Bloomington/London, 1969.

Bascom, William, and Gebauer, Paul. **Handbook of West African Art**. Milwaukee, 1953.

Bassani, Ezio. **Il vassoio dell'oracolo di ifa di Ulm e le statuette del culto 'abiku'**, in **Africa, Rivista trimestrale di studi e documentazione dell'Istituto Italo-Africano**, XXXVIII, 4, 1983, p. 580.

Bassani, Ezio. **Scultura africana nei musei italiani**. Bologna, 1977.

Bassani, Ezio. **Una bottega di grandi artisti Bambara**, in **Critica d'Arte**. Florence, 1978.

Bastin, Marie-Louise. **Art décoratif Tshokwe**, vols I, II. Lisbon, 1961.

Biebuyck, D. **Lega Culture: Art, Initiation and Moral Philosophy among a Central African People**. Berkeley, 1973.

Bodrogi, Tibor. **Art in Africa**. New York, 1968.

Boston, J. S. **Ikenga Figures among the North-West Igbo and Igala**. Lagos/London, 1977.

Brain, Robert, and Pollock, Adam. **Bangwa Funerary Sculpture**. London, 1971.

Čapek, Josef. **Umění přírodních národů** (Art of Primitive Nations). Prague, 1938.

Cole, H. M. **Art and Life among the Oweri Igbo**. Bloomington, 1982.

Cornet, Joseph. **Afrikanische Kunst, Schätze von Zaire**. Geneva, 1971.

Coronel, Patricia Crane. **Aowin Terracotta Sculpture**, in **African Arts**, XIII, 1, 1979.

Delange, Jacqueline. **Arts et peuple de l'Afrique noire**. Paris, 1967.

Dobbelmann, A. H. H. **Der Ogboni Geheimbund: Bronzen aus Südwest-Nigeria**. Afrika Museum, Berg en Dal, 1976.

Drewal, H. J. and M. T. **Gelede: Art and Female Power among the Yoruba**. Bloomington, 1983.

Eyo, E., and Willett, F. **Treasures of Ancient Nigeria**. London, 1982/3.

Fagg, Bernard. **Nok Terracottas**. London, 1977.

Fagg, William. **African Sculpture**. The International Exhibitions Foundation, Washington/New York, 1970.

Fagg, William. **African Sculpture from the Tara Collection**. Art Gallery, University of Notre Dame, 1971.

Fagg, William. **African Tribal Images: The Katherine White Reswick Collection**. Cleveland Museum of Art, Cleveland, 1968.

Fagg, William. **Nigerian Images**. London, 1963.

Fagg, William, and Elisofon, Eliot. **The Sculpture of Africa**. London, 1958.

Fagg, William. **Tribes and Forms in African Art**. New York, 1965.

Fagg, William. **Vergessene Negerkunst: Afro-portugiesisches Elfenbein**. Prague, 1959.

Fagg, William, and Pemberton, John. **Yoruba: Sculpture of West Africa**. 3rd ed., New York, 1982.

Fagg, William, and Plass, M. **African Sculpture**. London, 1964.

Fernandez, James. **The Exposition and Imposition of Order: Artistic Expression in Fang Culture**, in d'Azevedo (q. v.).

Fischer, Eberhard. **The West Guinea Coast: A Short Introduction to a West-African Art Province**, in **Critica d'Arte**, vol. XLVI. Florence, 1981.

Fischer, Eberhard, and Himmelheber, Hans. **Die Kunst der Dan**. Zurich, 1976.

Fischer, Eberhard, and Homberger, Lorenz. **Die Kunst der Guro, Elfenbeinküste**. Rietberg Museum, Zurich, 1985.

Foss, Perkins. **Urhobo Statuary for Spirits and Ancestors**, in **African Arts**, IX, 4, 1976, p. 12.

Fraser, Douglas. **Primitive Art**. London, 1963.

Frobenius, Leo. **Die Masken und Geheimbünde Afrikas**. Halle, 1898.

Fröhlich, H. V. W. **Exotische Kunst im Rautenstrauch-Joest-Museum**. Cologne, 1971.

Fry, Philip. **Essai sur la statuaire mumuye**, in **Objets et Mondes**, vol. X, Fasc. 1. Paris, 1970.

Garrard, Timothy F. **Akan Metal Arts**, in **African Arts**, XIII. 1, 1979.

Gaskin, L. J. P. **A Bibliography of African Art**. London, 1965.

Gerbrands, A. A. **Afrika: Kunst aus dem schwarzen Erdteil**. Recklinghausen, 1967.

Gillon, Werner. **Collecting African Art**. London, 1979.

Gower, Tess. **Art of the Mende from Sierra Leone**. Exhibition Catalogue. Glasgow, 1980.

Griaule, M. **Masques dogons**. Paris, 1938.

Grunne, Bernard de. **The Terracotta Statuary of the Inland Delta of the Niger and Mali**. Munich, 1982.

Haselberger, Herta. **Bemerkungen zum Kunsthandwerk in der Republik Haute Valta**, in Zeitschrift für Ethnologie, vol. 94, book 2, Brunswick, 1969, pp. 171 to 246.

Herold, Erich. **Zur Ikonographie der 'aku-onu' Masken (Jukun, Nigeria)**, in Abhandlungen und Berichte des Staatlichen Museums für Völkerkunde. Dresden, 1975, p. 77.

Herrmann, Ferdinand. **Afrikanische Kunst aus dem Völkerkunde Museum der Portheim-Stiftung**. Berlin/Heidelberg/New York, 1969.

Himmelheber, Hans. **Deutung bestimmter Eigenarten der Senufo-Masken**, in **Baessler-Archiv**, N. F., XIII, 1965, p. 73.

Himmelheber, Hans. **Negerkünstler: Ethnographische Studien über die Schnitzkünstler bei den Stämmen der Atutu und Guro im Innern der Elfenbeinküste**. Stuttgart, 1935.

Himmelheber, Hans. **Negerkunst und Negerkünstler**. Brunswick, 1960.

Hirschberg, Walter. **Die Künstlerstrasse: Auf Studienreise durch Kamerun**. Vienna, 1962.

Holas, Bohumil. **Arts de la Côte-d'Ivoire**. Paris, 1966.

Holas, Bohumil. **Die Kunst der Elfenbeinküste: Die Kunstschätze des Museums von Abidjan**. Vevey, 1969.

Holas, Bohumil. **L'image du monde bété**. Paris, 1968.

Holas, Bohumil. **Masques ivoiriens**. Paris/Abidjan, 1969.

Holas, Bohumil. **Sculptures ivoiriennes**. Abidjan, 1969.

Holý, Ladislav. **Afrikanische Plastik**. Prague, 1967.

Horton, Robin. **Kalabari Sculpture**. Lagos, 1965.

Imperato, Pascal James. **Bamana and Maninka Twin Figures**, in **African Arts**, VIII, 4, 1975.

Jones, G. J. **The Art of Eastern Nigeria**. Cambridge, 1984.

Kandert, Josef. **Exotické slonovinové řezby 16. a 17. století** (Exotic Ivory Engravings of the 16th and 17th Centuries), in **Časopis Národního muzea v Praze**, Historical Series, No. 2, 1985, p. 82.

Kecskési, Maria. **Kunst aus dem alten Afrika**. Innsbruck/Frankfurt-am-Main, 1982.

Kjersmeier, C. **Centre de style de la sculpture nègre africaine**, vols I—IV. Copenhagen, 1935—38.

Korabiewicz, W. **Sztuka Afryki w zbiorach polskich**. Warsaw, 1966.

Krieger, K. **Westafrikanische Plastik**, vols I—III. Berlin, 1965—69.

Krieger, K., and Kutscher, G. **Westafrikanische Masken**. Berlin, 1960.

Lamp, Frederick. **Cosmos, Cosmetics, and the Spirit of Bondo**, in **African Art**, XVIII, 3, 1985.

Laude, Jean. **African Art of the Dogon: The Myths of the Cliff Dwellers**. New York, 1973.

Lebeuf, J. P. **L'Art ancien du Tchad: Bronzes et céramiques**. Paris, 1962.

Lebeuf, J. P. and Annie. **Les arts des Sao**. Paris, 1977.

Leiris, M., and Delange, J. **Afrika: Die Kunst des schwarzen Erdteils**. Munich, 1968.

Leuzinger, Elsy. **Africa: The Art of the Negro People**. London, 1960.

Leuzinger, Elsy. **African Sculpture: A Descriptive Catalogue**. Zurich, 1963.

Leuzinger, Elsy. **The Art of Black Africa**. Greenwich, 1972.

Luschan, Felix von. **Die Altertümer von Benin**. Berlin, 1919.

Maggs, Tim, and Davison, Patricia. **The Lydenburg Heads**, in **African Arts**, XIV, 2, 1981.

Mansfeld, Alfred. **Urwald-Dokumente: vier Jahre unter den Crossflussnegern Kameruns**. Berlin, 1908.

McIntosh, Susan and Roderick. **Finding West Africa's Oldest City**, in **National Geographic**, vol. 162, No. 3, 1982, pp. 396—418.

McIntosh, Susan and Roderick. **Terracotta Statuettes from Mali**, in **African Arts**, XII, 1977.

McLeod, M. **The Asante**. London, 1981.

Meauzé, Pierre. **African Art: Sculpture**. London, 1968.

Meauzé, Pierre; Noll, Colette, and N'Diaye, Francine. **Sculptures africaines dans les collections publiques françaises**. Paris, 1972.

Meek, C. K. **A Sudanese Kingdom**. London, 1931.

Menzel, Brigitte. **Goldgewichte aus Ghana**. Berlin, 1968.

Messenger, John C. **The Carver in Anang Society**, in d'Azevedo (q. v.).

Meyer, Piet. **Kunst und Religion der Lobi**. Rietberg Museum, Zurich, 1981.

Morigi, Paolo. **Raccolta di un amatore d'arte primitiva**. Bern, 1980.

Newton, Douglas. **The Nelson Rockefeller Collection: Masterpieces of Primitive Art**. New York, 1978.

Nicklin, Keith. **Skin-Covered Masks of Cameroon**, in **African Arts**, XII, 2, 1979.

Olbrechts, F. M. **Les arts plastiques du Congo Belge**. Brussels, 1959.

Olderogge, Dmitri. **The Art of Africa: Negro Art from the Institute of Ethnography**. Leningrad/London, 1969.

Oliveira, Ernesto Veiga de. **Escultura Africana no Museu de etnologia do Ultramar**. Lisbon, 1968.

Paulme, Denise. **Les Sculptures de l'Afrique noire**. Paris, 1956.

Paulme, Denise. **Une société de Côte-d'Ivoire... les Bété**. Paris, 1962.

Perrois, Louis. **Arts du Gabon**. Arnouville, 1979.

Rattray, R. S. **Religion and Art in Ashanti**. Oxford, 1927.

Read, C. H., and Dalton, O. M. **Antiquities of Benin and from other Parts of West Africa in the British Museum**. London, 1899.

Robbins, Warren M. **African Art in American Collections**. New York/Washington/London, 1966.

Roy, Claude. **Le m'boueti des Mahongwe**. Paris, 1967.

Sarpong, P. **The Sacred Stools of the Akan**. Ghana, 1971.

Schädler, Karl-Ferdinand. **Afrikanische Kunst in deutschen Privatsammlungen**. Munich, 1973.

Schweeger-Hefel, Annemarie. **Holzplastik in Afrika**. Vienna, 1960.

Schweeger-Hefel, Annemarie. **Masken und Mythen: Sozialstruktur der Nyonyosi und Sikomse in Obervolta**. Vienna, 1980.

Schweeger-Hefel, Annemarie. **Plastik aus Afrika**. Vienna, 1969.

Segy, Ladislas. **African Sculpture Speaks**. New York, 1952.

Shaw, Thurstan. **Igbo-Ukwu**, vols I, II. London, 1970.

Sieber, Roy. **Sculpture of Northern Nigeria**. Museum of Primitive Art, New York, 1961.

Sousberghe, L. de. **L'art Pende**. Brussels, 1958.

Stoll, Mareidi and Gert. **Ibeji: Zwillingsfiguren der Yoruba** (Twin Figures of Yoruba). Munich, 1980.

Sydow, Eckart von. **Handbuch der westafrikanischen Plastik**. Berlin, 1930.

Sydow, Eckart von, and Kutscher, Gerdt. **Afrikanische Plastik**. Berlin, 1954.

Talbot, P. A. **In the Shadow of the Bush**. London, 1912.

Thompson, Robert Farris. **Black Gods and Kings: Yoruba Art at UCLA**. Bloomington/London, 1971.

Torday, Emil, and Joyce, Thomas A. **Notes ethnographiques sur les peuples communément appelés Bakuba ainsi que sur les peuplades apparentées: Les Bushongo**. Brussels, 1911.

Trowell, Margaret. **Classical African Sculpture**. London, 1954.

Trowell, Margaret, and Nevermann, Hans. **African and Oceanic Art**. New York, 1968.

Wassing, René S. **The Arts of Africa**. London, 1970.

Willett, Frank. **African Art: A Concise History**. New York, 1971.

Willett, Frank. **Ife in the History of West African Sculpture**. New York, 1967.

Williams, Drid. **The Dance of the Bedu Moon**, in **African Arts**, II, 1, 1968.

INDEX OF AFRICAN TRIBES AND LANGUAGE GROUPS

African tribes are known by many synonymous names, with numerous variations in spelling. This book uses the forms most commonly employed in contemporary accounts of African art. The most important synonyms have been given both in the text and in the list that follows. In the case of the Bantu tribes, art historians use either names with the Bantu plural prefix Ba- (in the western half of the continent) and Wa- (in its eastern half), or dispense with these and give only the root of the name: Bakuba or only Kuba, Wamuera or just Muera (or Mwera), and so on. The present author prefers the full Bantu names, on the grounds that roots are not used by themselves in Bantu languages, being no more than philological units.

So if the reader does not find the name of a tribe in the list, he will probably find it by joining one of the two prefixes to it. In a few exceptional cases the unprefixed name is almost universally used — Makonde rather than Wamakonde, Zulu instead of Amazulu — and we have followed suit; the full name however, is given as a cross-reference in the list.

INDEX OF AFRICAN TERMS

INDEX OF AFRICAN NAMES AND GEOGRAPHICAL TERMS